INVASIONS OF INDIA FROM CENTRAL ASIA

INVASIONS OF INDIA

FROM

CENTRAL ASIA

DEMETRIUS C. BOULGER

GYAN

Published by

Gyan Publishing House
5, Ansari Road
Daryaganj, New Delhi-110002
Phone: 011-47034999, 9811692060
E-mail: books@gyanbooks.com

Distribution Network
gyanbooks.com
India, USA, Canada, UK, Australia

ISBN: 978-93-7225-467-9 (PB)

First Published, 1879

2nd Impression 2025

Printed at: Gyan Press, Delhi.

INVASIONS OF INDIA FROM CENTRAL ASIA
Author: DEMETRIUS C. BOULGER

THE INVASIONS OF INDIA.

INVASIONS OF INDIA

FROM

CENTRAL ASIA.

LONDON:
RICHARD BENTLEY AND SON,
Publishers in Ordinary to Her Majesty the Queen.
1879.

PREFACE.

To understand the history and present position of India, it is absolutely necessary to have some acquaintance with the history of Central Asia. For from Central Asia (known as Scythia, Tartary, or Turkestan in past times) India has always been ruled in historic, and presumably in prehistoric, times.

Some have supposed Bactria, or Balkh, to have been the site of the Garden of Eden. In long past ages, the Aryans are thought to have held an extensive empire in the mountains of the Hindoo Kush. From thence they invaded India, and their descendants form the military, sacerdotal, and mercantile class of Hindoos in India to this day. The Brahmin, the Rajpoot, and the Buniah are the descendants of Aryans of Bactria. The lower castes and the servile class are the descendants of the people they subdued.

But the Aryan masters of India in their turn were subdued from Central Asia in historic times. They were conquered by the race that we call Tartars. The fierce and rude soldiers of Turkestan have ruled India for the last eight hundred years, since A.D. 1002.

Alexander the Great conquered India in 324 B.C. He followed the road which so many Tartar invaders have since taken—through Persia, Kandahar, and Ghuzne, through Afghanistan to the Indus. But the Greek invasion was a mere passing inroad, and left little mark on the people of India. This is the first historical invasion of India recorded.

The next invader was Mamood of Ghuzni, in A.D. 1002. He was a Turk, who, from the mountains ot Afghanistan, formed a magnificent empire. He ruled not only India, but Bokhara, Kashgar, Khorassan, and other provinces of Central Asia. The invasion of Mamood of Ghuzni was a long and lasting evil. His soldiers were from Turkestan. By the Koorum Valley he made thirty inroads into the rich, level, unwarlike land of Hindustan. He destroyed the fanes of the Hindoos, carried away the inhabitants into hopeless slavery, and subjected the afflicted land to every misery, and every degradation. From this time the Tartars of Central Asia, finding the invasion of India so easy, so profitable, and, in their idea, so meritorious an act in a religious point of view, have continually poured down to plunder the plains of India.

I have used the word 'Tartar.' It is used to describe numerous races of Central Asia, much as the word 'Frank' is applied by Asiatics to all Europeans. No tribe of Central Asia ever called themselves Tartars. It is said that the vanguard of Genghis Khan were called 'Tatars,' from Tatar Khan, the brother of Moghul Khan, a remote ancestor of the Moghuls. But their enemies in Europe called them Tartars, asserting they that came from Tartarus. The invasion of Europe by Genghis Khan in 1238, caused the greatest consternation. The Moghuls were then the master race of Turkestan. Starting from thence they conquered China, India, Georgia, Circassia, Astrachan, Livonia, Moscow. From their conquest of Russia, through Poland, they reached Germany, and even the shores of the Baltic. For two hundred years the Moghuls (Tartars) ruled Russia. *Si vous grattez le Russe; vous trouvez le Tartare,* says the proverb. Gibbon remarks of the Moghul occupation of Russia: 'A temporary ruin in other countries was less fatal than the deep and perhaps indelible mark which servitude of two hundred years has imprinted on the character of the Russians.'

The once master races called Tartars in Europe were either Moghuls, Turks or Usbegs, races kindred to each other.

The third invasion of India from Central Asia was also

a mere passing inroad, that of the Moghuls under a brother of Genghis Khan in 1303. It brought to India all the horrors that Russia, Hungary, and Germany experienced from the same barbarians—razed cities, wholesale massacres, hopeless slavery. In consequence of this invasion, all the races of Central Asia are called Moghuls by the people of India to this day—Turk, Turcoman, Usbeg, and Persian are to them Moghuls, as all Europeans are Franks.

The fourth invasion of India was that of the Turks under Tamerlane, when Delhi was sacked and its inhabitants ruthlessly massacred, in 1398.

The fifth invasion of India from Central Asia was under Sultan Baber, in 1525; the sixth, under Nadir Shah, 1739; the seventh under Abdulla, a Turcoman, in 1761. Soon afterwards British rule was established, and the invasion of India from Central Asia ceased. It is of these last invasions that this work treats.

The history of India teaches that in past ages whoever held the crown of Turkestan held that of India also, if not in his hand at least within his grasp. Turkestan has gone through the following revolutions, which have left indelible marks not only on India but on Europe.

The earliest record of Turkestan that history gives is that of the Huns under Attilla, in 450 A.D. The Huns lost their supremacy in Central Asia, which was acquired by the Avares, or Geougens. The Khan of Geougen was killed by the Turks in 545 A.D. The Turks who were his slaves and workers in iron, rose on their masters under Bertezana, their first leader. The Turks of Constantinople were a branch of this race of Central Asia. Four hundred families marched from the Oxus in 1299; they gained Asia Minor by conquest, and entered Europe in 1353.

The Turkish supremacy in Turkestan fell before the all-conquering Moghuls under Genghis Khan in 1224. The Turks, however, recovered their supremacy in Central Asia, under Tamerlane, in 1383. Tamerlane, like Genghis Khan, was a world-wide conqueror, ruling Turkestan, Kipzak (the Cossack country), Russia, Asia Minor, Syria, Egypt, Armenia, Georgia, and conquering India. He left to his descendants twenty-seven crowns, including that of the Crimea. But one hundred and twenty years later, in 1506, the possessions that he had acquired were lost by his descendants to a new tribe of Moghuls, the Usbegs, who have ruled Turkestan for the last three hundred and seventy years, and who have fallen to the Muscovite in our day.

The Turks of Central Asia, of Samarcand, like the Turks of Constantinople, ceased to be a rude, wandering tribe. Among the beautiful mountains of Southern Turkestan, in a temperate climate, with every gift of nature lavished in profusion, Samarcand rose, decked with the spoil of a thousand cities of Asia Minor, Syria, and of India. Samarcand, the city of Tamerlane, was such a city as Cairo, Constantinople, Bagdad, or Delhi. It was full of splendid mosques, built by workmen brought from India and Damascus, beautiful gardens, magnificent palaces; full of trade, and full of wealth.

Samarcand was celebrated for its manufactory of paper; and from thence also came Kermizi, crimson velvet, the cramoisy of the old ballads. The mulberry abounds in Turkestan, and considerable quantities of silk were manufactured, and all the fruits of Southern Europe grow there in profusion.

The Turks of Samarcand had an extensive literature. Their language is the parent of Osmanli Turkish; they can boast of poets, geographers. historians, astronomers, and endless theological writers on the tenets of the Moslem creed. Two of their books, the 'Institutes of Tamerlane' and the 'Life of Sultan Baber,' have been translated into English.

The martial spirit of the Turks, their despotic government, their unjust laws of land, their barbarously cruel punishments, were not drawn wholly from the Koran, though fostered and preserved by it, but from the laws of Genghis Khan—a work they looked upon as semi-divine. The Moghuls obtained many of their ideas, practices, and cruelties from the Chinese, with whom they were brought much in contact, from the circumstances of their geographical position.

The Russians are the heirs to the Tartar supremacy in Europe and Central Asia, we are the heirs of the same race in India.

CONTENTS.

THE TURKISH INVASION OF INDIA, UNDER SULTAN BABER, IN 1525.

CHAPTER I.

FROM KABUL TO PESHAWUR.

CHAPTER II.

FROM PESHAWUR TO DELHI.

CHAPTER III.

THE TURKS AS RULERS OF INDIA.

CHAPTER IV.

THE DEATH OF BABER.

CHAPTER V.

THE HISTORY OF NOOR MAHAL.

CHAPTER IV.

AURUNGZEBE.

THE PERSIAN INVASION OF INDIA, UNDER NADIR SHAH, IN 1739.

CHAPTER I.

THE COURT OF THE GREAT MOGHUL.

CHAPTER II.

THE BATTLE OF PANIPUT.

CHAPTER III.

THE SACKING OF DELHI.

CHAPTER IV.

THE RISE OF THE BRITISH POWER IN INDIA.—1756.

THE ENGLISH INVASION OF KABUL, IN 1839.

CHAPTER I.

CHAPTER II.

CHAPTER III.

THE

TURKISH INVASION OF INDIA,

UNDER SULTAN BABER, IN 1525.

CHAPTER I.

FROM KABUL TO PESHAWUR.

Usbegs — Sultan Baber — The invasion of India — Turks and Moghuls—Jellalabad—The river Kabul—The Kheiber Pass.

In 1525, the Usbegs held the position in Central Asia that the Russians do now. They were the advancing, encroaching power. They had come from the north and taken the great cities of Khiva, Bokhara, Herat, even lordly Samarcand.

The Turks, Moghuls, and Usbegs were kindred races. The Usbegs, a branch of the Moghuls, called themselves thus after a favourite leader, Usbeg Khan. But the Usbegs surpassed any other tribe of the day, in Central Asia, in fighting qualities. Their tactics were better, their cavalry superior, and they had a soldier of genius as a leader, Sheibany Khan. City after city fell to the Usbegs; from Khiva to Herat there was not a city left unsacked. These Usbegs, under Sheibany Khan, had made many khans of Central Asia throneless fugitives; among them Zehir-ul-deen Muhammed Baber (Baber means 'the Tiger'), a descendant of Tamerlane, and also a descendant of Genghis Khan.

Baber was born to the throne of Ferghana, or Transoxiana, now the Russian province of Khokan; but the ever-successful Sheibany Khan had taken from him his throne, his home, his country. No depths of humiliation had been spared him. Baber's fortunes, for many years, had sunk so low, that he wandered barefooted, tentless, among the mountains of Khorasan, with about twelve ragged, starving, but faithful followers. There was only one tent among all the fugitives, and that Baber gave up to his mother. His favourite sister had fallen into his enemies' hands, and was in the harem of Sheibany Khan.

But Baber conquered his overwhelming difficulties by his energy, ability and courage. After many years spent in the bitter school of adversity, he gained the throne of Kabul, the Switzerland of Asia.

In 1525, Baber was ruler of that beautiful, but poor country. He was strong and powerful. He had attached to his interests and his standard many good officers, many of the leading men and free-lances of Central Asia. He determined to invade India; partly because the Usbegs had followed him to the gates of Kabul, and had taken the fortress of Khandahar. So Sultan Baber went forth to conquer a new throne; 'Leaving behind me,' as he said, 'my old and inveterate enemies the Usbegs, and placing my foot on the stirrup of resolution, and my hand on the rein of confidence in God.' He invaded India in the winter of 1525.

For twenty years this invasion of India had been Baber's most cherished dream. In his autobiography he writes: 'From the time I conquered the country of Kabul, which was in 1507, till the present time, I had always been bent on subduing Hindustan. Sometimes, however, from the misconduct of my Amirs (nobles) and their dislike to the plan, sometimes from the cabals and opposition of my brothers, I was prevented from prosecuting any expedition into that country, and its provinces escaped being overrun.

'There was no one left, great or small, noble or private man, who could dare to utter a word in opposition to the enterprise. I had attached myself in a peculiar degree to the affairs of Hindustan, and in the space of seven or eight years entered it five times at the head of an army.' *

Baber wrote his own autobiography in a dialect of the Turkish language. It was translated into Persian, and also into English, fifty years ago, by Dr. Leyden. It is a most curious book. In simple language, Baber gives graphic descriptions of his wars, his friends, his enemies, his motives, his pleasures, his sorrows. He gives also a very truthful account of the geographical features of the countries he conquered, and of their inhabitants. We will allow Baber to tell the tale of the Turkish invasion of India from Kabul in his own words, whenever the thread of the narrative will admit of it. It was a

* Baber's 'Memoirs,' p. 309.

conquest pregnant with momentous consequences. The civilisation of India is Turkish to this day. Until the year 1857, his descendants continued to rule in Delhi.

The Amirs (nobles) of Baber's court disapproved of the invasion, daunted by the perils and dangers. Nothing but the almost supernatural influence of the king's master-spirit made them consent to accompany him. There were great difficulties to be overcome before Baber could carry out his ambitious project; difficulties so great that they would have deterred an ordinary man.

Baber had only ten thousand horsemen with whom to invade India. Sultan Ibrahim, King of Delhi, was known to have one hundred thousand regular troops, and one thousand war elephants. He had immense hoarded wealth; he could hire a large force of mercenaries and call out all the noted chivalry of Rajpootana. Before reaching Delhi, the capital of India, a strong fortified city, there were walled cities and fortresses to be taken, manned and held by war-loving and armour-clad Pathans.

Between Kabul and India lay ranges of high mountains, inhabited by war-like tribes only half subdued, who, in case of a Turkish defeat, might cut off the return of the beaten army to Kabul in the rugged Kheiber, or the lofty Khoord Kabul Pass. The Pathans were Afghans, who lived and ruled in India. Before Baber's invasion, India had been three times overrun and conquered from Afghanistan. But Baber was brave, and such traits of character as the following had made him an adored leader.

Returning from Herat, in Korasan, to his capital of Kabul, he had to lead his troops across those ranges of mountains that hem Kabul in on every side from the outer world. It was night; the way was lost among the mountains; a heavy snowstorm set in.

'Every man,' wrote Baber in his 'Memoirs,' 'was obliged to dismount and halt where he happened to be. Many men waited for morning on horseback. Some desired me to go into a cavern, but I would not go. I felt that to be in a warm dwelling, while my men were in the midst of snow and drift, *would be inconsistent with what I owed them, and a deviation from that companionship in suffering that was their due.* It was right that whatever their sufferings and difficulties were, and whatever they might be obliged to undergo, I should be a sharer with them. There is a Persian proverb that "Death in the company of friends is a feast." I continued, therefore, to sit in the drift, in a sort of hole in the snow, which I had cleared and dug out for myself, till evening prayers, when the snow fell so fast that—I had remained all the while crouching down on my feet—I now found that four inches of snow had settled on my head, lips, and ears. That night I caught a cold in my ear.'*

A cavern was found at length in the mountains, and was reported 'very extensive, and sufficiently large,' says

* Baber's 'Memoirs,' p. 211.

Baber, 'to receive all our people.' Only when his men entered before him did he consent to take shelter in what he calls a warm and comfortable place.

The following character of Baber is given by Ferishta, the Persian historian :

'He was a prince of great humanity, and carried his generosity to such excess that it bordered upon prodigality. With respect to the first, he so often pardoned ingratitude and treason, that he seemed to make it a principle to render good for evil. He thus disarmed vice, and made the wicked the worshippers of his virtue.'*

'He was of the sect of the Hanefites' (one of the four orthodox sects of the Mohammedans), 'in whose doctrines and tenets he was perfectly versed, yielding more to the evidence of reason than to the marvellous legends of superstitious antiquity. He was not, however, forgetful of that rational worship which is due to the Creator, nor a despiser of those laws and ceremonies which are founded upon sound policy for the benefit of the superficial judges of things. With respect to his military character, he seems to have had few that could equal him. He rendered the most dangerous enterprises easy by his undaunted courage and perseverance, which rose above all difficulties, and made him more the object of admiration in adversity than in the height of his prosperity. The Hanefites are called by Arabian writers the followers of

* Dow's translation, vol. ii. p. 138.

reason, and those of the three other sects, followers of tradition.'*

Baber was well-made, above the middle height, with a pleasant, intelligent face. In the miniatures extant at the present time, Baber is thus represented to us. He wears, in Oriental fashion, the usual kaftan, with the addition of long riding-boots; his head is swathed with a snowy-white turban, and his whole presence is stately and commanding. His eyes are large, dark, and piercing, and surmounted by highly-arched and marked eyebrows; and his glance is keen and penetrating. There is a likeness of Baber extant, in a book once the property of his son, and now the property of the Government of India, and to be seen in the library of the Government College, Agra. The book is a beautiful specimen of Oriental penmanship, and is profusely illustrated with pictures, in good drawing, of castles, battles, and sieges. These illustrations resemble medieval illuminations, or miniatures, from the fineness of the painting, and are in fairly good perspective.

'There are four roads,' writes Baber, 'that lead from Kabul to India; in all of these there are passes more or less difficult. One of these is by the way of Lamghauat, and comes by the hill of Kheiber, in which there is one short hill pass; another road leads by Bangash, a third by Naghz, the fourth by Fermul.' The Lamghauat road is the present road from Kabul to Peshawur, and it was

* Sale's 'Koran,' p. 110.

by that that Baber, his horsemen, baggage, and cannon marched. This route has a melancholy interest to the English. It was the scene of the Kabul massacre in 1842, when a British army, of four thousand fighting men and twelve thousand camp followers, was cut to pieces.

'On Friday, the 1st of Sefer, in the year 932, when the sun was in Sagittarius' (A.D. 1525, November 17th), 'I set out on my march to invade Hindustan,' to use Baber's words. On that day the king, followed by his Amirs, all mounted on Turkoman and Tipchäk horses, both men and horses clad in armour, rode across the river Kabul, which is fordable, and across the rich valley of Kabul, flat and level for ten miles; then stopped at Bootkhat, and encamped on the banks of the river Dehyakub that night. Bootkhat is at the foot of the great Khoord Kabul Pass, the mountains of which rise to the height of eight thousand feet. While encamped at Bootkhat, Baber received an embassy from the Sultan of Kashgar, his kinsman, and also 'privately' received letters from the 'Khanims' (the ladies). These ladies were his aunts, his mother's sisters, with whom he had spent much of his youth. One of them was married to the ruler of Kashgar.

Baber waited in camp some days at Bootkhat for the troops to assemble. These were mostly peasants from the provinces of Afghanistan, who had never before left their mountains for more than a month's forage.

As the strings of loaded camels arrived at the end of the first day's march, each tent was pitched with precision in its appointed and accustomed place. Day after day the camp moved from ten to twenty-five miles, which is considered the limits of an ordinary march. Baber's tents and those of the Amirs always occupied the same position, and their personal followers were always encamped around them.

In the ranks of Baber's army were to be found men of many races—Afghans, Hazaras, Arabs, Beloochees, Turks, and Moghuls. Amongst them were his old veterans, who had followed his fortunes for twenty years, and who were used to battles and sieges.

The leaders were nearly all Turks and Moghuls. The troops were armed—some with matchlocks, some with bows and arrows, in the use of which they were very expert. Besides the soldiers who collected at Bootkhat, there was an immense array of slaves, merchants, and camp followers: 'there were strings of long-haired male and female camels laden with tents, with awnings of velvet and purpet.' Baber had a large audience-tent; he also had two sets of smaller ones. Slaves, tent-pitchers—all were fighting men. Baber recounts how well his cook and butler fought on one occasion. Servants had been raised to the rank of Bey (lord), and had been given the honour of having horse-tail standards carried before them, and this for services rendered to Baber in former wars. This honour is known in Europe as a Pasha of three tails; these tails were often those of the yak of Tibet. There had been a great batch of new lords created before starting for Hindustan. Baber's advisers and companions in pleasure and arms were Turks from his native country of Transoxiana—Andijanians, as the Russians still call them.

He was accompanied also by Moghul Beys—his own relations on his mother's side. Baber did not love the Moghul race. 'All his villainy arises from his being a Moghul,' he wrote of a man he disliked.

These Moghuls were born horsemen; and their fierce charges in many Indian battles helped to gain that country to Baber. Chin Taimur Sultan, a Moghul, was a maternal cousin who did him good service in India.

A favourite verse of Baber's is this:

> 'If the Moghul race were a race of angels, it is a bad race;
> And were the name Moghul written in gold, it would be odious.
> Take care not to pluck one ear of corn from a Moghul's harvest;
> The Moghul's seed is such, that whatever is sowed with it is execrable.'

He mentions the Moghul race with aversion, partly because the Moghul troopers were given to mutiny and insurrection. He always speaks with pride of being a Turk, and of being of the family of Timour, Tamerlane, the great world-wide conqueror.

The kings of the dynasty Baber founded at Delhi, which ruled India for three hundred years, are each known in European history as 'the Great Mogul;' but the name was a misnomer, and arose from the people of India having but vague ideas of their foreign invaders. One of the first invasions of India, from Central Asia, had been by Genghis Khan, a Moghul; and all other invaders—Afghans, Turks, and Persians—received the one name known to the ignorant; exactly as all Europeans are Franks in the East, or Feringhee (Varangians, from the Varangian guard at Constantinople, in the time of the Eastern emperors).

Several of Babèr's commanders were his cousins, and also descended from Timour. Two—Sultan Mohammed Mirza, and Sultan Hussain Mirza—had been driven from Herat by the Usbegs. They did the Turks good service in several hard-fought battles in Hindustan.

The whole Turkish forces were not yet collected: some of the best troops were to meet them further on. The men were in first-rate order. 'Perhaps on no other occasion had I my men in such perfect discipline,'* writes Baber, when the Turks had not long before taken Khelat-ï-Ghilzi. In it was found immense booty and wealth. For twenty years, ever since Baber had held Kabul, he had been used, every year, to undertake a 'little war' against the tribes who lived among the hills—Mammands, Ghilzies and others, who had for centuries defied the authority of the King of Kabul, and he had brought most of them to obey his authority. These steep mountains and fierce tribes proved a good school for teaching the Turks the art of war.

* 'Memoirs,' p. 227.

On the 22nd November, the Turks began the ascent of the stupendous Khoord Kabul Pass; the road, for a distance of five miles, runs through precipitous mountain ranges, and is shut in by high beetling rocks, into whose gloomy recesses the sun rarely penetrates. The mountain road rises to an altitude of eight thousand, five hundred feet; the steep hill-sides are clad with pine-trees, and occasional holly-trees. The road ascends through miles of rock until it reaches Jugduluk.

In these splendid Alpine solitudes Baber received the first fruits of the gold of Ind. The governor of the town of Lahore sent him about one thousand pounds sterling. 'The greater part of this sum,' writes Baber, 'I despatched, through Mulla Ahmed, one of the chief men of Balkh, to serve my interests in that quarter.' * This sum was much thought of. Kabul was a poor country; its revenue amounted only to about thirty-three thousand pounds, at that time.

At Jugduluk the British army, in 1842, ceased to exist; they were all massacred in the snow by the Ghilzie tribes. A few officers reached Gundermuck, but only one man reached Jellalabad. The distance between Kabul and Jellalabad is fifty miles.

The Ghilzies did not attack Baber on this occasion; they still inhabit this part of the mountains. On a former occasion they attacked him. The hill-tribes of Afghanistan, in Baber's time, were exactly what they are

* 'Memoirs,' p. 290.

now, and exactly what the English found them to be in 1842.

'The Ghilzies and other tribes,' says Baber, 'formed the plan of obstructing our march through the hill-pass of Jugduluk, and drew up on the hill which lies to the north, beating their drums, brandishing their swords, and raising terrific shouts. As soon as we had mounted, I ordered the troops to ascend the hills and attack the enemy, each in the direction nearest to him. Our troops accordingly advanced, and making their way through different valleys, and by every approach they could discover, got near them, upon which the Afghans, after standing an instant, took to flight.' Baber says of them: 'they are robbers and plunderers even in peaceable times.' *

On November 24, the Turks arrived in a more smiling country at Gundamuk; they encamped there under the shade of lofty plane-trees and dark cypresses. In this valley there also grew bitter almonds, mulberry-trees, willows, wild roses and wild lavender.†

On the 26th November, they left the mountain passes, and reached a semi-tropical climate at Jellalabad. Here there was a walled city; and from the low altitude of this valley, oranges, citrons, even the banana, grew in the beautiful gardens which Baber had planted and irrigated artificially sixteen years before. ‡

* 'Memoirs,' p. 232. † Burnes' 'Kabul,' p. 1.
‡ Baber's 'Memoirs,' p. 291.

At Jellalabad Baber was detained, much against his will, waiting for the remainder of the troops. They were under the command of his son Humayon, who was but eighteen years of age. Humayon's mother was Baber's favourite wife (who she was is not known); he mentions her often, but always under the pet name of 'Maham,' and she had great influence over him. He had not been fortunate in his other matrimonial enterprises; he quarrelled bitterly with his first wife, a cousin of the house of Timour.

His feelings on the subject were strong, as may be seen by the following Persian verses:

> 'A bad wife in a good man's house,
> Even in this world, makes a hell on earth;
> May the Almighty remove such a visitation from every good Moslem.'

Baber was kept waiting eight days for his dilatory son. The king killed the time, drinking in his favourite pleasure-garden at Jellalabad, with congenial spirits.

'In these memoirs,' writes Baber, 'I have already repeatedly described the limits and extent of the Bagh-i-Wufar (the Garden of Fidelity), its beauty and elegance. The garden was in great glory. No one can view it without acknowledging what a charming place it is. During the days that we stayed there, we drank a great quantity of wine at every sitting, and took regularly our morning cup. When I had no drinking parties, I had maajun parties' (the maajun is a medicated confection which produces intoxication). 'In consequence of Humayon's delay beyond the appointed time, I wrote him sharp letters, taking him severely to task, and giving him many hard names.' *

Jellalabad was called Adinapur at that time; it had a fort in which lived the governor of the province of Nauganuhar. The 'Garden of Fidelity' was opposite the fort. Baber took great interest in this garden; on one occasion he writes: 'Next morning I reached Bagh-i-Wufar; it was the season when the garden was in all its glory. Its grass-plots were all covered with clover; its pomegranate-trees were entirely of a beautiful yellow colour. It was the pomegranate season, and they clustered upon the trees. The orange-trees were green and cheerful, loaded with innumerable oranges; but the best oranges were not yet ripe. Its pomegranates were excellent, though not equal to the fine ones of our country; all the people in the camp had pomegranates in abundance.' Baber gave away the fruit of the orange-trees also. 'I stayed till the first watch, and bestowed the oranges on different persons. I gave Shah Hassan the oranges of two trees; to several Beys (lords) I gave one tree, and to several two trees.' This garden Baber had planted himself, and laid out about sixteen years before; it was divided by two roads, which crossed each other. 'It was beautifully situated on an eminence among mountain scenery; there were reservoirs of water

* 'Memoirs,' p. 278.

to irrigate it; and from it, towering to the sky, could be seen the perpetual snows of the "White Mountain," the "Sufed Koh."'

The country of Kabul grows abundance of grapes, which are made into wine; the inhabitants also make a kind of beer from millet. Baber, though in most respects a devout Mussulman, drank to excess; his 'Memoirs' are full of amusing anecdotes of his drinking parties. This is a picture of his private life and friends.

'On one occasion,' he writes, 'after bed-time prayers, we had a drinking-party. Dervesh Muhammed Sârbân was present at these parties. Though young, and a soldier, yet he never indulged in wine. He always rigidly abstained from it. Kutluk Khwajeh Gokultash had for a long time renounced the profession of arms and become a Dervesh. He was very aged, and his beard had become white, but he always joined us at our wine in these jovial drinking-parties. "Does not the hoary beard of Kutluk Khwajeh make you ashamed?" said I to Muhammed Dervesh. "Old as he is, and white as is his beard, he always drinks wine. You, a soldier, with a black beard, never drink! What sense is there in this?" It never was my custom, as I did not think it polite, to press anybody to drink who did not wish, so that this passed as a mere pleasantry, and he was not induced to take wine.' *

In these jovial parties, in the 'Garden of Fidelity' at

* 'Memoirs,' p. 273.

Jellalabad, a week had passed, when at length Prince Humayon and his troops arrived. 'I spoke to him with considerable severity on account of his long delay,' writes Baber. Another division of the army arrived from Ghusni under Khwâjeh Kilân—an able officer.

'The whole forces being now united' (Dec. 3rd), Baber writes, 'we marched, and halted at a new garden, which I had laid out between Sultanpur and Khwajeh Kustrum.'

On Wednesday, December 6th, Baber embarked on a raft or flat-bottomed boat on the river Kabul, his favourite way of travelling. 'Drinking all the way, till we reached Kosh-Gumbez, where I landed and joined the camp.'* The road from Kabul to India, *viâ* the Kheiber Pass, runs for sixteen miles along the Kabul river. From Jellalabad to Peshawur, the river Kabul, though a rapid torrent, can be navigated by the rafts of the country. The rafts are of peculiar construction. 'About eighty skins are used for each raft, but only a fourth part of these are inflated. The rest are stuffed with straw, spars are placed across, and the whole bound together with a floating frame-work. When the paddles are used, the motion of the raft is circular, the great object being to keep it in the force of the stream.'†

These rafts can perform the journey from Jellalabad to the plain of Peshawur in fifteen hours; but, from the difficult nature of the navigation, it is generally necessary

* 'Memoirs,' p. 291. † Sir Alex. Burnes' 'Kabul,' p. 277.

to moor for the night, and this is usually done at the town of Talpoora. Considerable care and dexterity are required to avoid the projecting rocks, and the whirlpools which they form.

On one occasion, about a year before, Baber met with an accident. 'When the raft struck, the shock was so violent, that Kukh-dem, Tengri Kuli, and Mir Muhammed Saleban, three Amirs, were tossed into the river, and were dragged into the raft again with much difficulty. A china cup, with a spoon and cymbal, fell overboard.' Soon after, the raft struck again. 'Shah Hassan Shah Bey went over on his back. While falling, he laid hold of Mirza Kuli Gokultash, and drew him along with him. Dervesh Muhammed Sarban likewise tumbled into the water. The former kept swimming in his gown and dress of honour, till he reached the shore. On disembarking from the raft we passed the night in the raftsmen's house. Dervesh Muhammed Sarban made me a present of a cup of seven colours, like that which had fallen overboard.'* These two nobles followed Baber to India. Mirza Kuli Gokultash was an old and faithful adherent of thirty years. In many a day of disaster and difficulty against the Usbegs, he had stood by Baber; and on one occasion saved his life at the risk of his own. Dervesh Muhammed Sarban was a young man at the time. A new favourite, he had the courage of his opinions, as we have seen, and would not drink. His influence, with that of

* Baber's 'Memoirs,' p. 273.

Sheikh-Zein a year later, and the keen reproaches of his own conscience, made Baber abandon this habit of intoxication, to which he had so completely given himself up, that on his march from Kabul to India he was rarely a day sober.

With open *naïveté*, the king recounts how unpleasantly some of his drinking-parties ended. 'The boat had a level platform above, and I and some others sat upon the top of it,' Baber writes. 'A few others sat below the scaffolding. Towards the stern of the ship, too, there was a place for sitting.' On one occasion Baber and twelve of his principal nobles had a drinking-party in this boat. Some of them became 'mad drunk.' 'Baba Jan, one of the musicians, getting drunk, talked very absurdly. Whatever exertions I could make to preserve peace were all unavailing; there was such an uproar and wrangling. The party became quite burdensome and unpleasant, and soon broke up.'* But to continue the march of the Turks.

'On the 7th December, after putting the troops in motion,' says the diary, 'I again embarked on a raft, and took a maajun' (a medicated confection of opium, which produces intoxication). 'We had always been accustomed to halt at Kerik Arik. On coming over against Kerik Arik, though we looked in every direction, not a trace of the camp nor our horses was visible. It came into my head that as Gurm-Cheshmeh' (the hot springs at

* Baber's 'Memoirs,' p. 259.

the head of the Kheiber Pass) 'was near at hand, and was a shady, sheltered spot, the army had probably halted there. I therefore went on to that place. On coming near Gurm-Cheshmeh, the day was far spent. Without stopping there, I went on all the next night and day, having made them bring the raft to an anchor only while I took a sleep. About the time of early morning prayers, we landed at Yedeh Bir, and at sunrise the troops began to make their appearance. They had been for two days encamped in the territory of Kerik Arik, though we had not observed them.'*

The Turks marched through the Kheiber Pass, unopposed, halting *en route* at Ali Musjid.

* 'Memoirs,' p. 291.

CHAPTER II.

FROM PESHAWUR TO DELHI.

Peshawur—The King of Delhi—The March to Delhi—The Battle of Paniput—Delhi—The fall of Agra—The Koh-i-noor.

BABER arrived at Peshawur, in India, on the 10th of December, having taken three weeks to perform a journey of about two hundred miles, but which he had on other occasions performed in six days. Peshawur was at that time called Bekram, and was an outlying province of Kabul. The Turks had built a fort there. Baber was now in Hindustan, 'the Gurmsil, or country of warm temperature.' Immediately on reaching it, he writes, 'I beheld a new world. The grass was different, the trees different, the wild animals of a different sort, the birds of a different plumage, the manners and customs of the Ils and Uluses (the wandering tribes) of a different kind. I was struck with astonishment, and indeed there was room for wonder.' Whilst at Peshawur, Baber and his courtiers hunted the wild rhinoceros. Peshawur was an ancient Hindoo city. Near it was a celebrated place of Hindoo worship, called Gurh-Katri. Baber, with his usual curiosity, visited it, and thus describes it: 'There are nowhere else in the whole world such narrow and dark hermits' cells as at this place. After entering the doorway and descending one or two stairs, you must lie down, and proceed crawling along, stretched at full length. You cannot enter without a light. The quantities of hair, both of head and beard, that are lying scattered about, and in the vicinity of the place, are immense.'* These excavations are very ancient, and are of Buddhistic origin. The hair lying scattered about was what had been cut off and left by the pilgrims as votive offerings.

Until the Turks should reach the very heart of the Indian Empire at Delhi, they had no very serious opposition to fear. The whole of the Punjaub, now a rich agricultural country watered by five great rivers, was then an almost uninhabited waste, except for a few strongly-defended and walled cities, in which the unwarlike Hindoos could live in some security from their bad neighbours, the highlanders of Kabul. 'The Moghuls of Balkh and Kabul, every year, used to make raids on the Punjaub, and for this reason this country remained depopulated for a long time, and very little agriculture was carried on. Rai Ram Dio Bahti, of Patiyala, rented the whole Punjaub from the Governor of Lahore for nine hundred thousand takas'† (about two thousand pounds of our money).

The two strongest fortresses of the Punjaub, Lahore

* 'Memoirs,' p. 264.

† 'The Ornament of the Assembly,' p. 122.

and Sialkote, were already in the hands of the Turks, and had Turkish garrisons. Baber had taken them some years before in one of his numerous inroads into India.

The king had strengthened his position as much as possible by diplomacy. Many of the discontented nobles of Ibrahim's court had been gained over. Among these were Allaodeen Lodi, and Dowlet Khan Lodi, kinsmen of Sultan Ibrahim. The Rajpoot chief of Udipore had also promised Baber assistance.

'This day' (Dec. 12th), 'when we stayed at Peshawur, I sent for several Beys and noblemen who were about my person, as well as for the paymasters and Diwans; and having nominated six or seven of them as superintendents, appointed them to attend at the Nilab passage to conduct the embarkation, and to take down the name of every man in the army, one by one, and to inspect them. That same night I had a defluxion and fever. The defluxion ended in a cough; every time I coughed, I spat blood. I was considerably alarmed, but, praise be to God! it went off in two or three days.'*

'We made two marches from Bekram, and after the third, on Thursday the 12th, we encamped on the banks of the river Sind, or Indus.

'On Saturday, the first day of the first Kebi (Dec. 16th), we passed the Sind, and having also crossed the river Kechkot halted on its banks. The Beys, paymasters, and Diwans, who had been placed to super-

* 'Memoirs,' p. 293.

intend the embarkation, brought me the return of the troops who were on the service; great and small, good and bad, servants and no servants, they amounted to twelve thousand persons.'

This Turkish force was divided into three commands—one under Baber himself, one under his young son Humayon, and one under his trusted old comrade-in-arms, Khwajeh Kilan. Two of his cousins, one of the race of Tamerlane, Muhammed Sultan Mirza and Chin Timor Sultan, had high commands. Abdal-Aziz was master of the horse. Ustad Ali Kuli, from Khorasan, and Mustafa, the cannoneer, a Turk from Constantinople, commanded the artillery.

The King of India at the time was Sultan Ibrahim Lodi, an Afghan by race from Kohistan. The house of Lodi had been reigning for sixty years—since 1450. Three kings of that name had ruled—Behloh Lodi, Sekander Lodi, and Ibrahim. Ibrahim had inherited his throne from his father and grandfather. 'This prince, contrary to the maxims and policy of his father and grandfather, behaved himself with insupportable pride and arrogance to his friends and family. One foolish expression of his was that kings had no relations, but that everybody should be the slaves of royalty. The Omrahs (nobles, plural of Amir), of the tribe of Lodi, who had always been honoured with a seat in the presence, were now constrained to stand before the throne, with their hands crossed. They were so much disgusted with this insolence, that they privately became his enemies.' By this haughtiness, and by more substantial injuries, Ibrahim Lodi had alienated his brother Alla-odeen, and his kinsman, Dowlet Khan Lodi, who was governor of Lahore. They had been in treasonable negotiation with Baber; but they had broken faith with Baber when he arrived in person in India, as they had done with Ibrahim, their lawful ruler.

Baber continued his advance on Delhi. On the 30th December he reached Perserur; on the 31st, Kilanur, a town between the Kavi and the Biah. From thence he went to a valley called 'Dun,' and took a castle of Dowlet Khan Lodi, in which he found a valuable library. Ten days were expended on this successful expedition; the traitor, Dowlet Khan Lodi, a very old man, fell into the hands of the Turks, and soon afterwards died. From Dûn, they came to the Rupur on the Sutlej, and from thence to Sirhind, a place of great importance. It was a walled town, six miles round, containing a fort, a fine mosque, and fine gardens; on the east side was a large lake. Two marches beyond Sirhind, at Chiter, a small town on the river Kagar, near Thanaser, Baber 'had information that Sultan Ibrahim, who lay on this side Delhi, was advancing, and that the Shekdar of Hissar-Firozeh, Hamid Khan Khasl-Khail, had also advanced ten or fifteen kos towards us, with the army of Hissar-Firozeh and of the neighbouring districts.'*

* 'Memoirs,' p. 301.

On February 25th the Turks reached Umballa. On the 26th Prince Humayon attacked Hamid Khań, the Shekdar of Hissar-Firozeh (Shekdar is a military governor of a district), and took him by surprise. 'Our troops,' writes Baber, 'brought down one hundred or two hundred of the enemy, cut off the heads of the one half, and brought the other half alive into camp, along with seven or eight elephants. Bey Merak Moghul brought the news of this victory of Humayon to the camp at this station on Friday the 18th of the month. I directed a complete dress of honour, a horse from my own stable, with a reward in money, to be given to him.'*

On Monday (March 5th), Humayon reached his father's camp, which was still at the same place, 'with a hundred prisoners and seven or eight elephants, and waited on me. I ordered Ustad Ali Kuli and the matchlock men to shoot all the prisoners as an example. This was Humayon's first expedition, and the first service he had seen. It was a very good omen. Some light troops having followed the fugitives, took Hissar-Firozeh, which, with its dependencies and subordinate districts, yielded a kror' (about £25,000 sterling).

On the 12th of March the Turks reached Shahabad. 'We now began also to receive repeated information from Ibrahim's camp that he was advancing slowly, a kos or two at a time, and halting two or three days at each encampment. I, on my side, likewise moved on to meet

* 'Memoirs,' p. 302.

him; and, after the second march from Shahabad, encamped on the banks of the Jumna, opposite to Siraweh.' The invaders crossed the Jumna by a ford. Baber used to sail on the river in a boat.

Now Baber was reaching the crisis of his fate; either he would find a grave in a foreign land, or come out of the impending conflict victorious. On the 12th of April the Turks arrived within two marches of the city of Paniput, which lies about fifty miles from Delhi. 'At this station,' writes Baber, 'I directed that, according to the fashion of Rum' (that is, of the Ottoman Turks), 'the gun-carriages should be connected together with twisted bulls' hides, as with chains. Between every two gun-carriages were six or seven tûras of breastworks.' (These tûras were branches of trees, interwoven like basket-work, it is supposed.) 'The matchlock-men stood behind these guns and tûras, and discharged their matchlocks. I halted five or six days in this camp, for the purpose of getting the apparatus arranged. After every part of it was in order and ready, I called together all the Amirs and men of any experience and knowledge, and held a general council. It was settled that, as Paniput was a considerable city, it would cover one of our flanks by its buildings and houses, while we might fortify our front by tûras, or covered defences, and cannon; and that the matchlock-men and infantry would be placed in the rear of the guns and tûras.'* This council was held

* 'Memoirs,' p. 304.

at two days' march from Paniput. The Turks moved forward two marches on the 12th of April, and reached that city. 'On our right were the town and suburbs. In my front I placed the guns and tûras which had been prepared. On the left, and on different other points, we dug ditches, and made defences of the boughs of trees. At bowshot-distance spaces were left large enough for a hundred or a hundred and fifty men to issue forth. Many of the troops were in great terror and alarm ; trepidation and fear are always unbecoming. Whatever God Almighty has decreed from all eternity cannot be reversed ; though, at the same time, I cannot greatly blame them. They had some reason ; for they had come two or three months' journey from their own country ; we had to engage in arms a strange nation, whose language we did not understand, and who did not understand ours' (Persian). 'We are all in difficulty, all in distraction, surrounded by a people, by a strange people. The army of the enemy opposed to us was estimated at one hundred thousand men ; the elephants of the emperor and his officers were said to amount to nearly one thousand. Ibrahim Lodi possessed the accumulated treasures of his father and his grandfather in current coin, ready for use. It is a usage in Hindustan, in situations similar to that in which the enemy now were, to expend sums of money in bringing together troops, who engage to serve for hire. These men are called Bedhindi. Had he chosen to adopt this course, he might have engaged one or two hundred thousand more troops. But God Almighty directed everything for the best. Ibrahim Lodi had not the heart to satisfy even his own army, and would not part with any of his own treasure. Indeed, how was it possible that he should satisfy his troops, when he was miserly to the last degree, and beyond measure avaricious! He was a young man of no experience; he was negligent in all his movements. He marched without order, retired or halted without plan, and engaged in battle without forethought. While the troops were fortifying their position in Paniput and its vicinity with guns, branches of trees, and ditches, Dervesh Muhammed Sarban' (this, it may be remembered, was the young soldier who would not drink) 'said to me, "You have fortified our ground in such a way that it is not possible he should ever think of coming here." I answered, "You judge of him by the Khans and Sultans of the Usbegs. It is true that, the year in which we left Samarkand and came to Hissar, a body of the Usbeg Khans and Sultans, having collected and united together, set out from Derbend"' (a celebrated hill pass), '"in order to fall upon us. I brought the families and property of all the Moghuls and soldiers into the town and suburbs, and, closing all the streets, put them in a defensible state. As these Khans and Sultans of the Usbegs were perfectly versed in the proper time and season for attacking and retiring, they perceived that we were resolved to defend Hissar to the last drop of our blood, and had fortified it under that idea; and, seeing no hopes of succeeding in their enterprise, they fell back by Bundah Cheghâniân. But you must not judge of our present enemies by those who were then opposed to us. They have not ability to discriminate when it is proper to advance, and when to retreat." God brought everything to pass favourably. It happened as I foretold.'*

For the next seven or eight days, Ibrahim Lodì allowed Baber to remain unmolested at Paniput, and to strengthen his position there. Several minor attacks were made by the invaders; and in one of these, Muhammed Ali Jeng-Jeng, one of Baber's favourite officers, was wounded by an arrow, but not mortally.

In the course of the night of the 20th of April, 'We had a false alarm for nearly one geri (twenty-four minutes); the call to arms, and the uproar continued. Such of the troops as had never before witnessed an alarm of the kind were in great confusion and dismay.'†

In a short time, however, the alarm subsided. On the morning of the 21st of April, the battle was fought that gave India foreign masters for many centuries, and a form of government that it still retains.

'By the time of early morning prayers, when the light was such that you could just distinguish one object from another, notice was brought from the patrols that the enemy were advancing, drawn up in order of battle. We, too, immediately braced on our helmets and our armour, and mounted.'

* 'Memoirs,' pp. 304, 305.

† 'Memoirs,' p. 305.

Baber records the names of the officers who commanded at Paniput, to the number of forty-three. On this, as on all occasions, he records the services he received from the men about him with generous appreciation.

The right division was led by Prince Humayon, accompanied by Khwajeh Kilan (the follower who had attended Baber's fortunes for so many years). In this division also were Sultan Muhammed Duldai, Baber's cousin, from the great city of Herat and Hindu Bey, a man of local experience ; he had for many years served in Northern India as Turkish governor of Lahore. The left division was commanded by Muhammed Sultan Mirza, a prince of the house of Timour, Baber's cousin, with instructions that, as soon as the enemy approached sufficiently near, it should take a circuit and come round upon their rear, a favourite tactics with the Usbegs.

'When the enemy first came in sight, they seemed to bend their force most against the right division. I therefore detached Abdul-Aziz, who was stationed with the reserve, to reinforce the right. Sultan Ibrahim's army, from the time it first appeared in sight, never made a halt, but advanced right upon us at a quick pace. When they came closer, and, on getting view of my troops, found them drawn up in order and with the defences that have been mentioned, they were brought up and stood for a while, as if considering whether to halt or advance. They could not halt, and they were unable to advance with the same speed as before. I sent orders to the troops stationed as flankers on the extremes of the right and left divisions, to wheel round the enemy's flank with all possible speed, and instantly to attack them in rear; the right and left divisions were also ordered to charge the enemy.'* The Moghul flankers accordingly wheeled upon the rear of the enemy, and began to discharge arrows at them. Mehdi Khwajeh (Baber's son-in-law), who commanded them, was in danger of being taken 'by a body of men with one elephant. Ustadi Ali Kuli discharged his guns many times in front of the line to good effect; Mustafa, the cannoneer on the left centre, managed his artillery with great effect.'† The calibre of this artillery is doubtful. Baber mentions elsewhere cannon that took five hundred men to draw; and of a gun, cast by Ustal Ali Kuli, which carried sixteen hundred paces. The battle continued for two or three hours, 'the enemy made several poor charges,' 'they were huddled together in confusion, and, while totally unable to advance, found also no road by which they could flee.'

'The sun had mounted spear-high when the onset began, and the combat lasted until midday, when the enemy were completely broken and routed, and my friends victorious and exulting. By the grace and mercy of Almighty God, this arduous undertaking was ren-

* 'Memoirs,' p. 306. † Ibid. p. 307.

dered easy for me, and this mighty army, in the space of half a day, laid in the dust.' Sultan Ibrahim was found lying dead, on a spot where five or six thousand men were slain; his head was brought to Baber, more than one Rajpoot Rajah was killed. Many elephants and Pathan Amirs were also taken. The same night, without a minute's delay, Prince Humayon and Khwajeh Kilan, with three or four other nobles, and some troops, were despatched to take the Fort of Agra, seventy miles away, the place where Ibrahim Lodi generally lived; while Baber himself marched for the great city of Delhi.

Delhi for three thousand years had been a great city; it was contemporaneous with Nineveh and Babylon. The city of Delhi of that day was called Firosabad; it was six miles round. On the rocky hill, which extends on one side of the city, was a citadel, built by King Feroze a hundred years before the Turkish invasion. At the Bagdad gate was a large brass bull, taken from the Hindoos by Ibrahim's father. On another side of the city was King Feroze's other palace, in which stood another trophy of war, a large monolith of stone, surmounted by the Moslem emblem of the Crescent, shining in brass; on it were inscriptions in the Pali tongue, which recalled a long-forgotten king, Asoka, the King Alfred of Hindoo history. He was a Buddhist, who impressed on his people kindness to kindred, the preservation of animal life to the extent of not killing them even for food, courtesy and gentleness to all men, which remained characteristics of the Hindoos, ages after King Asoka and his gentle Buddhist creed were forgotten by them.

Many mosques were in the city; one, the 'Black Mosque,' is still standing, grim and dark. A smaller mosque, which also still exists, a hundred years before had so much struck Baber's great ancestor, Tamerlane, that he took the workmen away to Samarcand to erect one like it in that city.

Baber expresses no surprise at the strength, splendour, and extent of the mausoleums, palaces, and gardens that strike Europeans of the present day with wonder and surprise. The cities of Samarcand and Herat, which he describes in his diary, must have exceeded even Delhi in splendour.

One of the features of the architecture of the time was that the buildings were decorated and ornamented with encaustic tiles of the most beautiful shades of light and dark blue, on which were drawn beautiful and most artistic designs. In Persia and Samarcand, mosques of the same period were also decorated with these blue encaustic tiles.

The forty miles covered with remains of palaces, mosques, gardens, mausoleums, caravansaries, wells, bridges, around Delhi are the most wonderful and beautiful ruins in the world. Such is the opinion of Fergusson, the great writer on architecture. Bishop Heber said of the Mohammedan builders in India, that 'they built like giants, and finished like jewellers.' This tersely describes the extraordinary strength of the masses of wrought stone and their delicate finish, a strength that has withstood five centuries of neglect. These Saracenic builders used no wood in their buildings; their cement is as hard as iron, and this is the reason of its stability. Their delicate carving was learnt from the Hindoos, who executed the Saracenic designs. The Moslem creed admits of no representation of human life. By the more rigid Moslems, even pictures of butterflies and flowers are considered idolatrous. The Hindoos, like the Greeks, of whom they were the forefathers, idealised nature.

Baber entered Delhi, the capital of India, by the south; it took him two days to march from the field of Paniput. He went over an ancient bridge, which still stands, and passed by the handsome mausoleum of Secunder Lodi, and visited the sights of the place, as so many conquerors have done since. He wandered to the Kootub, that strange, tall, unrivalled pillar, which was raised to call the faithful to prayer in the splendid mosque, open to the blue heavens, below; a mosque built of carved stones, from the ruined fanes of the Hindoo idols. He visited the palace of Alla-o-deen (an early Pathan king), an unrivalled work of art, now in ruins, all except one gateway. It is one of the best representations of the form and design of the Moslem conquerors, with the wonderful carving of the patient and industrious Hindoo.

Baber also saw a grave which to this day is kept up and visited: the grave of Nizam Ed-din Aulia. This man was supposed to be the founder of the Thugs, possibly to have been connected with the Old Man of the Mountain, the head of the assassins. The palace of Nizam Ed-din still stands in ruins, massively built, without arches, near the spot where he lies. Near the grave of the author of so many political murders, stands the grave of the poet Khousroo, whose songs are still heard in the mouths of the peasantry of India.

Baber also visited the palace of his vanquished foe, built round a lake, and his gardens, the ruins of which still remain. But the house of Lodi, during their tenure of power for sixty years, had mostly lived at Agra; and to Agra, leaving the capital of India, Baber hastened. His last day at Delhi was spent in his usual manner, in a boat on the river Jumna, where he drank 'arak' with his friends.

Baber was justly proud of his great victory, and writes of it thus:

'The most high God, of His grace and mercy, cast down and defeated an enemy so mighty as Sultan Ibrahim, and made me master and conqueror of the powerful empire of Hindustan. From the time of the blessed Prophet (on whom, and on his family, be peace and salvation!) down to the present time, three foreign kings had subdued the country and acquired the sovereignty of Hindustan. One of these was Sultan Mahmud Ghazi, whose family long continued to fill the throne of that country. The second was Sultan Shehabeddin Ghuri; and for many years his slaves and dependents swayed the sceptre of these realms. I am the third; but my achievement is not to be put on a level with theirs; for Sultan Mahmud, at the time when he conquered Hindustan, occupied the throne of Khorasan, and had absolute power and dominion over the Sultans of Khwarizm, and the surrounding chiefs. The King of Samarcand, too, was subject to him. If his army did not amount to two hundred thousand, yet, grant that it was only one hundred thousand, and it is plain that the comparison between the two conquests must cease. Moreover, his enemies were Rajahs. All Hindustan was not at that period subject to a single emperor; every Rajah set up for a monarch on his own account in his own petty territories. Again, though Sultan Shehabeddin Ghuri did not himself enjoy the sovereignty of Khorasan, yet his elder brother, Sultan Ghiaseddin Ghuri held it. In the Tabakat-e-Nasiri (a very good history of the Mussulman world) it is said that on one occasion he marched into Hindustan with one hundred and twenty thousand Cataphract horse. His enemies, too, were Rais and Rajahs. A single monarch did not govern the whole of Hindustan. When I marched into Behreh, we might amount to one thousand five hundred, or two thousand men at the utmost. When I invaded the country for the fifth time, overthrew Sultan Ibrahim, and subdued the empire of Hindustan, I had a larger army than I had ever before brought into it. My servants, the merchants and their servants, and the followers of all descriptions that were in the camp along with me, were numbered, and amounted to twelve thousand men. The kingdoms that depended upon me were Badakhshan, Kundez, Kabul, and Kandahar; but these countries did not furnish me with assistance equal to their resources, and indeed some of them, from their vicinity to the enemy, were so circumstanced that, far from affording me assistance, I was obliged to send them extensive supplies from other territories. Besides this, all Mawer-alnaher' (Baber's native country, Transoxiana) 'was occupied by the Khans and Sultans of the Usbegs, whose armies were calculated to amount to about one hundred thousand men, and who were my ancient foes. Finally, the whole empire of Hindustan, and Behrer to Behar, was in the hands of the Afghans. Their prince, Sultan Ibrahim, from the resources of his kingdom, could bring into the field an army of five hundred thousand men. At the time some of the Amirs to the east were in a state of rebellion. His army on foot was computed to be a hundred thousand strong; his own elephants, and those of his Amirs, were reckoned as nearly a thousand. Yet, under such circumstances, and in spite of this power, placing my trust in God, and leaving behind me my old and inveterate enemy, the Usbegs, who had an army of a hundred thousand men, I advanced to meet so powerful a prince as Sultan Ibrahim, the lord of numerous armies, and the emperor of extensive territories. · I bestowed the office of Shekdar' (military collector) 'of Delhi on Wali Kazil.' (He was the officer who commanded the flanking party of Moghuls at Paniput. The Shekdar was an officer, who received the revenue, and also commanded the troops.) 'I made Dost the Diwan of Delhi, and directed the different treasures to be sealed and given into their charge.'*

On the 26th, six days after his great victory, Baber started on his march to Agra, sixty miles away, and passed by Toghlakabad. There is there a very strong fortress, and the splendid mausoleum of the Afghan ruler who reigned in the year 1412.

Moulana Mahmud and Sheikh Zin, two priests, went from Toghlakabad into Delhi for Friday prayers, and read the Kutbeh in Baber's name, distributed some money among the Fakirs and beggars, and then returned back. The reading the Kutbeh (the king's titles and genealogy) is a religious service usual on a new king coming to the throne.

On the 4th of May Baber reached the outskirts of Agra, and went to the palace of Suliman Fermuli, a Pathan noble of Ibrahim's court. The next day he went to the palace of Jilâl Khan Jighat, another Indian Bey, nearer the fort. Baber found that the strong fort of Agra was in the possession of the Hindoo troops of Bikermajit, Rajah of Gwalior, 'his family and clan.'

* 'Memoirs,' pp. 308, 309.

Bikermajit himself had been 'sent to hell' (the charitable mode in which a good Mussulman signifies the death of an infidel), fighting at the side of Ibrahim at the fatal field of Paniput. Baber states that, 'When Humayon arrived, Bikermajit's people attempted to escape, but were taken by parties Humayon had placed upon the watch, and put into custody. Humayon did not allow them to be plundered. Of their own free-will, they presented to Humayon a peshkesh' (tribute), 'consisting of a quantity of jewels and precious stones. Among these was one famous diamond which had been acquired by Sultan Alaeddin. It is so valuable that a judge of diamonds valued it at half the daily expense of the whole world. It is about eight miskals' (672 carats). 'On my arrrival, Humayon presented it to me as a peshkesh, and I gave it back to him as a present.'*

This stone is the Koh-i-noor, now in the possession of her Majesty. It remained in Baber's family for two hundred years, when, in 1739, it was taken by Nadir Shah. The English took it from Runjeet Singh's family, 1848; when the British army presented it to her Majesty. The Indians have a superstition that the owner of it is unfortunate.

* 'Memoirs,' p. 308.

CHAPTER III.

THE TURKS AS RULERS OF INDIA.

The Treasurer of Ibrahim—The discontent of the Turks—Baber poisoned—The Battle of Sikri—Turkish Victory—The Rajpoots.

The day after his arrival in the fort of Agra, May 11th, Baber began to examine and distribute the treasure of Sultan Ibrahim. He was living in Sultan Ibrahim's palace. 'I gave Humayon seventy lacks (£700,000), and over and above this treasure a palace, of which no account or inventory had been taken. To some Amirs I gave ten lacks (£100,000), to others eight lacks, seven lacks, and six lacks. On the Afghans, Arabs, Baluches, and others that were in the army, I bestowed gratuities from the treasury suited to their rank and circumstances. Every merchant, every man of letters—in a word, every person who had come in the army along with us, carried off presents and gratuities which marked their great good fortune and superior luck. Many who were not in the army also received ample presents from these treasures; as, for instance, Kamran (Baber's brother in Kabul) received seventeen lacks; Muhammed Zeman Mirza (a cousin, son of the Sultan of Khorasan), fifteen lacks; Askeri, Mirza, and Hindal (sons of Baber in Kabul); in a word, all my relations and friends, great and small, had presents sent to them in silver and gold, in cloth and jewels and captive slaves. Many presents were also sent for the Beys in our old territories and their old soldiers. I sent presents for my relations, and friends to Samarcand, Khorasan, Kashgar, and Irak. Offerings were sent to the Sheikhs (or holy men) in Khorasan and Samarcand, as likewise to Mekka and Medina. To the country of Kabul, as an incentive to emulation, to every soul, man or woman, slave or free, of age or not, I sent one shahrokhi (the value tenpence or elevenpence) as a gift.'*

Væ victis! While these rejoicings were going on among the captors, the adherents of hapless Sultan Ibrahim suffered from the Turkish conquerors. Baber continues: 'Among the officers of superior importance in the fort were Malek Dad Karani, Mulli Surdek and Firiz Khan Miswani (Afghan), who, having been convicted of some frauds concerning the treasure, were ordered for punishment.'† This was the inhuman punishment of the bastinado, still common in Turkey and Persia, and wherever the Moslem creed is paramount. The bastinado consists of inflicting a number of blows on the bare feet, by which the recipient is often crippled, or even killed outright. Among the Turks, under Baber's family, this punishment was

* 'Memoirs,' pp. 304. † Ibid., p. 308.

traditional; Tamerlane even had it inflicted on his sons. Tamerlane also was guilty of the inhumanity of impaling people; this last-mentioned barbarity also was until lately a legal punishment in Turkish lands. Baber was even guilty of the great barbarity of flaying men alive. 'When Malek Dad Karani was carried out to be bastinadoed, much intercession was made for him; the matter was not settled for four or five days, when, according to the desire of his intercessors, I pardoned him, and even conferred on him some marks of favour. I also permitted all his adherents to retain their property.'*

Ibrahim's mother was conducted with all her effects to a palace, which was assigned for her residence, about a kos (two miles) below Agra. Landed property was given her to the amount of seven lacks (£70,000) a year. Firishta says she became the greatest favourite of Baber's seraglio. She was a Hindu princess probably, and a clever woman. Her son, Sultan Ibrahim, the late ruler, had not been Sikunder Lodi's eldest son, but, through his mother's influence, he had been declared by Sikunder Lodi heir to the throne. In Mohammedan countries the king on his death-bed wills away the throne, and primogeniture is not always regarded.

Baber gave away all the contents of the treasury. He reserved not a single dinar for himself. 'This generosity, which bordered upon prodigality, fixed upon

* 'Memoirs,' p. 308.

him the name of "Collindar," whose custom it is to keep nothing for to-morrow,' writes Ferishta.* The following year Baber was in want of money, and raised the taxes thirty per cent.

It was now the middle of May. Agra is an intolerably hot place. The rays of the sun are terrible, the wind blows in fierce blasts like the breath of a furnace; the city is full of glare, heat and dust. When the hot weather sets in, the inhabitants shut themselves up in underground cellars, and never move out of their houses until the sun has set; even indoors the thermometer rises to 106 degrees in the shade. Sunstrokes are very common, and many of Baber's men suffered from them, as they incautiously exposed themselves, not knowing the danger. Baber himself did not feel the heat of India to the same extent as his followers. He maintained that the heat was as nothing compared to that of Ballik and Candahar. 'It happened too,' he adds, 'that the heats were this year uncommonly oppressive. Many men about the same time dropped down, as if they had been affected by the Simûm wind, and died on the spot.'

'On these accounts not a few of my Beys and best men began to lose heart, and to object to remaining in Hindustan. Some even began to make preparations for their return. If the older Beys, who were men of experience, had made these representations, there would have been no

* Dow's translation, vol. ii. p. 124.

harm in it; for if such men had communicated their sentiments to me, I might have got credit for possessing at least so much sense and judgment as, after hearing what they had to urge, to be qualified to decide on the expediency or inexpediency of their opinions, to distinguish good from evil. But what sense or propriety was there in eternally repeating the same tale in different words, to one who himself saw the facts with his own eyes, and had formed a cool and fixed resolution in regard to the business in which he was engaged? What propriety was there in the whole army, down to the very dregs, giving their stupid and unformed opinion? It is singular that when I set out from Kabul this last time I had raised many of low rank to the dignity of Bey, in the expectation that if I had chosen to go through fire and water they would have followed me, back and forward, without hesitation, and that they would have accompanied me cheerfully, march where I would. It never entered my imagination that they would be the persons to arraign my measures, nor that, before rising from the council, they should show a determined opposition to every measure, and plan, and opinion which I proposed and supported in the council and assembly. Though they behaved ill, yet Ahmedi Perwanchi (secretary) and Wali Zazin (the Moghul) behaved still worse. From the time we left Kabul till we had defeated Ibrahim and taken Agra, Khwajeh Kilan had behaved admirably, and had always spoken gallantly, and given such opinions as befitted a brave man; but a few days after the taking of Agra all his opinions underwent a complete change. Khwajeh Kilan was now, of all others, the most determined on turning back. I no sooner heard this murmuring among my troops than I summoned all my Beys to a council. I told them that empire and conquest could not be acquired without the materials and means of war; that royalty and nobility could not exist without subject and dependent provinces; that by the labours of many years, after undergoing great hardships, and measuring many a toilsome journey, and raising various armies, after exposing myself and my troops to circumstances of great danger, to battle and bloodshed, by the Divine favour I had routed my formidable enemy, and achieved the conquest of the numerous provinces and kingdoms which we at present held; "and now what force compels me, and what hardships oblige us, without any visible cause, after having worn out our life in accomplishing the desired achievement, to abandon, and fly from, our conquests, and to retreat back to Kabul, with every symptom of disappointment and discomfiture? Let not any one who calls himself my friend ever henceforward make such a proposal. But if there is any among you who cannot bring himself to stay, or to give up his purpose of returning back, let him depart." Having made them this fair and reasonable proposal, the discontented were of necessity compelled, however unwillingly, to renounce their seditious purposes. Khwajeh Kilan not being disposed to remain, it was arranged that as he had a numerous retinue he should return to guard the presents. I had but a few troops in Kabul and Ghuzni, and he was directed to see that these places were all kept in proper order and amply supplied with the necessary stores. I bestowed on him Ghuzni, Gerdez, and the Sultan Masaudi Hazaras. I also gave him the Perganna of Kehram in Hindustan, yielding a revenue of about £800 or £1,000 sterling. Khwajeh Mir Miran was likewise directed to proceed to Kabul. The presents were entrusted to his charge, and put into the immediate custody of Mulla Hassan Siraf and Noukeh Hindu. Khwajeh Kilan, who was heartily tired of Hindustan, at the time of going wrote the following lines, in Turki, on the walls of some houses in Delhi :

'"If I pass the Sind safe and sound,
May shame take me, if I ever again wish for Hind."

'When I still continued in Hindustan, there was an evident impropriety in his composing and publishing such vituperative verses. If I had previously cause to be offended at his leaving me, this conduct of his doubled the offence. I had composed a few extempore lines in Turki, which I wrote down and sent him.

'"Return a thousand thanks, O Baber! for the bounty of the merciful God
Has given you Sind, Hind, and numerous kingdoms.

If unable to stand heat, you long for cold :
You have only to recollect the frost, and cold of Ghuzni."'

There were not only the intolerable climate, the disgust and insubordination of the soldiery, but other dangers to be faced, which Baber thus recounts :

'When I came to Agra, it was the hot season. All the inhabitants fled from terror, so that we could not find grain nor provender, either for ourselves or our horses. The villages, out of hostility and hatred to us, had taken to rebellion, thieving, and robbery. The roads became impassable. I had not time, after the division of the treasure, to send proper persons to occupy and protect the different Pergannas and stations' (counties and towns). 'There was a strong mutual dislike and hostility between my people and the men of the place. The peasantry and soldiers of the country avoided and fled from my men. Afterwards, everywhere, except only in Delhi and Agra' (which had been taken, as we have seen, by coup-de-main), 'the inhabitants fortified different posts, while the governors of towns put their fortifications in a posture of defence, and refused to submit or obey.'* Many of the Indo-Afghan nobles had, from their two hundred years' residence in India, become half Hindoo. They had intermarried with the Hindoo princes; some of those who passed for Afghans were completely Hindoos by race, renegades either from

* 'Memoirs,' pp. 335—337.

necessity or in a few cases from conviction. All the cities within a radius of two hundred miles around Baber, under their Afghan-Hindoo leaders, prepared to stand a siege; and to the last opposed the Turkish invaders. The Pathan nobles who refused to submit or to obey Baber were Kasim Sambali, in Sambal, Nizam Khan in Biana. Biana was a strong castle in the hilly country of Miwat, and but thirty or forty miles from Agra. 'The Rajah Hassan Khan Miwat in Miwat, that infidel, was the prime mover and agitator in all these confusions and insurrections,' writes Baber. 'Muhammed Zeitun was in Dhalpoor, Tatar Khan Sarangkhani (Lord of Sarang) was in Gwalior, Hussain Khan Lohani in Raberi, Kutab Khan in Etawa, and in Kalpi Ali Khan. Kanauj (Oude), and the whole country beyond the Ganges, was entirely in possession of the refractory Afghans, such as Nasir Khan Lohani, Maaruf Fermuli, and a number of other Amirs, who had been in a state of open rebellion for two years before the death of Ibrahim. At the period when I defeated that prince, they had overrun and were in possession of Kanauj and the countries in that quarter, and had advanced and encamped two or three marches on this side of that city.'

Baber's position at Agra was one of extreme danger and difficulty; his army was on the verge of mutiny. His intimate friends, his most trusty advisers and officers, had turned against him; provisions were short, the tropical heat simply unendurable to those hardy mountaineers, who were dying from sunstroke and sickness. The enemy were in walled towns and strong castles all around Agra. But the greatest danger of all was, that the Hindoo nations of Rajpootana were rising to drive away the Turkish invaders. Amid these dangers, it is hardly to be wondered at that Baber's army and Baber's officers longed to leave India, and enjoy the fruits of the pillage of Agra and Delhi in their cool and beautiful mountain homes in Kabul. But no entreaties, no persuasion, no threatening dangers could make their leader abandon the splendid kingdom he had so nearly gained. Baber stayed in Agra; he built palaces and made watercourses, and laid out gardens. So did Khalifeh the vizier, Sheikh Zin, and Yunis Ali. So many costly buildings were reared, that one side of the river Jumna was called Kabul by the inhabitants of the country. Strange fate of India! It is held, but never loved by its foreign conquerors. Baber did not at heart like the country more than his followers, or than many of its present English rulers. He remained at Agra, however, virtually unmolested for ten months. 'Shortly after coming to Agra, I passed the Jumna with this object in view, and examined the country, to pitch upon a fit spot for a garden. The whole was so ugly and detestable, that I repassed the river quite repulsed and disgusted. In consequence of the want of beauty, and of the disagreeable aspect of the country, I gave up my intention of making a charbagh (a pleasure-garden); but as no better situation presented itself near Agra, I was finally compelled to make the best of this same spot. In time, going on without neatness and without order, in the Hindoo fashion, I produced edifices and gardens which possessed considerable regularity; in every garden I sowed roses and narcissuses regularly, and in beds corresponding with each other. We are annoyed with three things in Hindustan—one is heat; another, strong wind; and the third, dust. Baths and running water are the means of removing all three inconveniences.'*

'Hindustan is a country that has few pleasures to recommend it.' Baber's opinions are nearly the same as those of most English officials at the present day. He says, 'The people are not handsome. They have no idea of the charms of friendly society, of frankly mixing together, or of familiar intercourse.' (This arises from the prejudices of caste, the iron rule by which only people of the same tribe may eat or drink together, or intermarry.) 'They have no genius, no comprehension of mind, no politeness of manner, no kindness or fellow-feeling, no ingenuity or mechanical invention in architecture; they have no good horses, no good flesh, no grapes or musk-melons, no good fruits, no ice, no cold water, no good food or bread in their bazaars, no baths or colleges, no candles or torches; a gang of dirty fellows whom they call Dentis carry a kind of torch. These

* 'Memoirs,' p. 341.

filthy Dentis bring in their torches, which they carry up to their master, and then stand holding them close by his side. The chief excellence of Hindustan is that it is a large country, and has abundance of gold and silver. Another convenience of Hindustan is that the workmen of every profession and trade are innumerable; for any work there is always a set ready, to whom the same employment and trade have descended from father to son.'* Baber mentions that he employed daily two thousand stonecutters.

Besides building palaces and making gardens, the king devoted these nine months of peace to a study of the birds, fish, and animals of India: on all of which subjects he gives a clear and interesting account in his 'Memoirs;' and also of the fruits and of the flowers, of the manners and habits of the people, and of the ruling families. No better description of India is to be found than that given by this soldier of fortune.

During the month of December, 1526, Baber's life was attempted by poison. Towards the end of November, Prince Tahmasp of Persia sent an embassy and 'several curiosities of the country as presents, among these two Circassian female slaves.' Of one of these Baber became enamoured. Ibrahim's mother, who until then had been first favourite, became jealous, and attempted to poison Baber. This is the reason given by Ferishta, Baber himself is silent as to the lady's motive. The cook,

* 'Memoirs,' p. 333.

at the instigation of Ibrahim's mother, put some poison into a stew of hare and carrots. Baber ate some of the stew, and was ill; the remainder was given to a dog, who died after eating it. As a precaution against poison, it was the custom to have all the dishes tested by a 'taster' before they were placed before the king. Ibrahim's mother was tried and convicted. Baber gives this account of the trial:

'On Monday, being a court day, I directed all the grandees and chief men, the Beys and Viziers, to attend Diwan (council). I brought the two men and the two women, who being questioned, detailed the whole circumstances of the affair in all its particulars. The taster was ordered to be cut to pieces. I commanded the cook to be flayed alive. One of the women was ordered to be trampled to death by an elephant, the other I commanded to be shot with a matchlock. The lady I directed to be thrown into custody. She, too, pursued by her guilt, will one day meet with due retribution.'* He writes to Kabul, after recovering from the effects of the poison: 'Thanks be to God! there is now no remains of illness. I did not fully comprehend before that life was so sweet a thing. The poet says:

'"Whosoever comes to the gate of death, knows the value of life."

'Whenever these awful occurrences pass before my

* 'Memoirs,' p. 349.

memory, I feel myself involuntarily turn faint. The mercy of God has bestowed a new life upon me, and how can my tongue express my gratitude? Having resolved with myself to overcome my repugnance, I have written fully and circumstantially everything that happened. Although the occurrences were awful, and not to be expressed by the tongue or lips, yet by the favour of Almighty God other days awaited me—they have been passed in happiness and health. That no alarm or uneasiness might find its way among you, I have written this on the twentieth of the first Kabia, while in the charbagh (Dec. 25th, 1526). As the ill-fated lady had been guilty of so enormous a crime, I gave her up to Yunis Ali and Khwajeh Asad, to be put under contribution. After seizing her ready money and effects, her male and female slaves, she was given to Abderrahim's charge to be kept in custody. Her grandson, the son of Ibrahim, had previously been guarded with the greatest respect and delicacy. When an attempt of so heinous a nature was discovered to have been made by the family, I did not think it prudent to have a son of Ibrahim's in this country. He was sent to Kabul. The cooks who had mixed the poison, and the taster who had been negligent, were brought to trial.'*

A month after this attempt, Baber's position in India became most critical. The threatened attack on Agra by the Rajpoots, the Hindi-Pathan Amirs, took place,

* 'Memoirs,' p. 348.

and all the Rajpoot chiefs from Rajpootana joined the Pathans. The Rajpoots were under the Rajah of Udipore, Rana Sanka the Pagan, as Baber always calls him. The house of Udipur (still existing, independent and powerful) claims a pedigree of two thousand years. The Rajpoots were kings of India at the time of Alexander the Great's invasion. Living in a mountainous country, they maintained, and still maintain even under the English, a semi-independence. Rana Sanka had overthrown the once powerful kingdom of the Afghan Moslems at Mando; where ruined mosques and beautiful palaces still show the taste, wealth, and splendour of the Pathans. Having paled the splendour of the crescent there, the Rajah of Udipore hoped to rid his country of the Turkish invaders altogether.

During the nine months that Baber had spent in India, some few Pathan nobles had joined him, but not many. 'On Monday (February 11th) I began my march to the holy war against the heathen,' Baber writes. 'Having passed the suburbs of Agra, I encamped on the plain, where I halted three or four days, to collect the army and communicate the necessary instructions. As I did not place great reliance on the men of Hindustan, I employed their Amirs in making desultory excursions in different directions.'* Information arrived that Rana Sanka, the head of the great house of Mewar, had reached Biana, about fifty miles from Agra. There he

* 'Memoirs,' p. 351.

had met a detachment of Turkish troops; several of Baber's officers had been killed by the Rajpoots, and those that returned were panic-struck. 'Kismi-Shah Mausur Birlâs, and every man that came from Biana, I know not whether from fear or for the purpose of striking a panic into the people, bestowed unbounded praise on the courage and hardihood of the Pagan army.' In another skirmish, Abdal-aziz lost a number of men, and the Rajpoots took his horse-tail standard; three more officers of importance fell. 'In consequence of the bold and unexpected advance of the Pagans, joined to the result of the engagement that had taken place at Biana, aided by the praises and encomiums passed on them by Shah Mausur Kismi, and those who came from Biana, there was an evident alarm diffused among the troops; and the defeat of Abdal-aziz completed the panic.'* At this time the Turks fortunately were reinforced by a party of five hundred men from Kabul, mostly fighting men; among them was Kazim Hussain Sultan, grandson of Hussain Mirza of Herat, and also, writes Baber, 'Muhammed Sherif the astrologer, a rascally fellow. Whilst the army was yet in the state of alarm and panic that has been mentioned, in consequence of past events and of ill-timed and idle observations that had been spread abroad, that evil-minded wretch, Muhammed Sherif, instead of giving me assistance, loudly proclaimed to every person whom he met in camp that at this time

* 'Memoirs,' p. 351.

Mars was in the west, and that whosoever should engage coming from the opposite quarter would be defeated. The courage of such as consulted this villainous soothsayer was consequently still further depressed. Without listening to his foolish predictions, I proceeded to take such steps as the emergency seemed to demand, and used every exertion to put my troops in a fit state to engage the enemy.'*

The small body of Turks had good cause for panic. A large army of Rajpoots were marching on them. To use the words of Zein the priest:

'And at this time many heathen of eminence, who never before in any war had assisted him (Rana Sanka), actuated by hatred to the armies of the faith, increased his villainous array, so that ten independent princes, as, for instance, Silah-ed-din (Pathan) possessed thirty thousand horse; Raul Udi Sing Nagari, ten thousand horse; Medini Rai (Hindoo), ten thousand horse; Hassan Khan Mewati (Pathan), (who had ruled in Miwat two hundred years, a great antagonist of Baber's); Barmul Idri (Hindoo), four thousand horse; Nirput Hada, seven thousand; Sittervi Kichi, six thousand; Dherm Deo, four thousand; Nirsing Deo, four thousand; Mahmud Khan Lodi, uncle of Ibrahim, who, though he possessed no country nor perganna, yet he had gathered about him ten thousand horse, who adhered to him in hopes that he might succeed in establishing his pretensions; insomuch that the total numbers of all these wretches, who

* 'Memoirs,' p. 353.

were separated from the fields of salvation and bliss, was two hundred and one thousand. These haughty Pagans advanced in hostile array to war with the people of Islam, and to destroy the religion of the Chief of Men, on whom be praise and blessing.'*

Sikri, about sixteen miles from Agra, was the place which the Turks fixed on to defend. Baber had built a palace there, and laid out a garden ; he had chosen that spot to fight, because water was obtainable, and the ground was hilly.

'There was a deep tank' (square pond) 'on our left,' writes Baber. 'I encamped there to have the benefit of the water. We fortified the guns in front, and connected them by chains. Between every two guns we left a space of seven or eight gez' (fifteen or sixteen feet) 'which was defended by a chain. Mustafa Rumi (Otto-man Turk) had disposed the guns according to the Con-stantinople (Rumi) fashion. He was extremely active, intelligent, and skilful in the management of artillery. As Ustâd Ali Kuli was jealous of him, I had stationed Mustafa on the right with Humayon.' Ustâd means a schoolmaster, and was applied to any man of science. Ustad Ali Kuli had lately cast a gun successfully at Agra, which carried sixteen hundred paces. 'In the places,' continues Baber, 'where there were no guns, I caused the Hindustani and Khorasani pioneers and spadesmen to run a ditch.'*

* 'Memoirs,' p. 360. † Ibid., p. 353.

Baber also sent out to collect bowmen of the Doab and Delhi. These he sent out to plunder the country of Miwat. He sent Sheikh Jemali (Hindi-Amir), accompanied by Mulla Turk Ali, lately arrived from Kabul, with these bowmen, 'to ruin and plunder Miwat.' Similar orders were given to Maghfur Diwan, who was instructed 'to proceed to ravage and desolate some of the bordering and remote districts, ruining the country, and carrying off the inhabitants into captivity. They did not, however, appear to have suffered much from the proceedings,' adds Baber.

The panic in the Turkish camp at Sikri continued. 'A general consternation and alarm prevailed among great and small. There was not a single person who uttered a manly word.' Panic and alarm was painted on every face, dejection and gloomy apprehension pervaded the whole Turkish camp. The world-renowned courage and gallantry of the Rajpoots of Rajpootana was well known to the invaders. They were coming 'in number like the leaves of the forest, like an innumerable army of locusts.' These Rajpoots had retained their creed and independence for five hundred years, against other Moslems, Moghuls, Afghans, Persians, and other races kindred to the Turks, who had often tried but had totally failed to conquer them. Rana Sanka, in eighteen pitched battles, had defeated the house of Lodi.

Baber says: 'At length, observing the universal discouragement of my troops, and their total want of spirit,

I formed my plan. I called an assembly of all my Amirs and officers, and addressed them: "Noblemen and soldiers! Every man that comes into the world is subject to dissolution. When we are passed away and gone, God only survives unchangeable. Whoever comes to the feast of life must, before it is over, drink from the cup of death. He who arrives at the inn of mortality must one day inevitably take his departure from this house of sorrow—the world. How much better it is to die with honour than to live with infamy!

'"'With fame, even if I die, I am contented;
Let fame be mine, since my body is Death's.'"'

(These last lines are from the Shahnamah of Ferdousi.)

'" The Most High God has been propitious to us, and has now placed us in such a crisis that, if we fall in the field we die the death of martyrs; if we survive, we rise victorious, the avengers of the cause of God. Let us then, with one accord, swear on God's holy Word that none of us will even think of turning his face from this warfare, nor desert from the battle and slaughter that ensues, till his soul is separated from his body." Master and servant, small and great, all with emulation, seizing the blessed Koran in their hands, swore in the form that I had given. My plan succeeded to admiration, and its effects were instantly visible, far and near, on friend and foe.'*

On the 16th of March, 1527, the decisive battle be-

* 'Memoirs,' p. 357.

tween the Turks and Rajpoots was fought. By the advice of Hussain Kâlifeh, the Vizier, the Turkish position at Sekri had been strengthened and strongly fortified. A ditch was dug round it. The Turks were only just entering into this strongly entrenched camp when the news arrived that the Rajpoots were advancing. 'Having dragged forward our guns, and advanced our right, left, and centre, in battle array, for nearly a kos' (a mile and a half), 'we reached the ground that had been prepared for us. Many tents were already pitched, and they were engaged in pitching others, when news was brought that the enemy's army was in sight. I immediately mounted, and gave orders that every man should without delay repair to his post, and that the guns and lines should be properly strengthened.'*

The battle of Sikri was a repetition of the battle of Paniput. The Turks were strongly entrenched. Humayon commanded the right wing; the left was commanded by Mohammedi Gokultash; Baber himself was in command of the centre. There were, as before, two flanking parties of Moghuls. The great-guns of Ustad Kuli Ali and Mustafa, and the fire of the matchlock-men, did great execution. The same Amirs as before distinguished themselves, together with several Pathan Amirs. Alla-o-deen, the brother of the late Sultan Ibrahim, and eight or ten other Pathan nobles, are mentioned. Among the Turks also was Malikdad-e-Kirrani, who so nar-

* 'Memoirs,' p. 358.

rowly escaped the bastinado. The ambassador from Persia was present, and Chin Taimur Sultan performed good service by a charge. The Rajpoots were defeated. The priest Zein thus writes: 'The warriors of the Faith, who were in the temper of self-devotion, and prepared to submit to martyrdom, heard, from a secret voice, the glad tidings, "*Be not dejected nor sorry; ye are exalted.*"* And the right and left of the army of the Faithful having driven the right, left, and centre of the Infidels into one place, the indications of the superiority of illustrious holy warriors and the exaltation of the standards of Islam began to be evident; and in the course of one hour, these damnable heathen and those atheistical wretches, being desperate and astonished at their condition, finally resigned their lives to despair, made an attack on the right and left of our centre, and, having advanced their greatest force on the left, had nearly reached it; but the holy warriors, distinguished by valour, exhibiting the fruits of excellence, planted the tree of their arrows on the ground of the breast of every one, and cast them all out like their black fortune. In this situation of things the breezes of success and victory blew on the garden of the Good Fortune, and the glad tidings came, "*Of a truth we have displayed on thy account a splendid victory.*"† The mistress Victory, whose world-adorning countenance, decked with waving ringlets, and with "God will aid you with mighty aid," had been

* From the 'Koran.' † Ibid.

hid behind a veil, as the ornamented Bride of Futurity, now gave her aid, and came to greet the Present. The vain Hindoos, discovering their dangerous state, were scattered abroad like teased wool, and broken like bubbles of wine.'*

The Rajpoots fought with their accustomed courage. Kraul Udi Sing, of Udipore; two noted Chohan Rajpoots—Rai Chanderbehan Chohan and Manikchand Chohan; and Dulpat Rai and Gangu, Kerm Sing and Rao-Rikersi, 'and a number of others, leaders of great clans, men of high rank and pride, measured the road to Hell, and from this house of clay were transferred to the Pit of Perdition.' Of the Pathan Amirs, Hassan Khan Mewati was killed by a matchlock-shot. The Rajpoot account of this battle agrees with the Moslem account, only they state that they were betrayed by a traitor in their own ranks.

'Having defeated the enemy,' says Baber, 'we pursued them with great slaughter. Their camp might be four miles from ours. On reaching it, I sent on Muhammedi Abdal-Aziz, Ali Khan, and some other officers, with orders to follow them in close pursuit, slaying and cutting them off, so that they should not have time to reassemble. In this instance I was guilty of neglect; I should myself have gone out and urged the pursuit, and not have intrusted that business to another. I had got about a kos (nearly two miles) beyond the enemy's camp, when I

* 'Memoirs,' p. 366.

turned back, the day being spent, and reached my own camp about evening prayers. Muhammed Sherif, the astrologer, whose perverse and seditious practices I have mentioned, came to congratulate me on my victory. I poured forth a torrent of abuse upon him, and when I had relieved my heart by it, although he was heathenishly inclined, perverse, and extremely self-conceited, and an insufferable evil speaker, yet, as he had been my old servant, I gave him £350 as a present, and dismissed him, commanding him not to remain within my dominions.'* A tower of the heads of the Infidels was constructed on the field of battle; the dead and wounded Hindoos were lying on the road as far as Ulwar and Miwat. Elias Khan, a Pathan, who had headed a rebellion in the time of Baber's difficulties while awaiting the Rajpoot attack at Sikri, was taken by the Turks, and flayed alive.

After this signal victory over the Rajpoots, Baber took the title of Ghazi—'Victorious over the Infidel.'

Rana Sanka, of Mewar, Baber's adversary (now represented by the house of Udipore), was the head of the great Rajpoot republic of small states, who, in strong mountain-fortresses, held their creed and their independence in the mountains of Rajpootana. He was as much a hero as Baber himself; he had succeeded to the throne in 1509; and, as we have said, he was victorious in eighteen pitched battles against the Pathan kings of Delhi and Malwa.

* 'Memoirs,' p. 368.

There are portraits still extant of Rana Sanka; he was of middle stature, but great muscular strength, fair in complexion, with unusually large eyes, which appear peculiar to his descendants. He exhibited at his death but the fragment of a warrior—one eye was lost in a broil with his brother, an arm in an action with the Lodi king of Delhi, he was a cripple owing to a limb being broken by a cannon-ball, and he counted eighty wounds from the sword and the lance in various parts of his body. Had he been succeeded in Rajpootana by a prince possessed of his foresight and judgment, Baber's descendants might not have retained the sovereignty of India.

Baber's enemy, the Rajpoot, was quite as civilised, enlightened and brave as his invaders, the Turks of Kabul; but he was less fanatical than the Moslems. His creed, like the Jewish, admitted of no converts; a man must be born a Rajpoot—he could not become one.

'The Rajpoot to this day remains the same singular being; concentrated in his prejudices, political and moral, as in the days of Alexander; desiring no change himself, and still less to cause any in others. Whatever be the conservative principle, it merits philosophic analysis.'

The Rajpoot government was feudal: the feudal form of government is indigenous, universal, and immemorial. The peasant was a yeoman; each city, each commune, was virtually independent. The land was divided into tithings and hundreds by the laws of Menu, and the king's share well defined. 'Let the king receive his annual revenue through collectors, but let him observe the divine ordinances and act as a father to his people' (Text 80). 'To protect the people and honour the priests are the highest duties of kings, and insure them felicity' (Text 88). 'From the people he must learn the theory of agriculture, commerce, and practical arts.' The divine legislator of the Hindoos expressly declares that a 'king addicted to vices, which tend to misrule, may lose even his life from public resentment' (Text 46). Duties of kings: 'Should the king, be near his end, through incurable disease, he must bestow on the priests all his riches accumulated from legal fines, and, having duly committed his kingdom to his son, let him seek death in battle, or, if there be no war, by abstaining from food.' The annals of the Rajpoots affords instances of obedience to this text of the divine legislator. One fifth of the soil was assigned for the support of the temples, their ministers, the secular Brahmins, bards, and genealogists.

The Rajpoots of the time of Baber were proficient in music, could all read and write, use the bow and ride, and speak the truth. The wisdom of their ancestors, which they greatly revered, was to be found in the Vedas, the laws of Menu, the classic poems of Vyasa and Valmika. The poems of Chund, which are considered historical, consist of sixty-nine books, containing

100,000 stanzas; and they have been translated into English by Colonel Tod.

There were copper mines in Rajpootana, which have long been worked. The architecture was good, strong, richly carved; and the Moslem conqueror of India learnt much from the Indians. The Rajpoots have been celebrated for patriotism and high courage; and, from their invincible spirit, they were never subdued by the Turks. In after ages, at the Turkish Court of Delhi, of seventy-six feudatory princes, the Rajah of Udipore, the descendant of Rana Sanka, ranked, from his high lineage and traditions, first of all. It is said that the princes of Rajpootana, though nominally subject to the Queen of England now, have vowed fealty to this house, their lords-paramount for eighteen hundred years.

Abulfuzil, the great Mohammedan writer of the time of Acbar, thus writes, and this evidence from one of rival creed is valuable:

'The Hindoos are religious, affable, courteous to strangers, cheerful, enamoured of knowledge, lovers of justice, able in business, grateful, admirers of truth, of unbounded fidelity in all dealings. Their character shines brightest in adversity. Their soldiers know not what it is to fly from the field of battle; but when the success of the combat becomes doubtful, they dismount from their horses and throw away their lives in payment of the debt of valour.'

The valour and unquenchable spirit of independence

have enabled the princes of Rajpootana to remain independent in their castles, perched like eyries on the mountain-tops, to the present day.

This battle at Sikri, between Hindooism and Mohammedism, is only one incident in a struggle that has lasted eight hundred years; and the Hindoo creed is still as young and as unsubdued as when Mahmoud of Ghusni attacked the Rajpoots. After nine hundred years of Moslem rule, and one hundred of British, the Rajpoot is unchanged. His ancestors can boast of an antiquity which was old when Greece and Rome existed. They gave civilisation to Egypt and Babylon.

The worship of the Rajpoot, like that of the Vedas, is sun-worship. The warrior of the early ages sacrificed his horse to this luminary, and dedicated to him the first day of the week. The sacred standard bears the image of the sun. Their two great races call themselves the 'children of the sun' and 'the children of the moon.'

The Rajpoot amusement is to spear wild boar, which they eat, and they drink wine from a skull at the saturnalia of the Holi. Another of their festivals is 'the worship of the sword.' The prince of the house of Udipore is armed with a two-edged sword, an enchanted weapon, said to be fabricated by the Vulcan of the Hindoos; and the Rajpoots worship their weapons with fasting, ablution, and prayer, at certain festivals. The Dassera is also a military festival, during which, with songs of praises, they celebrate the glories of the past and the fame of national military heroes and chieftains.

These details of the Rajpoot belief are given by Colonel Tod, an Englishmen who lived among them and studied their books.

CHAPTER IV.

THE DEATH OF BABER.

Humayon's return to Kabul—The taking of Chanderi—Baber's death—Turkish rule—The Turks driven from India.

BABER proposed following the Rajpoots back into their hilly and beautiful country of Rajpootana. 'I sent for the Turki and Hindi Amirs,' he writes, 'and consulted them about proceeding against the country of these Pagans. That plan was, however, abandoned, in consequence of the want of water on the road and the excessive heat of the season.'

In May, Humayon and many of the Turki Amirs joyfully returned to Kabul. 'Before the battle' (of Sikri), Baber writes, 'they had been seized with a longing for home. I made with them an agreement that they should return. Besides, Kabul was very imperfectly defended. On these accounts, I finally resolved to send off Humayon to Kabul.' Medhi Khwajeh, Baber's son-in-law, also thankfully received leave to return.

On his way back to Kabul, Humayon 'repaired to Delhi, and there opened several of the houses which contain the treasure, and took possession by force of the contents. I certainly never expected such conduct from him, and, being extremely hurt, I wrote some letters containing the severest reprehension.'

This conduct was so unlike Humayon's usual behaviour, that probably he believed that his father could never hold India, and that the money would be lost.

Baber spent the next few months of the intolerably hot weather in Agra. His constitution could not stand the change from the cool and healthy climate of the north. In August he fell ill, and remained ill until December.

In consequence of a vow, Baber began another 'holy war' against the Hindoos, and attacked the strong fort of Chanderi. It was beyond Kalpi and in Malwa, and it belonged to Rana Sanka. Medini Rao held the place with four or five thousand Hindoos. 'In a short time the Pagans, in a state of complete nudity, rushed out to attack us, put numbers of my people to flight, and leaped over the ramparts. Some of our troops were attacked furiously, and put to the sword. The reason of this desperate sally from their works was, that, on giving up the place for lost, they had put to death the whole of their wives and women, and, having resolved to perish, had stripped themselves naked, in which condition they had rushed out to fight.' (This was a common practice of the Rajpoots, who never allowed their women to fall alive into Moslem hands.) 'Two or three hundred Pagans had entered Medini Rao's house, where numbers of them slew each other in the following manner: one person took his stand with a sword in his hand, while the others, one by one, crowded in, and stretched out their necks, eager to die. In this way many went to hell; and, by the favour of God, in the space of about one hour, I gained this celebrated fort.'* Baber intended to go on to attack Rana Sanka at Cheitore, south of Ajmere, but news came from some of his captains, which called him to Oude. There Baber did what so many Englishmen have since tried to do, 'settled the affairs of Oude.' In Oude he defeated the last of the Pathan Amirs of Sultan Ibrahim's court.

At the taking of Chanderi, a Pathan nobleman, a man of mark, joined the Turks. His name was Shere. 'After Shere had stayed some time in the Turkish camp, and observed their manners and policy, he one day told a friend that he thought it would be an easy matter to drive those foreigners out of Hindustan. His friend asked him what reason he had to think so? Shere replied, 'That the king Baber himself, though a man of great parts, was but very little acquainted with the policy of Hindustan; that if the Pathans, who were now at enmity among themselves, could be brought to concord, he imagined himself equal to the task of driving them away.' His friend burst into a loud laugh, and began to ridicule this vain opinion. Shere, a few days afterwards, at the king's' (Baber's) 'table, had some solid dishes set

* 'Memoirs,' p. 377.

before him, with only a spoon to eat them. He called for a knife, but the servant had orders not to supply him with one. Shere, not to lose his dinner, drew his dagger, without ceremony, and, cutting up his meat, made a hearty meal, without minding those who diverted themselves at this odd behaviour. When he had done, Baber, who had been remarking this matter, turned to the Vizier, Amir Kalifeh, and said, "This Afghan is not to be disconcerted with trifles, and is likely to be a great man." Shere, perceiving by these words that the king had been informed of his private discourse to his friend, fled the camp that night, and went to his own estate. Shere afterwards joined Mahmud Lodi, who, after the defeat of the Rajpoots, had retired into Behar, a province of Bengal.'* Shere, in the end, proved a dangerous enemy to the Turks.

In 1528, Baber visited the noted Hindu fortress of Gwalior. He made also a treaty with Rana Sanka's son, by which the unassailable Hindu stronghold west of Dhulpur, Rantambor, was made over to the Turks. 'I agreed with him, by the blessing of God, I would make him Rana in his father's place, and establish him in Cheitore.'

'At this crisis the treasures of Delhi and Agra, which had been collected by Sekander and Ibrahim Lodi, being expended, and it being necessary to furnish equipments for the army, gunpowder for the service of the guns, and

* 'Ferishta,' Dow's translation, p. 169.

pay for the artillery and matchlock-men, on Thursday, October 8th, 1528, I gave orders that in all departments, every man having an office should bring a hundred and thirty instead of a hundred to the Diwan (council) to be applied to the procuring and fitting out the proper arms and supplies. This seems an increase of the taxes thirty per cent., but was not drawn from the people direct, but from the officials.'*

News arrived of the birth of a son to Humayon at Kabul; the child was called Alaman (the protected). Baber writes on the birth of his grandson: 'Thanks be to God who has given you a child; he has given to you a child, and to me a comfort and object of love. May the Almighty always continue to grant to you and me the enjoyment of such objects of our hearts' desire! Indeed, the Almighty, from His grace and bounty, hath accomplished our desires in a manner not to be paralleled in the revolution of time.'† He gives Humayon good advice in this letter. 'I have formerly told you that you should live on the most confidential footing with Khwajeh Kilan; you may act in regard to him with the same unrestrained confidence that you have seen me do. You must attempt by the utmost courtesy of manner to gain the heart of Sultan Weis, and to have him about you, and to direct yourself by his judgment, as he is a prudent and experienced man. Twice, every day, you must call your brothers and Beys to your presence, not

* 'Memoirs,' p. 387. † Ibid., p. 391.

leaving their attendance to their own discretion, and after consulting with them about business, you must finally act as may be decided to be most advisable. You must pay every attention to the discipline and efficient state of your army.' It was by following this line of conduct that Baber had surrounded himself with the faithful band who fought his battles, and gained his splendid victories.

To Khwajeh Kilan, Baber writes by his same messenger as to an intimate friend, telling him of his loneliness and homesickness in the land of exile. 'How is it possible that the delights of those lands' (Kabul and Ferghana) 'should ever be erased from the heart? Above all, how is it possible for one like me? They very recently brought me a single musk-melon; while cutting it up I felt myself affected with a strong feeling of loneliness and a sense of exile from my native country, and I could not help shedding tears while I was eating it.'* Baber's wife, Maham, and his children were in Kabul. His daily life in India was a splendid and busy one. He had held several great royal receptions and courts in the garden of the charbagh, where his veterans and tried men, on these occasions, were given 'vests of honour and articles of value.'

Upon the battlefield of Sekri, Baber had made a vow that he would abstain from wine for the future. His drunken habits had long preyed upon his sense of self-

* 'Memoirs,' p. 401.

respect. 'At the age of forty I will grow sober,' he was wont to resolve, but the age of forty came without the sobriety. But the vow wrung from him upon the battle-field was rigidly respected, although he found great difficulty in 'resigning himself to the desert of penitence.' Four years after the battle he writes: 'My longing and desire for wine and social parties were beyond measure excessive; it even came to such length, that I have found myself shedding tears from vexation and disappointment. In the present year, praise be to God, these troubles are over, and I ascribe them chiefly to the occupation afforded to my mind by a poetical translation, on which I have employed myself. Let me advise you, too, to adopt a life of abstinence. Social parties and wine are pleasant, in company with our jolly friends and old boon companions. But with whom can you enjoy the social cup? With whom can you indulge the pleasures of wine? If you have only Shir Ahmed and Haidee Kuli for the companions of your gay hours and jovial goblet, you can surely find no great difficulty in consenting to the sacrifice. I conclude with every good wish.'

Mahmud Lodi, who had joined the Pagan forces at Sokri, the brother of Ibrahim Lodi, had set up a kingdom in the province of Behar, to the north of Bengal. The Turks, who, in the year 1529, were doubting in what direction to turn their arms, with their habit of undertaking a yearly campaign, thought of attacking Bengal;

but the Moslem ruler of Bengal had sent ambassadors and peaceful messages. They determined, therefore, to move out against Behar. Baber and his army marched south. He reached Chunar, passed Benares, and even went as far as Patna, mostly by river; but he never seems to have defeated Mahmud Lodi, or even to have reached him in the province of Behar. Before he could do so, Baber was recalled north by the dangerous position of his generals in Oude. Lucknow had been lost to the Turks.

In June of that year (1528) Baber received his favourite wife, Maham, as he calls her, the mother of Humayon. The ladies had taken six months to travel from Kabul to Agra. The reason Baber gave for bringing all his women to India was that it was a safer country than Kabul, 'in which there were seven or eight rulers.'

On December 26th, 1530, Baber died at Agra; for fifteen months before his death his journal ceases. The last words with which it closes paint the forgiving character of the man. Rahimdad, a Hindu of rank, had been left in charge of the important fortress of Gwalior. He proved a traitor. 'On Tuesday, (A.D. 1529), Sheikh Muhammed Ghus with Shebabeddin Khosrou came out of Gwalior, as intercessor for Rahimdad; as the man was a humble and saintly personage, I forgave, on his account, the offences of Rahimdad; and sent Sheikh Kuren and Nur Bey to receive the surrender of Gwalior.'*

Said Khan, ruler of Kashgar, had gained possession of

* 'Memoirs,' p. 425.

Badakshan, a part of the Kabul empire. It is said Sultan Weis, and the other Turki Amirs who were in Kabul, had invited him; and worst of all, Abdal-Aziz, the staunch adherent of Paniput and Sekri, excited revolts and commotions openly, when Humayon left Kabul to be by the side of his dying father in India.

In the meanwhile, a report reached Baber that Said Khan had gained possession of all Badakshan, a part of the Kabul empire. The unwelcome intelligence that daily arrived from that quarter preyed upon his mind, and helped to impair his declining strength. He sent instruction to Khalifeh, the Vizier, to set out in order to recover Badakshan; but that nobleman, who was Baber's prime-minister, knowing probably that the order was dictated by Humayon's mother, who had great ascendency over Baber, and who wished to remove from court a powerful enemy of her son, found means to excuse himself. Similar orders were then sent to Humayon, in whose government Badakshan was; but that prince also declined engaging in the expedition, under the pretence that his affection for his father would not permit him to remove so far from the presence. Mirza Suleman, the son-in-law of Sultan Weis, was then despatched, with instructions to assume the government of the country, and was at the time furnished with letters to Said Khan, complaining of his aggression.*

Humayon reached Agra 1530, neither sent for nor

* 'Memoirs,' p. 426.

expected; but the affection of his father and the influence of his mother procured him a good reception. His offence of leaving his province was forgotten; and after remaining some time at court, he went to his government of Sambal in Northern India. When he had resided there about six months, he fell dangerously ill. His father, whose favourite son he seems to have been, was deeply affected at the news, and gave directions for conveying him by water to Agra. He arrived there, but his life was despaired of. When all hope from medicine was over, and while several men of skill were talking to the emperor of the melancholy situation of his son, Abdul Baka, a personage highly venerated for his knowledge and piety, remarked to Baber, that in such a case the Almighty had sometimes vouchsafed to receive the most valuable thing possessed by one friend as an offering in exchange for the life of another. Baber exclaimed that of all things his life was dearest to Humayon, as Humayon's was to him; and that, as next to the life of Humayon, his own was what he most valued, he would devote his life to Heaven as a sacrifice for his son's. The noblemen around him entreated him to retract the rash vow, and, in place of his first offering, to give the diamond taken at Agra, and reckoned the most valuable on earth; that the sages had said, that it was the dearest of our worldly possessions alone that was to be offered to Heaven. But he persisted in his resolution, declaring that no stone of whatever value could be put in competition with his life. He three times walked round the dying prince, a solemnity similar to that used in sacrifices and peace-offerings, and, retiring, prayed earnestly to God. After some time he was heard to exclaim, 'I have borne it away!—I have borne it away!' The Mussulman historian assures us that Humayon almost immediately began to recover, and that in proportion as he recovered, the health and strength of Baber visibly decayed. Baber communicated his dying instructions to Khwajeh Khalifeh, Kamber Ali Bey, Terdi Bey, and Hindu Bey, who were then at court, commending Humayon to their protection. With that unvarying affection for his family, which he had showed in all circumstances of his life, he strongly besought Humayon to be kind and forgiving to his brothers. Humayon promised, and, what in such circumstances is rare, kept his promise. The request which he had made to his nobles was heard, as the request of dying princes generally are, only as a signal for faction. Khwajeh Khalifeh had conceived a strong dislike to Humayon, in consequence of some circumstances which are not explained; so that the court of the expiring conqueror became the scene of intrigue and cabal. Kalifeh, as prime-minister, possessed the chief authority among the Turki nobles. He did not wish that the succession should be with the children of Baber, and had pitched on Medhi Khwajeh, Baber's son-in-law, as his successor. Medhi Khwajeh was a brave but extravagant and wild young man, and had long been closely connected with Khalifeh. When it was known that Khalifeh was in his interests, and intended to raise him to the throne, the principal men in the army lost no time in paying their court to Medhi Khwajeh, whose succession was regarded as secure, and who began to affect the deportment of a sovereign prince. Everything seemed to promise that he was to be Emperor of Hindustan, when suddenly he was ordered by Khalifeh to remain in his house under a guard.*

The cause of this sudden change has escaped the researches of Abulfazl and Khûfi Khan, two Indian historians. It is explained, however, by a well-informed historian, who relates the anecdote on the authority of his father. 'It so happened,' says he, 'that Mir Khalifeh had gone to see Medhi Khwajeh, whom he had found in his tent. Nobody was present but Khalifeh, Medhi Khwajeh, and my father, Muhammed Mokino. Khalifeh had scarcely sat down an instant when Baber, who was at the last extremity, suddenly sent for him. When he left the tent, Medhi Khwajeh accompanied him to the door, to do him honour, and to take leave of him, and stood in the middle of it, so that my father, who followed, but out of respect did not push by him, was immediately behind. The young man, who was rather flighty and harum-scarum, forgetting that my father was present, as soon as Khalifeh was fairly gone, muttered to himself, "God willing, I will

* 'Memoirs,' p. 428.

soon flay off your hide, old boy!" and, turning round at the same instant, saw my father. He was quite confounded, but, immediately seizing my father's ear, with a convulsive eagerness, twisted it round, and said, hurriedly, "You Tajik! The red tongue often gives the green head to the winds." My father, having taken his leave, and left the tent, sought out Khalifeh, and remonstrated with him on his line of conduct, telling him that, in violation of his allegiance, he was taking away the sovereignty from Muhammed Humayon and his brothers, who were accomplished princes, to bestow it on the son of a stranger; and yet, how did this favoured man behave? He then repeated what had passed, just as it happened. Khalifeh, on the spot, sent off an express for Humayon, and despatched a body of Yesawels (special messengers) or aide-de-camps to Medhi Khwajeh, to inform him that the king's orders were that he should instantly retire to his own house. The young man had now sat down to dinner, which was still before him. The Yasawels communicated their message, and forced him away. Mir Khalifeh then issued a proclamation, prohibiting all persons from resorting to Medhi Khwajeh's house, or waiting upon him, while Medhi Khwajeh himself received orders not to appear at court.'*

Baber in the midst of these intrigues, with which he was probably unacquainted, expired at the Charbagh, near Agra, on the 6th of the first Jermadi, December

* 'Memoirs,' p. 428.

26th, 1530, in the fiftieth year of his age, and thirty-eighth of his reign as a sovereign prince. His body, in conformity with a wish which he had expressed, was carried to Kabul, where it was interred on a hill that still bears his name. He had reigned five years over part of Hindustan. Humayon ascended the throne on the 29th of the same month, without opposition, by the influence of Khalifeh.

Humayon mounted the throne of India after his father's death. 'He was a great astronomer, and took much delight in judicial astrology. He fitted up seven houses of entertainment, and named them after the seven planets. In each he gave public audiences, according to the ruling planet of the day. In the house of the Moon he met foreign ambassadors, travellers and poets. Military men attended him in the house of Mars. Judges, lawgivers, and secretaries were received in that of Mercury.'*

In 1539 Humayon was utterly defeated by the Pathan nobles, under Shere. The Turks were obliged to withdraw to Lahore, and from thence Humayon was driven away from India. Shere declared himself King of Delhi, and he and his family reigned thirty years, until 1554, when Humayon again marched from Kabul, and succeeded in re-establishing the House of Timour. Humayon died at Delhi in 1555, where a very beautiful mausoleum still stands over his remains. His son, the celebrated Akbar, succeeded Humayon, and he reigned in great

* Dow's 'Hindustan,' vol. ii., p. 142.

prosperity and splendour for fifty years, until 1605.

The Charbagh, where Baber died, still stands at Agra. His grave, a very simple one on a hillside, in a garden, is the favourite resort of the inhabitants of Kabul to this day.

Whether Pathan or Turk ruled India, it was still the same system, Moslem rule. The whole of Moslem polity is drawn from the Koran. The vanquished are allowed to adopt the Moslem creed, or to pay in lieu a poll-tax under penalty of death. In treating of Moslem government, one may recall the opinion of Montesquieu :

'Of all despotic governments, there is none which oppresses more than when the prince declares himself the proprietor of the soil and heir of all his subjects. It always follows that the cultivation of the earth is abandoned ; but if, besides this, the prince is a merchant, every species of industry is ruined.' . . . 'A government cannot be unjust without paying hands to exercise its injustice ; now it is impossible but these hands will be grasping for themselves. Peculation is, therefore, national in despotic states.'

Among the Moslems, 'the prince is not a merchant ;' trade is left in the hands of private individuals. But the prince does declare himself 'the proprietor of the soil, and heir of all his subjects.' The whole of the agriculturists of all countries where Moslem arms have prevailed, are tenants of the crown. They are at the mercy of the local land-agent (Pasha) who collects the agriculturists' rents, miscalled 'revenue.' The cultivation of the earth is abandoned, 'the *hands* (Pashas) of despotic government grasp for themselves,' and peculation is universal.

The Turkish race, a master race, have ruled Central Asia, India, Persia, Arabia, Syria, Egypt, Asia Minor, all Asia except China. Wherever they are lords-paramount 'the prince declares himself the proprietor of the soil.'

The Turkish form of government in some respects is not peculiar to the Moslem or Turkish race. Their constitution is this: Firstly, a military autocrat, also head of the faith; secondly, an aristocracy, not of *birth* but of *office*, chosen by the king; thirdly, the mass of the people, tax-payers, and mostly cultivators of the soil, except in cities, where traders have some privileges.

This system has many evils; but when the autocrat is a man of extraordinary genius, a Peter the Great, a Napoleon, or in the Eastern world an Akbar or a Baber, it has great powers for good. 'The hands,' the Pasha and bureaucrat, gain some of the energy and honesty of the head. But when the great man dies, and great men are always exceptional, the motive power of a military despotism is gone, and an effete autocrat is the worst ruler in the world, stamping his mediocrity on all his subordinates, who dare not be more able than he.

The Russians have retained the legacy of Tartar or Turkish government left them by their conquerors. They have an autocrat, an aristocracy of office, and the mass of the people are peasant proprietors. The English in India found the country under Turkish institutions, and have kept them, with a few modifications. I quote a few incidents Baber gives in his Diary, to show the nature of his civil and military government:

'Having learned that the troops had exercised severities towards the inhabitants of Behreh, and were using them ill, I sent out a party, who having seized a few soldiers that had been guilty of excesses, I put some to death, and slit the noses of some others, and made them be led about the camp in that condition. As I reckoned the countries that had belonged to the Turks as my own territories, I therefore admitted of no plundering or pillage.'* We may also insert the following anecdote, related by Baber himself, to show how he enforced personal courage and honour among his officers (Amirs). Baber was fighting some rebellious Afghan frontier tribe at the time. 'Hussain Hassan (an officer), without motive or reason, had spurred on his horse into the midst of the Afghans, and while he was laying about him with his sword, his horse being wounded with an arrow, threw him. He had no sooner risen than they wounded him in the leg with a sword, threw him down again, despatched him with their hangers and swords, and cut him to pieces. The Amirs stopped short and stood looking on, but gave him no assistance.'† Baber rode up himself

* 'Memoirs,' p. 257. † Ibid. p. 271.

soon after, with six officers; they attacked the Afghans. These forty or fifty Afghans were all shot or cut down to a man. 'After slaying the Afghans, we halted in a cultivated field, and directed a tower of skulls to be made of their heads. By the time I reached the road, the Beys who had been with Hussain came up. Being very angry, and resolved to make an example of them, I said, "As you, though so many in number, have stood by and seen a young man of such merit and distinction killed by a few Afghans, on foot, and on plain ground, I deprive you of your *rank* and *station*, take from *you your commands* and *governments*, direct your beards to be shaven, and that you be led ignominiously round the streets of the town, that no man henceforward give up a youth of such worth to so contemptible an enemy. On level ground you stood looking on, and never lifted an arm. Be this your punishment."'*

Baber conquered Kabul in 1507. He writes: 'I partitioned out the country of Kabul among those Beys only who had lately taken service with me. Ghuzni and its dependencies I gave to Prince Jehangin (Baber's brother). The Tuman (province) of Nangenhar, Manderaur, the Dereh Nur, the Dehreh Kuner Nurgil and Cheghanserai, I gave to Prince Naser (another brother of Baber). Those Beys and young officers who had followed me in my expeditions and dangers I rewarded; giving to one of them a village, to another an estate in land; but

* 'Memoirs,' p. 271.

to none of them did I give the government of a district. Nor was this the sole occasion in which I acted in this manner; but uniformly, whenever the Most High God prospered my undertakings, I always regarded and provided for those Beys and soldiers who were strangers and guests in the first place, and in a superior manner to the Baberians, and those who were of Andejan (his own countrymen).'*

Baber wrote: 'We crossed the Kheiber Pass and halted at the foot of it. The Khizer Khails had been extremely licentious in their conduct. Both on the coming and going of our army they had shot upon stragglers and such of our people as lagged behind or separated from the rest, and carried off their horses. It was clearly expedient that they should meet with a suitable chastisement. With this view, early in the morning we marched to the foot of the pass, and spent the noon at Deh Gholaman. About noonday prayers, we fed our horses, and despatched Muhammed Hussain Kordie to Kabul, with orders to seize all the Khizer Khails in the place; and to put their property under sequestration, and to send me an account of what was done. That night we continued marching until midnight, and halted a little beyond Sultanpore, from which place, after having taken a short sleep, we mounted again. The quarters of the Khizer Khail extended from Behar and Masikh-keram as far as Karasu. The morning had

* 'Memoirs,' p. 156.

dawned when we came up and charged them. Much property and many children fell into the hands of our troops; a few of the enemy gained a hill which was near at hand and escaped. Next morning we took some Gher Jhawels. The Veziri Afghans had been very irregular in paying their taxes. Alarmed at this example of punishment, they now brought three hundred sheep as tribute.'*

* 'Memoirs,' p. 277.

CHAPTER V.

THE HISTORY OF NOOR MAHAL.

The Palace of an Empress—The Sun of Women—Prince Selim—Baffled longings—Marriage.

THE story of Queen Noor Mahal is given as a curious picture of manners at the time the Turks of Delhi were at their zenith of wealth and strength. It is a picture also of how the Moslem treat their women. Akbar was the greatest hero of the line of Timour, but the influence of Noor Mahal and her family almost more affected the history of India.

Noor Mahal and her family, Usbeg Tartars, came from Central Asia; and threw all their powerful influence on the side of religious intolerance and cruel persecution. These persecutions of the Hindoos caused the decisive conflicts of the Hindoos and Mohammedans in the succeeding reign under Aurungzebe. Akbar was for union and conciliation with the Hindoos, but the rigid bigotry of all the descendants of Noor Mahal race very much affected the history of India.

About three hundred years ago, in the winter of the year 1590, you could have seen a procession of women's litters, with closed curtains, passing through the streets of Futtehpore Sikri. The litter-bearers were clothed in a livery of rich silk brocade, their heads surmounted with turbans of golden tissue ; the eunuchs in charge of the litters were bravely attired, and riding spirited horses. This procession was that of the ladies of the Lord High Treasurer, on their way to the harem of the great Emperor Akbar, where they hoped to pay their respects to that emperor's wife, Miriam Zumani. This lady was by birth a Hindoo princess, a daughter of the distinguished house of Jeypore, and she was also the mother of the heir-apparent to the throne, Prince Selim. The palace of this queen was known as the Golden House, and it deserved the title. It was minutely ornamented, like a mediæval illumination, with paintings of figures and fruits on a ground of blue and gold.

The litters were put down in front of this gorgeous house ; the men who carried them were sent away by the eunuchs. From the first litter emerged a tall slight woman with grey hair ; from out of the second stepped a lovely young girl, who, from the strong family likeness, was evidently the daughter of the first woman. They were the wife and daughter of Aiass Khan, Lord High Treasurer of Akbar ; and the other litters contained their suite.

They first passed the outer court of the queen's palace,

a gay scene, crowded with women, slaves, and eunuchs, who, from their gay-coloured clothing, looked like a tulip-bed. But the mind of the treasurer's wife was occupied in considering how she would perform her part in the complicated ceremonial of the 'Kudder-i-nishust-o-burkhast' (that is, the correct manner of rising and being seated) befitting the occasion.

The treasurer's ladies had been admitted into the queen's presence in a room decorated with all the graces of painting and of sculpture, and with the floor spread with thick carpets of silk and gold. The queen was seated on the ground, on a velvet cushion richly embroidered. A blaze of jewels was on her head and neck and arms. Her complexion was dark and swarthy; her eyes were large; her hair black as the raven's wing. The two ladies made low obeisances three times as they approached the queen, Aiass Khan's spouse, with as much grace as they could muster. Then Miriam Zumani, with a smile of ill-suppressed amusement but with an air of good-nature, motioned to the treasurer's wife to be seated. The queen was always extremely entertained by the visits of this lady, a foreigner of another creed and colour. The queen was swarthy, whilst the treasurer's wife, a native of far northern lands, was hardly darker than many English women. Her cheeks showed a healthy glow; her eyes were grey, with dark lashes; and her hair a dark-brown colour. It was not the fact of her being a foreigner which caused that smile of ill-concealed amusement on the face of Miraim Zumani: she was used enough to these foreigners, the conquerors of her native land. Her own husband, the great King Akbar, was one of these aliens; but it was the rusticity of the treasurer's wife, her uncouthness, and the broken way in which she spoke Hindustanee, which she had acquired late in life. Then her voice was so loud, her movements so free and *brusque;* then there were those thousand little breaches of the correct code of manners and *savoir-faire*—that under-breeding, which we all are so quick to observe when we meet with it in the wives of men who from small beginnings have raised themselves to high posts, dragging their wives up with them. For this free-born Usbeg Tartar woman had in the past lived among very different scenes from the gorgeous luxury and stillness of this palace of an Eastern queen. She had ridden thousands of miles by her husband's side, past the terrific glaciers and pathless mountains of the Hindu Koosh; she had known deadly peril with almost daily familiarity; she had known biting cold and burning suns, fatigue, hunger, poverty, and thirst. And though she had not that polish acquired in courts, she was the very embodiment of common sense, with possibly a shade of sycophancy.

Her husband Aiass Khan's slow but constant rise at court had, perhaps, not been a little assisted by that backstair influence that has done so much in political circles in other lands besides Hindustan.

But after describing the elder woman, we ought to bring before you Mihr el Nissa, 'the sun of women,' the treasurer's daughter, the famous heroine of Eastern romance, known afterwards as Noor Mahal, 'the light of the palace'—Noor Mahal, before sorrow and remorse had dimmed her beauty or broken her proud spirit. The brightness of an unclouded life hung about her, as she stood there smiling, childish, happy. She was clothed in glistening gauze and satin, dancing the dances of her native land, and singing the songs of Balkh for the amusement of the queen. Beauty is not a thing that it is possible to describe. You cannot catch effects of sunshine and shadow in a picture, or express in colours the smile on a loved face; and Noor Mahal's beauty was not the mere surface beauty of form and colour of which men tire in a week. It was a more ethereal attraction; you hardly knew in her whether you admired body or spirit. She had a tall figure, a 'cypress' waist, a walk more free and independent than most women—a walk acquired from her mother, and rare among the shuffling steps of women reared in the harem. Her head was small, and proudly carried on her shoulders, which sloped with pleasing curve. She had a small oval face, with regular features. Her every movement was unstudied grace, her every look a thought. She had dark, almond-shaped eyes, Eastern eyes, with their finely-pencilled eyebrows. They were hazel eyes, large and soft, as those of a gazelle—eyes that showed every movement of the soul within, that lighted up so brightly when she was pleased; that had a far-away misty look when she thought, and that flashed and kindled when she was angry, which was rare.

To Noor Mahal just now the future is bright, and the present full of happiness. The state, the wealth, the splendour of the palace were pleasing to the girl's sensuous, artistic nature; and she, in the unpractical dreams of youth, painted to herself that she would soon be the mistress of such a house—perhaps, who knew, of this very palace?

Little of the ill-placed shyness of youth infected Noor Mahal. She was happy, and had a secret cause of rejoicing. The 'Sun of Women' loved, and was beloved. How prettily anxious she was to please the kind-hearted queen, Miriam Zumani. She loved her as the mother of her lover; for the girl loved devotedly Prince Selim, the queen's son. And as she danced and sang, she was full of happy expectation; for she hoped that Prince Selim might enter his mother's apartments. To her great joy the prince by-and-by appeared.

Their eyes met. She ceased her dancing; and in accordance with imperative Eastern etiquette, she shyly drew her veil over her face. That veil of transparent tissue, glistening with gold embroidery, enhanced rather than concealed her beauty. That glance of recognition had not been lost on Prince Selim, when, for one moment, she had raised to his face those smiling dark eyes.

Yet Prince Selim had not a pleasing expression. Drink, vice, and cruelty were already written in his face. He was, however, of tall and handsome exterior, with great breadth of chest and length of arm. His complexion was of a ruddy nut-brown; his eyes ominously keen and piercing. He was splendidly dressed in red satin and sable fur; and a particular feature about him was that he wore small gold earrings, a badge of slavery. This was from a superstition attached to his birth, and he habitually styled himself 'Sheikh Selim's slave.' His father had been childless for many years; and when Prince Selim was born, his parents believed it was in answer to the prayer of Sheikh Selim, a holy man.

Opportunities of courtship are rare in the East. Prince Selim had met Noor Mahal several times in his mother's house, and had fallen madly in love with this beautiful woman. He vowed that he would wed her. But there was an obstacle in his path, an insuperable obstacle to a man of honour. She was a betrothed maiden, and a betrothal among the Moslems is considered as binding as a marriage. Noor Mahal had been affianced to a young Persian lord, Shere Afghan, the richest, most powerful, and most accomplished noble at Akbar's court, and the Persian would not give up his lovely bride even to the heir to the throne. His honour would be compromised at the very thought. In vain Prince Selim petitioned his all-powerful father to annul Noor Mahal's engagement. The Emperor Akbar was too honourable a man to commit an injustice, or to outrage public opinion, even in behalf of a son to whom he was tenderly attached. The cruel temper of Selim fretted and fumed at being denied the possession of the only woman he had ever seriously loved. For though he had been already married twice, these had been only alliances for state policy with neighbouring Hindoo houses.

There were also some peculiar circumstances attending the birth of Noor Mahal. Her father, Aiass Khan, was a poor Usbeg, of noble birth, from the mountains of Central Asia. He had been tempted to leave the bleak mountains of his native land by reports of the fortunes to be made on the sunny plains of Hindustan. He started on this venturesome journey accompanied by his wife. To add to the hardsbips, when far from human aid in a desolate wilderness, his wife gave birth to a daughter. Aiass Khan and his wife were starving; their only hope of saving their own lives was to press on to the habitations of men and abandon the newly-born child. It was a terrible sacrifice, but the mother consented, and they had placed the child asleep under a tree, when, in the far horizon, their eyes perceived some travellers approaching. These travellers proved good Samaritans to them, and the desert-born babe's life, so nearly lost, was preserved. This child was Noor Mahal, whose loveliness had entranced the heir to the throne of the Great Moghul.

The scene has changed; some months have passed, and Noor Mahal is in her own home at Agra, a mass of buildings overhanging the running river Jumna. An air of vexation and anger can be traced on her usually happy face as she listens to the words of wisdom that are being poured into her unwilling little ears by that united family conclave, where relations dare to say those truths which strangers shrink from uttering, and which are so unpleasant to hear.

There is Aiass Khan, Noor Mahal's father, the prosperous statesman, a small clerkly-looking man, dressed in plain white muslin. He is attenuated, with a worn face, and with a singular air of gentleness and mildness. He has a low-toned voice, and those courteous manners recommended in the Koran to true believers. There is the old mother, whom we have seen before; and there is Noor Mahal's brother, Asiph Khan, a thoughtful youth, of whom in these days we might say, '*Il a des moyens, et il ira loin;*' and there too is her married sister, with her little children playing about, a sister into whose head never entered ambitious dreams of sharing a throne, but who was well and happily married to a cousin, who also shared in the prosperity of this successful family by holding the command of a thousand horse.

'Thou wantest not wisdom or piety, little one,' began her father. 'The laws of rectitude require that thou shouldst conquer this inclination. May God keep thee verdant and blooming in the garden of this world, Mehr el Nissa! Thy happiness is my happiness!'

'No, no; you are all selfish and unkind,' answered the girl passionately. 'You only consider your own interests in this matter; you none of you care how much I suffer, or how miserable you make me.'

'Fie, fie!' cried the mother, in a chiding voice. 'Thou wert ever a headstrong child. An honourable death is preferable to a disgraceful life. Art thou not betrothed? Are we breakers of a covenant made with God? Are we sticklers at no crimes, like pagans? Thou art not free to wed. But if thou wert, would it be wise, for the short and fleeting vanities of this world, to enter that hell of hatred, intrigue, and jealousy—a royal harem? "A rival wife's face is hateful." Consider the furious wrath of Johd Bac (Prince Selim's principal wife), a king's daughter. Consider that thy days would be numbered. Remember the poison and the dagger.'

'Do you think I fear Johd Bac, or Prince Chusero's mother—ugly, black paganesses?' said the girl, with a pang of jealousy. 'I would mould Prince Selim like wax in my fingers. Empire is my destiny! Was I not called the "Sun of Women"?'

'Wealth and power,' put in the cautious brother, 'depend not upon skill, but are the gift of Heaven. It often happens in this world that the foolish and imprudent are honoured, and the wise despised. Thy head is turned by flattering words, my little sister. To think that thou couldst cope successfully with Johd Bac, the crafty daughter of Dody the Fat! And when thou fallest, as fall thou wouldst, thy whole family would be disgraced with thee.'

'Thou, Asiph Khan, my brother, dost thou not fear to live in the river and be at enmity with the crocodile? Thou, Asiph Khan, and thou, dear father, will incur the wrath of Prince Selim; and it is said that he is cruel in his revenge. His whole happiness depends upon this marriage, and so does mine. At the first smile of treacherous fortune, you all seem to throw caution to the winds in braving the anger of this all-powerful prince. If the king says at noonday he sees the moon, you should say that you see the moon and stars!'

'Little one,' said her father gently, 'on some subjects it is unprofitable to argue. For the king of kings, the guardian of mankind, the exalted King Akbar (on whom be blessings until the seventh generation), has ordered me to call the astrologers to fix on the first day that is auspicious for thy union with the excellent Shere Afghan. And thou, in a happy home, with a good husband and with children about thee, wilt forget this idle dream. By Allah and the holy Imaum! who are we that we should aspire to mate with the son of the king!'

Poor Noor Mahal saw crumbling before her the whole fabric of her gorgeous dreams—power, wealth, satisfied love and ambition—all that made the happiness of her life. She had always lived as the companion of her father and brother, clever men, two of the leading minds of the day. She lived in the bustle of a court, possessed of those talents which you more often see inherited by the daughters than the sons of clever men. She painted to herself her future in the dulness of a private harem, with no sphere, no scope for that activity of mind and intellect which was her very life.

'If I were Selim's queen, I would raise thee to the highest offices in the State, Asiph Khan.'

'And I,' answered her brother, 'would not wish to owe my rise to a woman. If it is the will of Allah, my own knowledge, industry, or my sword, will gain me advancement.'

'It is a sad thing to be born a woman,' answered the girl; 'name and fame can never be mine, and not even love, though that alone may be enough for some women's happiness. It is not enough for mine.'

'It is criminal to describe the faults of a great person,' said her elder sister cautiously, and looking round carefully that no listening slave was near. '"Curse not the king in thine heart, lest a bird in the air should carry the sound," came from the East. 'What but a terrible future could be thine, dear sister, with such a man as Prince Selim. He is drunken, cruel, ferocious. But three days ago he commanded one of his servants, for some slight fault, to be flayed alive before him. To think that such a monster is the son of the humane King Akbar, who cannot endure even to see a dead animal skinned!'

'It is not true—it is not true! Selim, my Selim, never committed such a barbarity.'

'It is true, Mehr el Nissa,' said her father gravely.

The treasurer, who understood what we call the political position, thought it doubtful whether Prince Selim would ever ascend the throne of that great empire, or that he could retain that throne gained by the virtues of his father. He was a debauchee with no self-control; and it was probable that, like his brother Daniel, he would rapidly drink himself to death. Prince Selim showed in most things a surprising want of statecraft. He was then urging his father to persecute and kill the Hindoos and destroy their temples. And the great Akbar answered in a letter: 'With all God's creatures I am at peace. Five parts of the human race are aliens to our faith. I should ill discharge the duties of my exalted station were I to withhold *my* compassion and indulgence from any of those God has entrusted to my charge; especially from men who are usefully engaged in the pursuits of science and of art, and the improvement of mankind.' And not satisfied with angering the people at large, Prince Selim would now offend the great Rajpoot lords, the defenders of the throne. These lords it had been the wise policy of the great Akbar's whole life to conciliate. Akbar, by marrying himself into the great Rajpoot house of Jugpore, had found the path of concord in thus uniting the conquerors and the conquered. The Hindoo lords were satisfied; the kingdom was at peace. And Selim, for the sake of Mehr el Nissa, was willing to plunge the country into war by offending these powerful lords.

A month had passed. The whole of the great city of Agra was astir; it was the wedding-day of the treasurer's daughter. For days there had been agitation in the treasurer's palace, a turmoil of which Noor Mahal was the centre. It was an Eastern wedding, the one supreme moment of an Indian woman's life, the one piece of splendour and excitement allowed her, when, amid crowds of friends, days of feasting, cartloads of finery and presents, numberless congratulations and ceremonies, she is united to a man she has never yet seen.

And Noor Mahal, 'too young to be wise, too generous to be cautious, too warm to be sober, too intellectual to be humble,' in the infinite sorrow of those days, began to understand her lot in life as a woman. To have no voice in her own destiny was a hard lesson to Noor Mahal, a haughty nature, with little patience and with strong ambitions. But iron walls of custom are too strong for delicate hands. All the populace of Agra, great and small, was astir, and turned out in gala apparel to see the grandeur of the wedding procession. Multitudes of sightseers crowded the flat roofs and balconies of the houses. In the procession there were lines of elephants with gold and silver howdahs, innumerable palanquins richly gilt and painted. There were hundreds of led horses with saddles embroidered with gold, and some set with jewels. There were companies of foot and horse soldiers, with coats of brilliant hue, and golden turbans. There was a forest of lances, of brocaded flags and embroidered pennants, and among them the much-coveted cognisance of the Royal Fish and Balls, which proclaimed the treasurer's exalted rank. Then the bridegroom, Shere Afghan, came on horseback, preceded by a troop of his own relations and friends; and there, in his place, was the treasurer himself, and the demure worldly-wise young Asiph Khan, and the good cousin Sady Khan, who had married Noor Mahal's sister.

Shere Afghan was a tall slight youth, with a thin, swarthy, hatchet face. It was a countenance of singular determination. He had a high nose, curved like the beak of an eagle, a small mouth of sinister firmness, large black fiery eyes, with strongly-marked brows. But as he rode in the marriage procession, his face was hidden by a fringe of gold that formed a sort of veil. Such was the custom. He was young, only twenty-five, only a few years older than Noor Mahal herself. But young as he was, he bore his budding honours thick upon him. Her parents had chosen wisely and well for Noor Mahal. He was already noted among Akbar's paladins for his unsullied honour, his fantastic bravery; noted among men who were all honourable and brave as the vaunted knights of chivalry.

This man and this woman, who were to be united for life that day, had never as yet met face to face, in accordance with the well-known Eastern custom. Go-betweens and female relations of both bride and bridegroom had told them all particulars about each other. It was a '*mariage de convenance,*' an alliance of equal rank and fortune, as all such marriages are in the East. Noor Mahal had been given a painted miniature of Shere Afghan's handsome high-featured face. From behind latticed windows, she had seen his tall figure and Persian cap pass in various court ceremonies; but neither he himself nor his picture had interested his affianced bride in the least, because her heart was set on evading this marriage; while Shere Afghan had become deeply enamoured of Mehr el Nissa from her likeness. He was also on terms of great intimacy with Asiph Khan and the good old treasurer. He knew (who in the world did not know) all about Noor Mahal, her singular beauty, her wit, her liveliness. He would have been a bold man who would have dared to broach the subject to Shere Afghan of giving up his lovely bride to the dissolute and worthless Prince Selim. Little that reckless brave spirit counted or cared for the enmity of the heir to the throne.

That evening, after endless and wearying ceremonials, the newly-wedded pair saw each other for the first time. Their first glance, according to custom, was in a looking-glass. Noor Mahal, who was seated by her husband and surrounded by her relations and friends, lifted a heavy veil of silver and brocade which completely concealed her person; and then the two looked into the mirror together.

In that looking-glass Shere Afghan saw a face beautiful but angry, and very pale.

'How hideous is thy black skin Persian cap!' were the first words that Noor Mahal exclaimed with childish peevishness. 'The sooner thou art attired in a more courtly and manly attire the better.'

'Fie upon thee, child!' cried her mother, scandalised. 'What an unmannerly speech!'

'A blow from the hand of her we love is as sweet as raisins,' answered the bridegroom gallantly.

A sorrowful wedding-day had Noor Mahal, foiled at once in her ambitions and her loves. And a still more sorrowful wedding-day had her true and noble husband.

PART II.

Noor Mahal in the palace—Murder of Shere Afghan—Neglect and success—Noor Mahal's unbounded power—Her reverses, widowhood and death.

TWELVE years have passed; and Noor Mahal was now no longer a young girl, but was still a beautiful woman. She was thinner, paler, more ethereal-looking than ever. She had lost the beauty of extreme youth, and although she was now thirty, she possessed elegance, grace, and thoughtfulness in an unusual degree. That second summer had arrived, in which some few women are as attractive as in their early loveliness. And time had passed—twelve years—time which heals the sorrows of the sorrowful, and ravishes the joys of the glad. And Noor Mahal was at length the wife of Prince Selim, the man she had first loved, and Selim had become king, under the title of Jehangire. No human being ever experienced the vanity of gratified wishes more completely than Noor Mahal. She was the wife of the man she once loved, and over whom she had dreamed that she could hold eternal sway. She was his wife, but a slighted, scorned, neglected wife, instead of being ruling sultana, as her aspiring mind had dreamed. 'The fat, the black, the paganess' Jodh Bae, the mother of Prince Selim's sons, the lady of royal birth, as Asiph Khan had so wisely foreseen, ruled as supremely as ever.

To Noor Mahal a mere pittance of income had been given. She was lodged in the smallest and worst apartments of the seraglio. Jehangire allowed her only two shillings a day for the support of herself and her slaves. Jehangire refused even to see her, though she had been received with kindness by her former patroness, Miriam Zumain. This sum she naturally found totally insufficient, and she supplemented it by her own needlework. Could anything be more galling to a spirit so proud, so finely touched as hers?

A royal harem is thus arranged. There are four classes of wives. There is a first and principal wife, who is usually her husband's equal in birth and wealth. At the time of her marriage, her husband makes large settlements upon her, and, in case of divorce, she retains this money. After her there are three other wives, ladies of a position a little less distinguished than that of the first wife. They also are ladies of good family. The third rank is composed of as many women as the husband likes. With these he contracts a 'nikka' marriage, which is made with less ceremony than the others. For the fourth kind of marriage a Mussulman can buy a slave, or take a prisoner of war. In theory, each of these ladies ought to be lodged, dressed, and treated according to her rank; but in practice, a favourite often usurps even the rights and honours of the first wife. And Noor Mahal, who hoped to be first and leading spirit, found herself in one of the lowest and most degraded positions.

Prince Selim, on reaching the throne, had proved a rancorous and implacable enemy to the fearless young Shere Afghan, and had determined upon his death. He persecuted him at first secretly; for, despot as he was, he feared public opinion. Some of these persecutions were so strange, so romantic, that if they had not been attested by eye-witnesses, they would seem incredible. On one occasion Shere Afghan destroyed a tiger, unarmed, before the king, who had planned this exhibition for his destruction. When recovering from his wounds, after this encounter with the tiger, at Jehangire's instigation an elephant was driven to crush him as he passed in his litter wounded. With one stroke of his sword, Shere Afghan cut off its ponderous trunk, and thus saved himself. Once forty robbers, emissaries of Jehangire, attacked Shere Afghan in his bedroom; half of these he disabled, the rest fled. Finding all these means fail, Jehangire tried stronger measures. Shere Afghan had retired to his landed estates in Bengal, with his wife, and lived as a private gentleman, far away from the court. He was very wealthy. There Noor Mahal bore him a daughter. The king appointed a new governor to Bengal, for the sole purpose of removing the unfortunate Shere, who met his fate in this way. Shere Afghan was paying a friendly visit to the new governor, and he had but two servants with him, when he was suddenly attacked. He killed six men with his own hand, the treacherous governor being the first man who fell to his avenging sword. Seeing that he must be borne down by numbers, he invited his assailants severally to single combat, but he begged in vain. Then he turned his face towards Mecca, and taking some dust in his hands, for want of water, threw it, by way of ablution, over his head, and stood seemingly unconcerned. Six bullets entered his body in different parts before he fell. His enemies had scarcely the courage to come near him until they saw him in the agonies of death.

Then Noor Mahal, like Mary Stuart, immediately married her husband's murderer. The marriage was by the nikka ceremony, in which the husband is represented by some part of his attire, such as his sword or his turban; and Noor Mahal dispensed even with waiting the three short months a widow ought to wait, according to the Moslem law. The reason she gave for this marriage was, that by it 'the courage and heroism of Shere Afghan should never be forgotten as long as the annals of Hindustan were read.' Noor Mahal started on her journey to meet her old love and her new royal husband. It was a long journey of from four to six months, by litter, and by river in barges. Thus she had plenty of leisure to think of the gallant soldier who had long braved a powerful king for her sake. A beautiful domed mausoleum, near Burdwan, still stands, and marks the grave of Shere Afghan.

Noor Mahal at length arrived at court, at the royal castle of Agra, where she was kindly received by her former patroness, Miriam Zumani; but her former lover, Prince Selim, the King Jehangire, refused even to see her. He turned away in silence whenever his mother mentioned the name of the widow of Shere Afghan. Noor Mahal was placed in the royal seraglio, but treated little better than a slave. This treatment, so different from all she had hoped, preyed upon her mind. She affected that it was grief for her husband's death. For four years Jehangire continued to ignore the existence of the woman he had once passionately loved. His conduct was not dictated by caprice. The redeeming feature in his character, cruel and drunkard as he was, was an occult love of truth and justice. When his mind was heated with the relation of acts of oppression, never rare in the East, he would often burst out with the expression, 'Who in my kingdom has dared to do this wrong?' He had a gold bell placed over his bed, which could be rung by any one who considered themselves wronged, to the call of which he answered himself. He caused a young man named Seef Alla, a special favourite of his own, to be trodden to death for oppressing a peasant. The court was ordered to go into mourning for two months for this youth, and his funeral was celebrated with great magnificence. 'I loved him,' said Jehangire, 'but justice, like necessity, should bind kings.'

The murder of Shere Afghan is perhaps the first open and shameless crime we hear of in the annals of the heroic race of Timour in India. Such a deed had never been laid to the doors of Jehangire's great ancestors—the good Akbar, the knightly Baber, the self-sacrificing Humayon. Jehangire's mind was tortured with a remorse which he neither could nor cared to conceal; and what is said also to have greatly preyed on his mind, was the death of the Governor of Bengal, who was one of his most valued friends. The deed too was unpolitic. Amongst Moslems, the head of the state is also the head of the church and the law. Jehangire was looked up to by millions as the 'Fountain of Justice,' 'The shadow of God upon earth.' A rigorous and impartial justice was the one fact that made the office of despot revered as well as feared among his subjects.

Noor Mahal's rooms were ill-suited to her former fortunes, both as daughter and widow of a nobleman. They were mean architecturally, and built round three sides of a small court; but they were adorned with extraordinary splendour and magnificence. The ground was carpeted with cloth of gold; the doors were hung with curtains of the richest embroidery, and in a style all new to the court of Agra. Everything that artistic genius, skill, taste and wealth could lavish was to be found in the obscure rooms of this despised wife and broken-hearted woman. They say if you shut one door to genius, it opens another for itself, and Noor Mahal illustrated this saying. She had such exquisite taste, such skill, such artistic instincts. The designs that adorned her room were her own; the materials were brought from Bengal; the workmanship was by the hands of her female slaves, under her personal direction; she showed her artistic and inventive talent not only in embroideries, but in planning new jewellery and in painting silk. No one in the Seraglio who would be in the fashion (and who of the female sex would be out of it?) thought of adorning herself, except in the work of Noor Mahal and her slaves; and so the rival wives and the numerous ladies would crowd to the little habitation in the remote court of this woman who had so sad a history, to consult with her and to make purchases of her marvellous needlework. All visitors she received with the most courteous attention and tact, even those she most disliked. What were small feminine jealousies to Noor Mahal; trifles could pain her no more; she had suffered shipwreck of life, of fame, of fortune. In spite of great intellectual gifts, she had failed in attaining all that makes life great, happy, or even honourable. She had parted with all, even to a good conscience; she had paid so much, and received nothing in return. The Seraglio was supposed to contain six thousand women, including females, slaves, and attendants—even women soldiers and guards. There were Chinese, Abyssinians, Hindoos, Circassians, all of whom had been assembled and were supposed to add to the state of the king. There remains in Jehangire's palace to this day, in Agra, the endless bewildering labyrinth of courts, of rooms, of streets, in which they were crowded, with here and there stately suites of apartments exquisitely carved and painted, that once belonged to some favourite lady or some principal wife.

And in this crowd Noor Mahal was alone. Her mother was dead; her rigidly virtuous father blamed her conduct; and as she had so completely fallen under the king's displeasure, the self-seeking Asiph Khan, and even her sister, had the discrimination to feel that it was wiser to keep aloof from one who could in no way assist them up the perilous ladder of court favour and court patronage. They remembered, also, how they had always considered Noor Mahal incautious and hot-headed.

Wherever King Jehangire turned his footsteps in the Seraglio, on every hand was to be found work from the hands of Noor Mahal and her slaves, on every side he heard reports of her witty sayings, her sweetness, her amiability, her extraordinary beauty, the wondrous hangings of her rooms, and this in the Seraglio, where the king heard many blamed and few praised. The Seraglio rang with the charms and the talents of this lady; and woman, who cannot suffer rivals in beauty more than men can endure rivals in talent, counted the once noted beauty as no longer dangerous. She had lost her youth; she dressed plainly; she courted solitude and seclusion; she mixed in no court intrigues; she joined no party politics; she was a mystery, an enigma to the simpler shallower natures by which she was surrounded.

For four years, though so near her, Jehangire had not seen this woman for whom he had sinned so deeply. He formed the sudden resolution that he would visit Noor Mahal, but he communicated his intention to no one.

The sun was shining in the shabby little court, as it almost always does in India, in front of Noor Mahal's rooms; above was the narrow strip of blue sky. Outside, her little girl, the child of Shere Afghan, richly attired in gold and crimson, wandered hither and thither like some strange bright bird. Noor Mahal was absorbingly busy, following her daily avocations, working among her slaves and maidens. What salve is there for a sad heart like an absorbing pursuit? In such, her restless and aspiring mind had found resignation if not contentment. There was a stir, a movement, a cry of voices, the bustling importance of eunuchs, which made all the busy workers pause,—'Make way for the king!' 'Salute the Asylum of the Universe!' reached their ears; and then, all unexpected, Jehangire stood before the woman whose life he had embittered. For one minute a flush rose to her face, cheeks, ears, neck; everything shared in the crimson glow, and then she turned deadly pale; she made the usual salutation of touching the ground, and raising her hand to her head. It was a minute too absorbing for words; the past was all before Noor Mahal. It is reported that in death your past life rises before you like a panorama; there are such minutes in life also. She remembered her girlish passion, the warnings of her family, Shere Afghan's cruel death, her years of solitude and heartless neglect. Why had Jehangire come? There was no escape for her from this despot's cruel and uncontrollable will, as cruel and as little to be evaded as the decrees of Fate. One word passing Jehangire's lips, men would have rushed forward to seize her, to brick her up alive, it might be, in the honeycomb of dungeons that was under their very feet. Jehangire's eyes were wandering with surprise over the physical features of the scene; the magnificence that filled him with astonishment, the wondrous adornments of the rooms, which he, with all the endless resources of his enormous empire, had never been able to purchase; for taste and artistic instincts and knowledge are not purchasable articles. But what astonished him most of all was the intensely gorgeous attire of the slaves who surrounded her. 'No sultanas he had ever seen surpassed them in the splendour of their silken brocades of Bagdad.' Noor Mahal was dressed in the plainest, simplest way; she was a woman who never looked inelegant; her dress of plain white muslin enhanced her loveliness, showed off her tall, slight, statuesque figure, her small head, the straight-cut perfect face, the sad, refined, pensive air. 'Age could not stale, nor custom change, her infinite variety.' Jehangire thought he had never seen any one so lovely.

'Why this difference between Noor Mahal and her women?' he asked; and Noor Mahal answered, with her usual tact, in her low, musical voice:

'These are slaves, and must dress as it shall please those they serve. These are my servants, and I alleviate their burden of bondage by every indulgence in my power. But I am your slave, O Emperor of the world! and must dress according to your pleasure, and not my own.'

The king seated himself on a sofa, and requested Noor Mahal to be seated by him. This one interview was sufficient to establish with greater power than ever her influence over Jehangire. When he rose to depart, with tears in his eyes, he begged her forgiveness for his long unkindness, and threw round her neck a necklace he wore, containing forty pearls, each pearl being valued at £4000. From the wretched quarters that had been allotted to her, Noor Mahal was removed next day to those of the favourite sultana, which she never left. For twenty years she ruled the king and the kingdom. No important offices of state were given away without her consent, no treaties with foreign states were concluded without her knowledge. She was given the very unusual honour of being called 'Shahi,' empress. Money was coined in her name, and Jehangire said: 'Gold had gained a new value since it bore the name of Noor Mahal.' She strengthened her power by surrounding herself with her relations. Her father became vizier; her brother, Asiph Khan, was raised to the first rank of the nobility; her relations poured in from Central Asia, and were provided for. No family rose so suddenly to high rank or more deservedly than the family of Chaja Aiass. Her father was not dazzled by the splendour of his high office. He was a man of great ability in public affairs, and he bore the highest character for honour and probity. The courtier-like young Asiph Khan, though without his sister's great abilities, had the qualities that render men popular—tact, courtesy, and a modesty of manner that disarmed rivalry. Noor Mahal's abilities soon rendered her absolute in government, in which in all lands women are considered incapable of bearing a part. Jehangire more than ever gave himself over to drink and pleasure, for, as he said, 'His wife had wit enough in her little finger to rule the whole kingdom, without his troubling his head about it.' This was the secret of her power over this sensualist; she was invaluable to him. Noor Mahal was a great builder. By her orders rose mosques and serais, gardens and fountains, in many cities; many of which still stand.

The part of the palace where she passed much of her brilliant life still stands in the castle of Agra. It is called the Jasmine Bower. It has of late years been repaired by the orders of the English viceroy, Lord Mayo. The Jasmine Bower still bears the stamp of the elevated and artistic mind of Noor Mahal. Her private rooms and her balcony are also to be seen on the high castle walls of Agra, and overlook the rushing river Jumna, sixty feet below. The view from the balcony is extensive and beautiful; the great city, with its hundred gardens, and its domes and minarets, lies stretched below. The whole of this part of the castle is of white marble, a material so suited to a warm climate. The architecture is Saracenic; there are few doors or windows; the whole is open to the warm, soft air, the blue sky, the perennial sunshine of India. The pillars of the balcony of the Jasmine Bower are of white marble, inlaid with Florentine mosaic, with cornelian and bloodstone, and even with rubies, emeralds, and turquoises. The designs of this inlaying are probably Noor Mahal's own; they are very artistic. The design on some columns is a winding garland of leaves. The walls and ceiling of her rooms were brilliantly painted and gilded. The floors are of inlaid marble. They open into a small court, paved with white marble, in which plays a fountain. These rooms are in close proximity to and overlook the hall of private audience, where all public affairs of moment were transacted. Forming a part of Noor Mahal's private rooms, is a curious underground palace, called 'The Palace of a Thousand Mirrors.' Here she found refuge from the burning heat of summer. The walls are covered with thousands of small pieces of looking-glass; water in a marble conduit runs into a square marble tank in the centre of the room; the water is so arranged that it falls in a small cascade over lamps. The whole place used to be brilliantly lighted, and the walls of mirrors reflected each object a thousand times. But lower still, and near the subterranean palace, which, when lighted up, must have looked like fairyland, are melancholy prisons and dungeons, gloomy and secret, whose dark walls must have witnessed unspeakable misery; for, in repairs undertaken by the English, skeletons have been discovered walled up in the massive walls, and other traces of diabolical cruelty.

We English happily hardly comprehend the position of an Eastern despot. Jehangire was sole judge and absolute arbiter of the lives and property of his subjects. The highest as well as the lowest were at his mercy. Jehangire was cruel with a barbarity undreamt of in these days. He impaled seven hundred men outside the city of Agra. They were followers of his son Chusero, who had been driven into an ill-judged revolt by his father's cruelty; and while one of this wretched band of Chusero's followers lived, the hapless young prince was daily led out to see the sufferings and hear the groans of these men, who suffered for their misplaced loyalty to him; and the mother of Chusero, one of Noor Mahal's rivals of long ago, poisoned herself sooner than live and see the misery of her son.

But for twenty years Noor Mahal kept this despotic ruler her slave. She even managed to free herself from one of the strictest Moslem customs. Sir Thomas Roe, an English ambassador, who was sent to India by James the Second, mentions that she used to drive in the streets of Agra, unveiled, with the king, in a bullock-coach, drawn by a beautiful and small breed of oxen, called Ghinees.'

The Easterns have a proverb to show how short-lived is prosperity. 'The moonlight,' they say, 'lasts but for four days.' At length the star of Noor Mahal's good fortune waned; she was in deadly peril, and this from her own follies and mistakes—mistakes that even a woman of genius will make from consulting her heart more than her head. We cannot wholly detach ourselves from our past. Noor Mahal's own daughter, the pretty child who had brought some happiness to her obscurity and disgrace, had grown up and had been married to Jehangire's fourth son, Prince Sheriar; and this child of the long-forgotten and hapless Shere Afghan, the pet and idol of her mother, was destined to be instrumental in clouding her mother's last days and ruining her ambition.

The heir to the throne was Shah Jehan, Jehangire's eldest son, an able man and distinguished soldier. Noor Mahal determined to deprive him of his birthright, and to secure the succession to his younger brother, Prince

Sheriar, and thus not only secure the throne for her daughter, but, as Prince Sheriar was weak and indolent, she hoped after her husband's death still to retain the power she had held indisputably for twenty years.

Shah Jehan was not a man to allow himself to be tamely injured; he was deeply attached to his father; but this intrigue drove him into the desperate remedy of rebellion. Noor Mahal's high-handed government had made many malcontents. Shah Jehan's rebellion was successful: he was joined by many nobles, many troops. He had gained Bengal and Behar, two of the richest provinces of the empire; it was impossible to say what his next success would be. Noor Mahal feared he would soon reach the walls of the palace at Agra. She, the king, and the courtiers were overwhelmed with anxious forebodings when Shah Jehan was totally defeated near Benares by one of Jehangire's generals, named Mohabit Khan one of the first soldiers of the day. From that minute Shah Jehan's cause was hopeless; fortune abandoned him, he fell dangerously ill, he was hunted from place to place, his misery was extreme.

Jehangire was dotingly fond of his children, in spite of all that had passed. The king loved his son; he made every allowance for the provocation he had received. Jehangire shed tears on receiving a letter from Shah Jehan; in answer, he wrote and begged him to return to the court, and promised that the past should be forgiven. But though a wretched fugitive, hiding for his life, Shah

Jehan dared not return. He feared his father's weakness; he feared the machinations of Noor Mahal: he knew her vindictiveness too well. He kept away for many years; in fact, he never returned to see his father.

Mohabit Khan, the successful general, a blunt, loyal soldier, became the hero of the hour. The people hailed him as the saviour of society: he had saved them from a civil war, from a revolution. The king showered honours on him; he was indebted to him for his throne. But Noor Mahal and Asiph Khan, spoilt by long years of uncontrolled power, long years of prosperity, hated him—hated him for his growing influence over the king.

Mohabit was accused of treason, of malpractices. He sent his son-in-law to court to explain his conduct. Jehangire was marching to Kabul with an immense retinue of troops and servants, to the number of thirty thousand souls. The court was lodged in splendid silken tents, some even embroidered in pearls. The young lord alighted from his elephant in the imperial square of the camp; but Mohabit's representative was suddenly seized, bastinadoed, covered with rags, and sent out of camp riding backwards on a sorry jade, amid the shouts of the whole army.

The great soldier Mohabit bore the affront with seeming patience; he was encamped about five miles from Jehangire's camp, and was guarded by five thousand Rajpoots, who were intensely devoted to their leader. Mohabit was by birth a Rajpoot, but an apostate. The opportunity for revenge soon presented itself, and he seized it. The greater part of Jehangire's army had marched in advance of the king; the army had crossed the only bridge over the river Jhelum. The king, Noor Mahal, the court, the ladies, the silken tents, the thousands of slaves, were on the other side of the river. Mohabit and his Rajpoots seized the bridge and burnt it, and thus divided the king from his army; he then made a sudden and unexpected dash upon the imperial camp. Jehangire's household guards made a slight resistance, but were soon overpowered. The king was taken; and in the confusion of the attack, Noor Mahal escaped, and fled to her brother Asiph Khan, who had crossed the river that morning with the imperial army.

'The next morning at dawn, Asiph began his march to rescue the king. When he came to the bridge, he found it burnt, he resolved to ford the river, but the water was so deep that many of his men were drowned. Those who gained the farther shore had to fight the enemy at a manifest disadvantage. They were cut down as fast as they ascended the bank. A succession of victims fell to the swords of the Rajpoots; the action continued for some hours, the rear of Asiph Khan's troops pressing into the river prevented the front from retreating. Noor Mahal was not a tame spectator on the occasion. Mounted on an elephant, she plunged into the stream with her daughter by her side; the young lady was wounded in the arm, but her mother pressed on.

Three of her elephant drivers were successively killed, and one elephant received three wounds on the trunk. Noor Mahal herself, in the meantime, emptied four quivers of arrows on the enemy. The Rajpoot troops pressed into the stream to seize her; but the master of her household, mounting the elephant, turned him away, and carried her out of the river, notwithstanding her threats and commands.'

Jehangire remained in the power of Mohabit; Noor Mahal, Asiph Khan, Prince Sheriar, and his wife fled northwards, with the remains of the imperial army. They took refuge at Lahore, a strong-walled and fortified city, where they remained until Jehangire recalled Noor Mahal to his side. She came; but when she arrived at Agra, she was conveyed to a prison; her husband had joined her enemies, and had even signed her death-warrant.

The reasons Mohabit gave for this extreme severity were: 'That nothing but the death of the empress will give peace to the realm; and you, O Emperor of the Moghuls, whom we regard as more than human, ought to follow the example of God, who is no respecter of persons. Noor Mahal has estranged from you the hearts of your subjects; the most cruel and unwarrantable actions have been done by her capricious orders. In every corner of the empire her haughtiness has been the source of public calamity; her malignity the ruin of individuals. She has even extended her views to the empire by favouring the succession of Sheriar to the throne, under whose feeble administration she hopes to rule India.'

When Noor Mahal was informed of her doom, all she answered was:

'Permit me once more to see the emperor, and to bathe with my tears the hand that has fixed my death-warrant.'

Jehangire, fearing his own weakness, would not see her alone. By his side stood Mohabit Khan, the impersonification of merciless justice. Noor Mahal was admitted, surrounded by Mohabit's Rajpoot guard. The sight of this woman, who had made the whole happiness of his life, who had hitherto shared his joy and his affliction, completely unhinged Jehangire. He burst into tears, and wept like a child.

'Will you not spare this woman, Mohabit Khan? See how she weeps!' he asked of the stern dictator by his side.

'The Emperor of the Moghuls,' said the chivalrous Rajpoot, 'should never ask in vain.'

Noor Mahal's life was spared. The friends of Mohabit greatly disapproved of his generosity, and he had bitter cause to repent it himself. Noor Mahal lived, not to thank her forgiver, but to revenge herself, and soon her busy spirit hatched mischief.

The court was in Kabul. She stirred up the fanatical Moslem rabble to attack Mohabit. He was in imminent peril. His Rajpoot followers were all wounded or slain.

For six months Mohabit was minister or Vizier (Noor Mahal's father had died some years before), and held supreme power. He took the sudden resolve to throw up his high office. He was a soldier, and not a statesman. To be the conscientious head of a despotism is no sinecure. He had had no designs himself upon the empire, but, for self-preservation, he had been obliged to act as he had done. He exacted and obtained from Jehangire the most solemn promises of oblivion for the past, and he restored Jehangire to all his former consequence and power. To show his sincerity, he dismissed the greater part of his guards and attendants. This conduct was noble, but he had gone too far to retreat. Gratitude is not so strong a passion as revenge; the weak forget favours, but the haughty never forget indignities.

Noor Mahal remembered her danger, and the disgrace she had suffered from Mohabit, and she applied to Jehangire for his immediate death. She urged these specious arguments, to strengthen her ignoble request: 'A man,' said she, 'who is so daring as to seize the person of his sovereign, is a dangerous subject. The lustre of royalty must be diminished,' continued Noor Mahal, 'in the eyes of the people, whilst he who pulled his prince from the throne is permitted to kneel before it in feigned allegiance.'

Jehangire was shocked at her proposal. He commanded her to be silent; she was silent, but did not drop her design. She resolved to kill by private treachery the man she had failed to bring to a public death. She placed one of her eunuchs behind a curtain, with orders to shoot Mohabit when he should next come to pay his respects to Jehangire. The king overheard her commands to the slave. He told Mohabit of the snare laid for his life, and said that 'though he was resolved to save him from public disgrace, his power was not sufficient to protect him from private treachery.' Mohabit escaped from the court. He was declared a rebel by Noor Mahal, a price was put upon his head; and she seized the whole of his property.

Asiph Khan strongly disapproved of his sister's violence to Mohabit, and remembered that when they were in his power he had acted very differently towards them. But Asiph Khan's power depended upon his sister. She was haughty and vindictive; so he was obliged to observe a cautious silence, for since Mohabit's flight she was more despotic than ever. At last he secretly joined the disaffected Shah Jehan and Mohabit. Shah Jehan had married his daughter; and he (Asiph) foresaw that, as father-in-law to the Sultan, his prospects would be better than under Prince Sheriar or Noor Mahal. Asiph Khan promised to send Mohabit a ring, as a signal for them both openly to espouse the cause of Shah Jehan, when the time was ripe. At this time Jehangire's health visibly declined, and, in the certainty of his approaching death, Asiph Khan saw it would be unnecessary to wrest the crown from him by force. Jehangire died on the ninth of

November, 1627, of asthma, on a journey from Cashmere to Lahore.

As soon as the king was dead, Asiph Khan sent the ring to Mohabit. In his father's will, Prince Sheriar had been declared successor to the throne, according to Moslem precedent. In point of fact, the succession was usually decided by a civil war, waged by the king's sons, until one had proved himself the strongest in battle.

Asiph Khan and the troops at once declared for Shah Jehan. Prince Sheriar determined to meet them in battle. The decisive engagement took place at Lahore.

'Prince Sheriar had crossed the Jhelum before the approach of Asiph, and drew up his forces upon the first appearance of the enemy. It was rather a flight than a battle. The raw troops of Sheriar gave way almost without a blow. He was not himself in the action. He stood on a distant hill, and fell into the current of retreat. He shut himself up in the citadel of Lahore, which was invested next day by the army of Asiph. The friends of Sheriar deserted him, and made terms for themselves. The unfortunate prince hid himself in a cellar of the harem. He was found, and dragged to the light, was blinded next day, and ultimately killed. Blinded because, according to the Koran, no blind man can be king.'

Thus faded Noor Mahal's last vision of power. She continued to live at Lahore for twenty years, and her daughter, Prince Sheriar's widow, lived with her. Twenty-five thousand pounds were annually paid to her out of the public treasury, a paltry sum for a woman whose privy purse had been the king's revenue of forty millions. She was too proud ever to speak of public affairs, and she gave herself up to study, retirement, and ease.

Shah Jehan became king; his reign was peaceable, rich and glorious. Mohabit was raised to the post of commander-in-chief; Asiph Khan was vizier, with the salary of one million sterling a year. His daughter was Shah Jehan's sole and dearly loved wife. She was as beautiful as Noor Mahal. It was over Asiph's daughter that Shah Jehan raised the Taj Mausoleum, that mass of white marble and mosaic, which to this day is one of the wonders of the world. Noor Mahal, according to the Moslem custom, built a splendid tomb for her husband, and she and her daughter also lie buried at Lahore.

On the death of her father, Noor Mahal had wished to erect a mausoleum over him of silver, but was reminded 'that all sublunary things are subject to change, and that even the empire of the Moghuls might not be eternal;' and that it would be wiser to make it of stone. She accordingly raised over his remains a beautiful three-storied building, which still stands near Agra. It is built of marble inlaid with mosaic.

The four sons of Shah Jehan were in Jehangire's camp, near Lahore, when he died. They had been sent by Shah Jehan as hostages; their names were Dara

(Darius), Suja, Aurungzebe, and Morad. Asiph Khan travelled from Lahore to Agra with them, where they arrived on the 22nd of March, 1628. Shah Jehan was celebrating the feast of the Norose when his children were restored to him, safe and well, after three years of sorrow and anxiety.

When Shah Jehan succeeded to the throne of Delhi,* Dara Sheko, his father's favourite son, was thirteen years of age, Suja was twelve, Aurungzebe was ten, Morad only four. Shah Jehan had also three daughters: Jehanara, a pretty, lively girl of fourteen; Rochenara was the name of the second; Suria Banu (she was of exquisite beauty) the name of the third. These seven children were all of one mother, Asiph's daughter. The education of Shah Jehan's sons was confided to Afzil Khan, a man of great literary talent, who had been Shah Jehan's own tutor. Afzil Khan was raised by his grateful pupil to some of the highest offices in the State, from which he drew emoluments to the amount of three hundred and seventy-five thousand pounds yearly.†

Shah Jehan's children were handsome, gifted, intelligent, and lively. Aurungzebe was less tall and handsome than his brothers. He was studious and silent, and from his earliest years, affected to be very devout. Dara and his sister Jehanara were inseparable friends and companions. Aurungzebe and his sister Rochenara were much attached to each other, even in childhood.

* Dow, vol. iii. p. 122

† Ibid. vol. iii. p. 175.

For twenty years, Shah Jehan and Arjemund Banu (the daughter of Asiph) led a happy and united married life, until she died in child-bed in 1631, leaving a fourth infant daughter. Eight of her children survived her. Her husband loved her devotedly, and built over her the splendid Taj Mausoleum, 'the highest compliment that was ever paid to a woman.'

Shah Jehan removed the court from Lahore and Agra to Delhi, and there he built a magnificent new city near Firozabad, the city of Baber's time. It is near the splendid remains of six old cities. For Delhi, or Induprustha, had been a place of importance for three thousand years. Shah Jehan's city is modern Delhi; the town walls are six miles round, with ten fine gates. The palace, or 'Red Castle,' is an inner defence or castle, the high walls of which are three miles round; one side is protected by the river Jumna.

In April, 1648, the king entered into his new palace, and for nine days unceasing feasting and revelry were kept up to celebrate the event. Inside the large area, protected by the high walls of the 'Red Castle,' were beautiful gardens, palaces, fountains, running water, courts; it was a city within a city. The new palace and town were plentifully supplied with water brought from a long distance by a canal. The new town had also some fine broad streets, which still exist. The nobles built palaces and laid out gardens, principally in a quarter called Dario-gunge. In the palace, the part occupied by the royal family, was, like that of Agra, mostly built of white marble, inlaid with mosaic work. It is believed the Mohammedan architects were assisted by Italians and Frenchmen in the mosaic work and in erecting these fine buildings. The designs of the palaces, however, are purely Saracenic, and, like those of the palace of Agra, are exceedingly beautiful. Much of the palace, and nearly all the houses of the Amirs, have been destroyed.

Bernier, a French physician, and several Jesuit priests, were at the court of Shah Jehan, and have left interesting accounts of its customs and amusements, of its wealth and splendour. Some of the king's kinsmen were converted to Romanism by the Jesuits, but Arjemund Banu, the queen, was a most bigoted Moslem. She considered Romanism to be idolatry or image-worship. Owing partially to her bigotry, the Portuguese were attacked, by Shah Jehan's orders, at Hooghly in Bengal. Three thousand of them fell into the hands of the Turkish Governor of Bengal, and were sold as slaves. Their churches were pulled down, their images and crucifixes were broken. This was the first time the house of Timour crossed swords with Europeans. An old church, built by the Portuguese, still stands at Hooghly in good preservation.

Mohabit was very punctilious about rank; and in the beginning of Shah Jehan's reign, he would on no occasion give place to the vizier, Asiph Khan, who on his side would not relinquish the precedence which he derived from his high office. Shah Jehan did not choose to interfere in the contest; they were both his benefactors. He, however, was at last prevailed upon to decide in favour of Asiph. He made the following excuse to Mohabit: 'That in all civilised governments the sword should yield to the pen.'*

Mohabit was made Nizam (viceroy) of the Deccan, a large southern province of the empire, which had been but lately acquired. In 1634, he died at Brampour, at a very advanced age. Asiph Khan was raised to the rank of Wakeel Mutaluck. He died at the age of seventy-two, his death being hastened by grief at the death of another daughter. Though he had sons of his own, by will he left an immense fortune to his grandson, Prince Dara, Shah Jehan's eldest son, the heir to the crown. 'The amount, in coin, in jewels, in plate, elephants and horses, amounted to four millions sterling. His estates, in land, according to the tenure in India, reverted to the crown.'†

Mohabit left two sons, Shastu Khan and Shah Nawaz, who both played important parts in the next reign, which was that of the celebrated Aurungzebe.

* Dow, vol. iii. p. 162.

† Ibid. vol. iii. p. 184.

CHAPTER VI.

AURUNGZEBE.

Hypocrisy of Aurungzebe—His long and prosperous reign—The fatal policy of religious persecution.

In the reign of Aurungzebe the decay of the house of Timour began. That monarch reigned from 1658 to 1707. He was, like so many of his ancestors, a good soldier, a good ruler, but, unlike them, he was a Moslem bigot, and he persecuted the Hindoos. Although he had waded to the throne through the blood of many relations, Aurungzebe gave to India prosperity and peace for a period of fifty years. He was a religious hypocrite, like Louis XI. of France, with much of that monarch's capacity as well as his bigotry. His tongue was smooth but his arm was strong. He was a great captain; the Turks of Delhi were not effete as soldiers as long as he lived. Aurungzebe was but eighteen when he commanded an army which drove the dreaded Usbegs out of a province of Kabul, Badakshan, and from the city of Balkh. From a command in the extreme northern frontier of the Indian Empire he was removed by his father, Shah Jehan, to quiet the southern and tropical province of the Deccan, lately acquired by the Turks. There Aurungzebe was equally successful against the Mahrattas, Rajpoots under a new name and under a new organisation, who were more than ever the inveterate enemies of the hated Turks of Delhi. The conquest of the Deccan, joined to persecution and insults to the Hindoo creed, had caused the rise of the Mahrattas. Another of Aurungzebe's successful campaigns was against the Yusefzais and other tribes of the Kheiber. They had made an inroad far into the plains of the Punjaub, under Mohammed Shah, a chief who, like many others of that country, claimed to be a direct descendant from Alexander the Great. Aurungzebe drove them back, defeated them in their inaccessible mountains, marched through three valleys, and burnt their villages. When Shah Jehan had a paralytic stroke, and his death was hourly expected, Prince Dara, the eldest son and the heir to the throne, directed the administration. Dara was the darling of his father, who was often heard to say 'that all his other children were not half so dear to him as Dara.' He was handsome, attractive, generous, brave, and very popular. He was idolised by the Amirs for his soldierly character, and by the Hindoos he was beloved for his toleration in religious matters. He had been educated to consider himself heir to the throne; the wealth of his grandfather, Asiph, had enabled him to live with a state and magnificence which had added to his popularity with the vulgar, and had helped him to outshine his other brothers. Arjemund Banu the Queen, Asiph's daughter, had on her death-bed made Shah Jehan promise not to marry again, 'that other sons might not dispute the throne with her children.' This promise Shah Jehan faithfully kept. And to her sons, young as they were, her last request had been, 'Remember me, and live in peace.' Everything seemed to promise a bloodless succession. It was the wish of the court, of the king, and of the country; but against it there were Aurungzebe's unprincipled ambition and the habit of fratricidal war, the time immemorial custom of ancient Asia. This fatal national custom the Turks had brought to India. Aurungzebe had great influence with the army of the Deccan; he easily persuaded his troops and officers to join his cause. The more intelligent joined from ambition. But to keep up appearances and to gain popularity, he caused it to be given out that Dara had usurped the authority of the king, that Shah Jehan was not ill, but that Dara had imprisoned him. To get this lie believed was not difficult to a prince of Aurungzebe's deep cunning. The distance between Agra and the Deccan was more than a thousand miles, the communication rare. Aurungzebe then made a tool of his younger brother, Morad. He told him '*Dara ought not to reign;*' he was a 'heretic,' on principle indifferent about all religion. For Dara had not only adopted the freethinking creed of his race, but was very liberal and enlightened in his ideas on all subjects. He had been in the habit of associating with the believers of many different creeds.

Dara had written a book which had given great offence to all the orthodox Mohammedans. It was called 'The Uniting of both Seas.' He endeavoured to reconcile the Brahmin religion with the Mohammedan, citing passages from the Koran to prove their points of contact. The book more than anything else lost him the empire.

A hundred swords leaped from their scabbards at this cry of 'The true Faith.' The easy toleration of Dara and Suja had raised them a host of secret enemies among the Amirs. By encouraging men of all religions, especially the Brahmins, they had offended the Mohammedans. The Turkish nobles, the Persian and Usbeg Amirs, soldiers of fortune who crowded the court from Central Asia, and filled all the high appointments, 'could not see without envy men of different persuasion from their own admitted into the confidence of princes who still professed the Moslem faith.'

Dara associated much with the Jesuit priests at the court, and Suja, another brother, was even accused of being a Christian.

Aurungzebe declared that the unorthodoxy of his elder brothers was sufficient reason to exclude them both from the succession. His own claims he would waive; he had no ambition, he had no wish to reign. 'As for me,' continued Aurungzebe, 'I have long since dedicated myself to the service of God. I desire only that safety and tranquillity which suits the fervency of my devotion. But I will, with my poor abilities, assist Morad to take possession of a sceptre which the united wishes of the people of Hindustan have already placed in his hand. Morad may then think of his faithful Aurungzebe, and assign him a quiet retreat, that he may pass the remainder of his life in the austerities of religion.'

The hot-headed Morad was altogether deceived by his brother's hypocrisy. Morad was outspoken to a fault, incapable of deceit himself, and by nature unsuspicious of others. He was brave, honourable, and courageous; but he was self-conceited and rash, and he was completely duped and blinded. He ascribed Aurungzebe's moderation to his own superior merits and a sincere zeal for 'the Faith.' Nor would the hot-headed youth listen to those friends who whispered words of warning. To mention to him the designs of his brother 'was a satire upon his penetration; to suggest to him caution was in his eyes an accusation of his courage.'

Therefore Morad and Aurungzebe united their cause and their arms. They marched from the Deccan on the city of Agra. Shah Jehan was still living, but much weakened in mind and body by his last serious illness. Dara, backed by all the resources of the crown, met his brothers in battle near Agra. His filial affection, which was true and sincere, made him dissuade Shah Jehan, in his weak state, from taking the field in person, although he wished to do so. This proved a fatal mistake, for if the king had appeared many of the troops of the Deccan would not have opposed him. The brothers met in battle not far from Agra. Aurungzebe's good generalship and Morad's personal courage won the day in a long and sternly-contested battle. Dara fled from the field. He had lost the crown of India. Shah Jehan held one heartrending interview with his favourite child. He recommended him to reach Lahore, *vià* Delhi, to collect troops in the Punjaub and in Kabul. Dara took his favourite wife and a few faithful servants, but had no means of carrying away his jewels and treasures. The hoarded wealth of Asiph fell into Aurungzebe's hands.

With many smooth and flattering words Aurungzebe soothed and calmed his aged father's indignation and that of his sister Jehanara; Rochenara sided with Aurungzebe. The latter, when upbraided by his father, pointed out that the blame rested with Morad alone, who was aspiring to the throne; that he himself was a man of piety, his only wish was to leave the world and go on a pilgrimage to Mecca. To his brother Morad he wrote at this juncture, "My wishes are now completely accomplished. I have contributed to raise a prince worthy of the throne of our ancestors, and I have but one favour to ask for all the fatigues I have undergone. This world has already overwhelmed me with its cares. I long to throw the burden away; I am tired of the vain bustle and pageantry of life. Permit me to make a pilgrimage to

Mecca.'* Morad tried to dissuade his brother from so distant a journey, but without success, and Aurungzebe began to make preparations for a pilgrimage that he never intended to take.

But when Morad was heavy with drink, he was seized, carried away on an elephant, imprisoned at Agra, and placed in the charge of Shastu Khan, Mohabit's son. He was ultimately killed in prison by his brother Aurungzebe's orders. Morad was a mere tool in his clever brother's hands. He had few friends and no zealous adherents, and the world accepted his disappearance with indifference. But Aurungzebe, who had so often and so publicly stated that he had no worldly ambition, could not with any consistency appear as a candidate for the throne. He instigated a body of noblemen and officers of the court to wait on him. They begged him to abandon his idea of going to Mecca, and not to leave them exposed to the resentment of Dara. Aurungzebe seemed disappointed, and even offended at their proposal. At length he suffered himself to be persuaded. 'You are resolved to sacrifice my love of retirement to your own ease. Be it so. God will, perhaps, give me that tranquillity upon the throne which I hoped to find in a cell; and if less of my time shall be employed in prayer, more of it will be spent in good actions. I should only have an inclination for virtuous deeds in my retreat, but as Emperor of India I shall have the power of doing them. These

* Dow, vol. iii. p. 269.

motives, and not the vain pomp of greatness, induce me to assume the empire.'*

Without any pomp or display Aurungzebe was crowned at Delhi, and the Khutbah was read in his name. Leaving Shah Jehan a strongly-guarded prisoner in the castle of Agra, under the charge of his son, Mohammed, a youth of eighteen, and of Shastu Khan, Aurungzebe, with his usual energy and activity, followed Dára to Lahore. After various vicissitudes and battles, Dara was taken, his wife having died before him from misery and hardships. Dara and his young son were brought prisoners to Agra, and Aurungzebe hesitated what to do with his unfortunate brother. He asked the advice of his lords and leading officers. The mob of Delhi and Agra had risen in Dara's favour, and had raised a tumult when they heard that he had been taken prisoner. 'Among the lords was one Hakim, a Persian, who, with a design to gain the favour of Aurungzebe, insisted that Dara should be put to death as an apostate from the faith of Mohammed. Aurungzebe pretended to be startled, and said, "The thing is determined. I might have forgiven injuries done to myself, but those against religion I cannot forgive." He immediately ordered a warrant to be issued to Nazir and Seif, two fierce Afghan chiefs, which empowered them to kill Dara that very night.'† He was murdered in prison, and his head was brought to Aurungzebe, who wiped the face with a handkerchief. When he recognised the hand-

* Dow, vol. iii. p. 275. † Ibid. vol. iii. p. 333.

some features of his brother he exclaimed, 'Alas! unfortunate man!' and shed some tears.

Suja, the sole surviving brother, defended himself in Bengal. The Portuguese of Hooghly had taken up his quarrel. They lent him men and artillery; but he was defeated, and fled to Burmah, where he and his three sons, his wife, and several daughters, perished miserably.

Shah Jehan remained a prisoner, and was most affectionately tended by his daughter Jehanara. They lived together seven years in the castle of Agra as State prisoners. His usurper son treated him with every outward respect and lip service, with every consideration, state, and luxury, but allowed him no voice in public affairs, though he often affected to ask his advice.

The power he had gained by such infamous means Aurungzebe used well. He was not only a great soldier, but a great administrator, a great reformer, and his enlightenment was extraordinary and his industry untiring; but all his efforts to benefit India were marred by his religious intolerance. Aurungzebe can be best described as a great 'Red-tapeist.' Form, order, method, were his idols. He rose at dawn, plunged into a bath, dressed, and retired to prayers in a beautiful little white marble chapel or mosque—the Pearl Mosque—which he had caused to be built in the Red Castle of Delhi. Returning into his apartment from the chapel, he spent half-an-hour reading a book of devotions. He then entered the hall of justice at seven o'clock in the morning, and decided cases until nine. He had a sum of money placed at his side on the bench, and he relieved the necessitous with his own hand. Charity to the poor is a cardinal point in the Moslem creed. At nine he retired to the harem to breakfast, after which meal he came out on a balcony which faced the grand square of the palace. Being a part of the harem, the balcony was called the 'place of privacy.'* His elephants, gorgeously caparisoned, and his stud of riding-horses passedin review before him, or sometimes he witnessed fights between tigers and other animals. These amusements were shared by the ladies, unseen, behind lattices. At eleven o'clock he made his appearance, surrounded by his sons, in the hall of public audiences—'The Hall of the Forty Pillars.' It was a daily levée. All the nobles, officers, and officials assembled, and stood, according to their official rank, below the throne. Strangers were introduced, ambassadors from foreign countries were received, and all was conducted with an orderly and rigorous etiquette.

In the square which opened on the public hall of audience, Aurungzebe, after the levée, reviewed troops; sometimes his own, sometimes those of free-lances and soldiers of fortune from Central Asia, or those of a Rajpoot prince who wished to enter his service. The lower nobility presented themselves in another square; artisans, with curious inventions and works of utility, in

* Dow, vol. iii. p. 428.

another; and huntsmen, with rare animals from different parts of the kingdom, in a fourth square.

At one o'clock the king retired to his private apartments, accompanied by some of the great officers of state. The disposal of offices was generally arranged then, and questions of promotion and of patronage. At half-past two o'clock Aurungzebe dined, and took a short siesta. At four o'clock he appeared in the balcony above the great gate of the palace to the general public, when those in the crowd who had wrongs or grievances unredressed might and did call out, 'Justice! justice!' and, at fitting time, their complaints were entered into by the king himself. This custom of sitting in 'the gate,' old as the time of the Jewish kings, was a great check upon the peculation of the officials. The poorest yeoman who had been overtaxed by any official, if he complained, which he often did, obtained immediate redress. It was this easy and simple public justice that rendered living under despotic pashas endurable.

At six Aurungzebe went to prayers in the Pearl Mosque, after which he retired to his private rooms, accompanied by his principal counsellors. The most important part of the day's work began at seven in the evening. Letters of moment were written, and Aurungzebe sat up to a very late hour discussing affairs of state, and settling weighty business. Official work was his amusement.

Some changes were allowed in this routine. Some days there was no public audience or levée; some days he did not appear in the hall of audience. Sometimes he reviewed the troops; sometimes he audited the accounts of the officers of the revenue, the details of which department he understood better than any man in his dominions. The whole court feasted on religious feast days, and on some days they prayed and fasted. These days of work, of eighteen hours a day, beginning at dawn and ending at midnight, produced reforms; regularity, and scrupulous justice, spread over all his wide-extended dominions of thirty-two provinces. In the judicial branch the following reforms were introduced. To corrupt a judge was rendered for the first time a crime. Facilities of appeal were given. If a judge's decree was reversed, Aurungzebe would not always allow the judge to screen himself on the score of an error of judgment. 'In so clear a case,' he would say, 'either the judge had not sufficient ability to perceive the truth, and therefore is unfit for the post, or he has taken a bribe, and he is unjust, and unworthy of the post.'*

An unjust judge, a peculating farmer-general, a general who had failed in the field, were immediately dismissed from their offices; but they were often kept on at court, hanging about the anterooms of the Red Castle, out of favour and out of office. They were also expected to appear at the daily receptions in the Hall of the Forty Pillars. Having lost their precedence with their office, they sat in the lowest place among their peers, until in

* Dow, vol. iii. p. 427.

time, if they had patience, and if their offence was not serious, they were re-employed. In every department Aurungzebe had an organised system of spies, who reported every irregularity; and this, and the facility of complaining to the king in public, rendered it nearly impossible that the officials should oppress the people without the king hearing of it. In a rude way, it was a union of the king and people against the bureaucrats, and against the rapacity of the officials. He knew that 'the hands' (the pasha) of a despotism would peculate, would oppress, and he tried to protect the people.

Aurungzebe wrote many letters with his own hand. He corrected the diction of his secretaries. He never allowed a letter to be despatched without critically examining it himself. Besides the language of Turki, which was his mother-tongue, he could write and read Persian and Arabic thoroughly. His style was plain and concise in all three languages. He did all he could to promote education. He founded and built universities and schools in all towns, and paid high salaries to the teachers. He opened public libraries, and had copies made of the books which he considered of value for these libraries. He assisted agriculture in many ways, and issued edicts 'that rents should not be raised on those who by their industry had improved their farms.' Capital punishment was almost unknown in his reign.

His ancestors had built palaces and gardens. Aurungzebe's great works were nearly all of public utility. He built staging-houses for post-horses, from Kabul to Aurungabad, in the Deccan, a distance of twelve hundred miles. These staging-houses were erected at intervals of not more than ten or twenty miles; post-horses were to be procured in them, and simple provisions, shelter, etc. This was to assist travellers. The road was kept up, ferries were placed at the great rivers, the small ones were bridged. He placed the same facilities of communication from Guzerat to Bengal, a distance of fifteen hundred miles.

Though he had no friends like the kindly Baber, and mistrusted all men, he permitted no drunkards, sensualists, or men of bad moral character at his court. Flatterers he hated; singers, dancers, musicians, he considered a useless race of people, and drove them from the palace. On festivals only he wore cloth of gold and jewels; on all other occasions he dressed very simply, but he changed his dress twice a day, 'being very cleanly in his person.' He led the life of a hermit in the midst of a court unequalled in its splendour. 'He insisted upon the officers of the court, from the proceeds of their large salaries, living with state and magnificence, and not hoarding their wealth for themselves. "The money is the property of the empire," wrote Aurungzebe, "and it must be employed in giving weight to those who execute its laws."'* It is stated that he embroidered and

* Sullivan's 'Princes of India.'

sold skull-caps, such as the Moslems wear, and by the proceeds of his own handiwork left sufficient money to pay for his funeral expenses, ordering a small and poor wooden tomb to be placed over his remains. He died in 1707, in Ahmudnugger, in the Deccan, in the ninetieth year of his age, and was buried without state, according to his orders. His grave is still to be seen at Ahmudnugger, plain and simple, under high spreading trees. He was succeeded by his son Bahadur Shah; but for ten years after his death there was civil war, a fratricidal war, among his sons. Lalla Rookh (Tulip-cheek), immortalised by Moore, was Aurungzebe's daughter.

'I came a stranger into the world,' he wrote to his son Azim Shah, 'and a stranger I depart. I know nothing of myself; what I am, and for what I am destined. The days which I have passed in power have left only sorrow behind them. I brought nothing into the world, and, except the infirmities of men, I carry nothing out. Though I have a strong reliance on the mercies and bounties of God, yet, regarding my actions, fear will not quit me. Come then what may, I have launched my vessel to the waves.' The letter ends by saying, 'The Begum (his wife) appears affected; but God is the only judge of hearts. The foolish thoughts of women produce nothing but disappointment.'*

Among the Hindoos of the Deccan had risen a heaven-born leader. At first only a robber-chief, he gradually

* 'Princes of India,' p. 406.

became a powerful king, though all the resources of the Turks, under Aurungzebe, were employed against him for years. This was Sivajee. He was a man of consummate courage and genius ; he called himself 'a protector of Brahmins, kine, and cultivators ;' that is, the priests, the peasantry, and sacred cattle. This was an ominous union of the people and the powerful sacerdotal class, and was a national rising against foreign rule. After fighting the Moslem for forty years, Sivajee, 'the mountain rat,' as Aurungzebe called him, died ; his son fell into the hands of the Turks, and was barbarously killed. Still the Mahrattas remained as powerful as ever, and found another leader in Ragogee Scindiah. Aurungzebe also bitterly persecuted the Sikhs, a new sect, a compromise between Mohammedanism and Brahminism, who were rising into power in the Punjaub.

The result of Aurungzebe's rule, able and conscientious though it was, was most disastrous to the Turks. Tolerant as Aurungzebe was at the beginning of his reign, as he advanced in life, at the age of eighty years, he commenced the most impolitic religious persecutions, which threw all India into a blaze. He defiled the most sacred Hindoo temples, at Muttra, Benares, and Ahmedabad ; he slaughtered the sacred animal, the cow, and built mosques on the most hallowed places. He tried to raise a capitation tax on all Hindoos throughout India. The Rajpoots flew to arms. Under Chitore and Joudpore, soon two hundred thousand Rajpoots were in arms.

Rajah Sing, of Joudpore, wrote the following eloquent protest, which sums up the Hindoo wrongs:

'May it please your majesty,—your ancestor, Mohammed Jelal-ul-Deen Akbar, whose throne is in heaven, conducted the affairs of the empire in equity and firm security for the space of fifty-two years. He preserved every tribe in ease and happiness, whether they were followers of Jesus or of Moses, of Brahma or Mohammed; of whatever sect they might be, they equally enjoyed his countenance and favour, insomuch that the people, in gratitude for the indiscriminate protection which he afforded them, distinguished him by the appellation of the "Guardian of Mankind." His majesty Mohammed Noor-ul-Deen Jehangire likewise, whose dwelling is now in paradise, extending for a period of twenty-two years the shadow of his protection over the heads of his people, was successful, by constant fidelity to his allies and a vigorous exertion of his arm in business. Nor less did the illustrious Shah Jehan, by a prosperous reign of thirty-two years, acquire to himself immortal reputation and the glorious reward of clemency and virtue. Such were the benevolent inclinations of your ancestors; whilst they pursued their great and generous principles wheresoever they directed their steps, conquest and prosperity went before them, and thus they reduced many countries and fortresses to their obedience.* At this juncture it is

* From a scruple of conscience, Aurungzebe determined to raise

told, east and west, that the Emperor of Hindustan, jealous of the poor Hindoo devotee, will exact a tribute from Brahmins, Jogies, Vyraghees, and Sannyasis (different orders of begging monks); that, regardless of the high honour of the race of Timour, he condescends to exercise his power on the solitary inoffensive anchorite. If your majesty places any faith in those books by distinction called divine, you will there be instructed that God is the God of all mankind, not the God of the Mohammedans alone. The Pagan and Moslem are equal in His presence; distinctions of colour are of His ordination; it is He who gives existence. In your temple, to His name, is raised a prayer; in a house of images, where a bell is shaken, still He is the object of adoration. To vilify the religion or customs of the men, is to set at naught the pleasure of the Almighty. When we deface a picture, we naturally incur the resentment of the painter; and justly has the poet said, "Presume not to arraign or scrutinise the various works of power divine." In fine, the tribute you demand from the Hindoos is repugnant to justice; it is equally foreign to good policy, as it must impoverish the country; moreover, it is an innovation, an infringement of the laws of Hindustan. But if zeal for your own religion has induced you to determine on this measure, the demand ought, by the

the poll-tax—tribute ordained in the Koran upon members of the Hindoo community, who had hitherto been untaxed.

rules of equity, to have been made first on Ram Sing, who is esteemed the principal among the Hindoos; then let your well-wishers be called upon, with whom you will have less difficulty to encounter; but to torment ants and flies is unworthy of a generous mind. It is wonderful that your ministers should have neglected to instruct your majesty in the rules of rectitude and honour.'

We have seen the rise of the Turkish power, which followed the invasion of India under Sultan Baber; we have seen the Turks of Delhi at their zenith of pride and wealth under Jehangire and Shah Jehan; we have seen how the Moslem bigotry of Aurungzebe alienated the subject race—the Hindoos; and now we have come to the fall of the Turkish Empire.

The house of Timour fell from those causes which occasioned the ruin of the house of Lodi two hundred years before. It fell from a fresh invasion of India from Central Asia—from the disaffection of the subject races—from the pitiless self-seeking of the Moslem aristocracy of office—from the Sultan, the centre of the whole social and military system, being an effete trifler instead of an able leader.

The invasion of Nadir Shah gave the deathblow to the house of Timour, though it survived in name for one hundred years.

THE

PERSIAN INVASION OF INDIA,

UNDER NADIR SHAH, IN 1739.

CHAPTER I.

THE COURT OF THE GREAT MOGHUL.

The feeble rule of Mohammed—The traitors Cuttulick Khan and Saadat—Their overtures to Nadir Shah—A great Durbar at Delhi.

THE following account of Nadir Shah's invasion of Delhi in 1739 is translated from the account given in 'Les Lettres Édifiantes,' by two Jesuit priests. One was living at Chandernagore at the time, and wrote an account of passing events to the head of his order in the Levant. The other Jesuit was Nadir Shah's doctor, and followed him in many campaigns. The Jesuits had a church and large mission and many converts at Delhi at the time.

Some of the facts are taken from Dow's history. Dow wrote at Delhi in the year 1765, and he gained his information from eye-witnesses and from reliable Persian manuscripts.

I have also consulted the works of another eye-witness—the secretary of Sirbullind Khan, Mirza Zuman. Sirbullind Khan was a distinguished Amir of the Court, and took a leading part in the public life of the day. The letters of Mirza Zuman were translated from the Persian by Mr. James Fraser in 1742, while he resided in India, and are published in his life of Nadir Shah.

Mohammed, the ninth Turkish King of India, the great-grandson of Aurungzebe, was not altogether unworthy of the race of great men from whom he sprang. He was brave, handsome, humane, courteous, generous, and well versed in Persian and Arabic literature, but he was a trifler and a sensualist. He only loved pleasure and amusement. He might have steered the ship of State in peaceful times, over a summer sea, but he was called to rule in an age of extraordinary difficulty and danger, so that he might have said with Hamlet—

> 'The time is out of joint;—O cursed spite!
> That ever I was born to set it right!'

When the iron grasp of the master-hand of Aurungzebe was removed by death, the Hindoos rose on every side under the new name of Mahrattas, so that when Mohammed came to the throne the whole land had burst into the flames of rebellion. Not only was the Mahratta outbreak to be resisted, but also the intrigues and quarrels among the Mohammedan nobles of Delhi.

In 1737 Mohammed had reigned twenty years. He was born in the purple. The early years of his reign were troubled by two Seyds (descendants of the Prophet), who aspired to power; but those difficulties had been overcome by a Pathan noble named Dowran, who had been rewarded by being made Amir-ûl-Omrah, one of the highest offices in the State.

Mohammed, unlike his ancestors, left the whole affairs of the State to his ministers, who did what they pleased in the kingdom. Behind the double defences of the city walls at Delhi and those of his impregnable palace 'the Red Castle,' Mohammed heard of the towns and villages of his provinces being sacked and burnt by the Mahrattas, but he never tried to protect his subjects. Like some modern Turkish pasha, ease, pleasure, and magnificence were his idols, and, however critical might be the state of the country, he could not be drawn from the marble palaces, the fountains, and the gardens of the red palace at Delhi. 'If there is a Paradise upon earth, it is this, it is this,' was illuminated in Persian upon the white marble walls of the 'Aesh Mahal' (the Palace of Pleasure) where he spent his life. He went, it is true, in stately procession every Friday to the great mosque in the middle of the town, but this was absolutely necessary. Inexorable etiquette obliged him also to hold public levées in the great Hall of Audience, to attend the Court of Justice, and to show himself on the balcony daily to the people; but these things wearied him, and to escape from the intolerable tedium of audiences, of state receptions, Mohammed used to reside for months together at Merowlie, a summer palace six miles from Delhi, near the tall monumental Kootub. There the great royal camp was pitched on high, rocky ground, whilst around it there were gardens, high-walled, private, and shady, where the ladies of the palace disported themselves in silver swings under the spreading trees. These gardens were artificially watered with running watercourses. There were also artificial lakes, on whose borders stood palaces, kiosques, and pleasure-houses; and in these Mohammed, with surroundings of fabulous luxury, led an Arcadian existence with his court and his ladies—an existence of unclouded pleasure, but 'of pleasure laughing at fame.'

Yet, if he would have opened his eyes to the truth, it was no time for idle ease. The Mahrattas had taken Ajmere, in Rajpootana, and were burning the villages up to the walls of Agra and Delhi. But the king would not meet them in battle. So low had the Türkish power fallen that Mohammed bought off his enemies and promised to pay them 'chouth,' a fourth of the revenue. And an enemy far more dangerous threatened India. Nadir Shah was on the northern frontier. He had taken Kandahar and Kabul. This peril the King of Delhi affected to despise. 'It was impossible,' he declared, 'that he meant to invade India.'

The two men of the greatest importance at the Court of Delhi in the year 1739 were Kimmer, the vizier, and Dowran Khan Amir-ûl-Omrah, commander of the forces. They were both devoted to the king, but they were 'favourites.' 'A favourite,' says the proverb, 'has no friends,' and he is very sure to have enemies. Many of the other Amirs hated and feared these two favourites. 'Dowran,' says an old writer, 'had such influence over the king that, in his royal master's name, he acted precisely as he fancied.' The other nobles were jealous of this overwhelming influence. Among all the silken-robed crew of courtiers there was no one who hated Dowran Khan with a more mean and rancorous hatred than an old Usbeg Amir, called Cuttulich Khan. He held nominally a higher place at court than Dowran, for he was Viceroy of the Deccan, and was known by the title of the Nizam. He had, moreover, at this time reached the extraordinary age of ninety, although his mental and bodily faculties were as vigorous as ever.

It was at this advanced age that Cuttulich Khan found himself supplanted by an upstart at the very court where he had been a man of mark for half a century. He hated this upstart Dowran, but there was besides a far deeper reason for this hatred.

The Nizam dreamed that his province of the Deccan, which was remote, and but lately acquired, might become independent of the Court of Delhi. At the age of ninety he could hardly be ambitious for himself, but he hoped that his son and his grandson might be kings of the Deccan. His enemy, Dowran, had become acquainted with this secret and unprincipled ambition, and was resolved to prevent its realisation. There was no want of grounds of complaint against the Nizam. For twenty years he had paid no revenue from his province, and it was he who had urged the Mahrattas to attack Delhi. He was one of the causes of their inroads. Another noble was also discontented, Saadat, Governor of Oude, and he also was preparing to rebel.

Dowran had penetrated the schemes of these traitor viceroys, and determined to deprive them of their lives and their government. He had ordered them up from their own provinces to the court at Delhi, and they cherished, in consequence, an implacable hatred against him. They did not feel strong enough to break at once into open rebellion, and were obliged to obey the king's commands, but they knew that *their destruction had been decided on.*

'Desperate evils bring forth desperate remedies.' To save themselves, these two Amirs invited the great Persian conqueror, Nadir Shah, to invade their country. They hoped that in the confusion that would ensue their fortunes, which were at a low ebb, might improve, or Nadir Shah might confer independence on them, as a reward for their assistance. Above all, they trusted that this foreign invasion would result in the ruin of the King Mohammed, as it would, most certainly, in that of his favourite, Dowran.

These traitor viceroys were as much foreigners in India as we English at the present time. Cuttulich Khan was an Usbeg. Saadat was a Persian. They were both mere adventurers, though they had reached the highest offices of the State.

The numerous distant provinces of the Indian Empire, nineteen in number, were governed by 'Nawabs,' viceroys, or satraps. These officials were military governors, who farmed the revenue for a certain sum, and reserved the overplus for their own use. When the king took the field, the nawabs or viceroys were obliged to repair to the imperial standard, though it was the custom for each nawab to erect his own standard, and to form a separate camp. The nawabs every morning attended at the royal pavilion, and received orders from the Amir-ûl-Omrah, 'the Captain-General.' It is perhaps needless to say that the King of Delhi's will was absolute in everything.

We have said that Dowran Khan was the king's favourite. 'He was, besides, "Captain-General" of the empire. In India the offices of paymaster-general and commander-in-chief were united. Dowran Khan had such influence in the State that he had engrossed to himself all ministerial power. Mohammed, the king, was fond of pleasure and amusement, and hated business.' Dowran appeared to assume no authority, but directed everything.

The proposal of the traitors to invade India reached Nadir Shah just as he had conquered the city of Kandahar. His reply to it was that 'he objected to the difficulty of getting through the defiles, of passing great rivers, and to the many encounters that he must expect to have with the Afghans and the warlike nations of those parts. He feared, moreover, the opposition he must expect from Nasir Khan, Governor of Kabul, and Zekaria, Governor of Lahore, to say nothing of all the forces of the King of Delhi.'

To this the traitors answered: 'His imperial majesty and favourite courtiers employ their time with wine and women, and that if Nadir Shah resolved to attack India he would find none of the great ones ready to take the field.' They promised, moreover, to win over the Governor of Kabul and the Governor of Lahore to their side, so that Nadir Shah should meet with no opposition. They asked Kimmer-ul-Din, the vizier, to join them. He was related by marriage to the old Nizam; but he replied indignantly that he would not join any plot detrimental to the public interest, and pointed out the infamy of sacrificing the country to private resentment.

As Mohammed's apathy and the Nizam and Saadat's treachery were to bear most bitter fruit, I will now ask the reader, in imagination, to visit the Court of the Great Moghul before its wealth, state, and splendour have passed away from the earth. I have chosen the time when the Viceroy of the Deccan and the Viceroy of Oude have arrived at Delhi, and, with their troops, are encamped outside the city walls. Let us suppose that the Nizam's elephant has entered the 'Silver Street,' the high street of a gay and lordly city. A channel of water ran down its centre, and on each side of the road were shady trees, forming boulevards. There was a great hurly-burly of people and traffic in the open shops of the bazaar.

The mass of the pedestrians were dressed in bright-coloured cloths, and amongst them a few veiled women were to be seen. Besides this everyday crowd, thronging the 'Silver Street,' making their way to the king's Durbar came the small ruling princes, the nobles, the officers, civil and military.

They were a strange and splendid sight. The King of Delhi's nobles formed one of the most powerful and wealthy official aristocracies that the world has ever seen. All who rode to the Durbar were well mounted and well accoutred. Their robes were of cloth of gold, brocaded silk, or velvet, bedecked with jewels; some, leaning back upon silken cushions, were borne in litters upon six men's shoulders, surrounded by attendants with peacocks' tails to keep off flies and dust; some were riding gaily-caparisoned horses; some were on elephants, and all were accompanied by a cortége of attendants and by men who rode in front to make way for them, and followed by well-mounted troopers, their household cavalry.

Beneath all this grandeur and prosperity, the Nizam's treachery, though unknown and unperceived, was inevitably working its way. An earthquake was about to swallow up these holiday-makers who trod so gaily through the familiar streets of their capital. The splendour of Delhi would soon simply be a tale to be told. War had never ravaged the new Delhi of Shah Jehan. It was full of colleges, mosques, caravanserais, palaces, merchants, traders, and shopkeepers. Its population was numbered at two millions of inhabitants, who trusted to their high walls, and feared no foreign invaders.

Modern Delhi was built about 1648 by Shah Jehan, Mohammed's ancestor. Its walls were seven miles in circuit, and it was entered by ten fine gates. Mohammed's palace, 'the Red Castle,' is a strongly-fortified citadel, looking more like a fortified city than a single palace. In the centre of the town, on a rock, rises the beautiful Jumma Musjid, the finest mosque in the East.

The Amirs at the time had palaces standing in fine gardens, artificially watered, and mostly built near the river. The town was composed of a dense mass of two-storied brick houses, with flat roofs. Delhi is still an important town, but it was then the capital of a great empire, a centre of political and commercial activity, of court favour and patronage, of pleasure, and amusement, and elegancies. It was full of dancing women and singing men, of actors, painters, and sculptors, and even of poets, historians, and theologians.

The city was divided by three great boulevards, broad and spacious thoroughfares. One of these, the Chandni Chouk, or 'Silver Street,' we have mentioned.

The people looked with interest and pleasure at the sight of the nobles passing. Special interest was directed to the pageant of the Nizams' procession. 'It is he of the Deccan,' 'It is he of Oude,' they cried, and the multitude failed not, especially those of the Moslem faith, to *salaam* as the old traitors passed on elephants. An equal interest was taken in Saadat, Governor of Oude, because he was known to be a good soldier, and had lately had a successful engagement with the Mahrattas, who were in ill-favour with the townspeople. The Mahrattas, the daily dread of open villages, had robbed up to the very town walls of Delhi: 'The infidels, pagans, thieves, and robbers, the oppressors of honest townsmen and helpless peasants,' as the Moslem inhabitants of Delhi called them.

The Nizam's elephant had made its way to the gateway of the citadel. Before them rose the frowning Lahore gate. Indian castles much resemble those of the Middle Ages in Europe. Contrasting with these red granite walls was the green of the flowering peach-trees which grew in a garden close to the ditch.

Scattered about were the numerous tents of the nobles and of the officers of the guard; at a still greater distance were the gardens of the palace.

The Nizam and Saadat made their way to the private Hall of Audience, especially set apart for the reception of the nobility, and we will follow them into King Mohammed's presence. The Hall of Audience is a very beautiful pavilion of white marble, supported on massive pillars of the same material, the whole of which, with the connecting arches, are richly ornamented with flowers of inlaid mosaic of agate and bloodstone, lapis lazuli and cornelian. The floor is of white marble; the top of the building is ornamented by four marble pavilions, surmounted with golden cupolas; the ceiling was covered with silver filigree work. All this, except the ceiling of filigree work, remains to this day, much as it was on the day of the interview of the Nizam with Mohammed, but for that State occasion the pillars of the hall were hung with brocade and cloth of gold. 'The roof of the hall was a canopy of flowered satin, fastened with red silk cords, which had great tassels of silk, mixed with threads of gold. The ground was spread with silken tapestries, and to accommodate the extraordinary concourse of people, a spacious tent had been joined to the hall. This tent was supported by three solid poles plated with silver, the size and thickness of a ship's mast. This large outer tent was crowded by the lesser nobility, and the common people without were prevented from entering it by silver balustrades and soldiers on guard.'

Mohammed Shah's throne deserves description. The pomp and vanity of this world never desired a more costly mass of splendour than the Peacock Throne. It was valued at twelve millions of our money. One of its chief gems was the Koh-i-Noor.

This throne was made by Mohammed's ancestor, Shah Jehan, in 1642. It had taken seven years to make. It was reported to have been designed by a French adventurer, Austin de Bourdeau, a jeweller, who, after defrauding several princes in Europe, took refuge with Shah Jehan in Delhi, where he made a large fortune.

'This work of art,' writes an eye-witness, 'had two

peacocks standing behind it, their tails being all expanded; the whole so overlaid with sapphires, rubies, emeralds, and other precious stones, as to represent the colours of life. The throne itself was six feet long by four feet broad, and it stood on six massive feet, which, with the body, were of pure gold, inlaid with rubies, emeralds, and diamonds. It was surmounted by a canopy of gold, supported by twelve pillars, all richly emblazoned with costly gems; a fringe of pearls ornamented the border of this canopy. On either side of the throne stood umbrellas, one of the Oriental emblems of royalty. They were formed of crimson velvet, richly embroidered and fringed with pearls. The handles were eight feet high, and studded with large diamonds. Between the peacocks stood a parrot of the ordinary size, cut out of one emerald. The finest jewel in the throne was a ruby, which had fallen into the hands of Timour when he plundered Delhi in the year 1398. Jehangire diminished the beauty and lustre of the stone by engraving upon it his own name and title, and when he was reproved for this piece of vanity by Noor Mahal, he replied: "This stone will perhaps carry my name farther through time than the empire of the house of Timour." This stone has been lost. A large ruby, cut into a little cup, with Jehangire's name on it, came into the hands of an English firm of jewellers in Calcutta some twenty years ago, and, if the missing ruby, it might still be traced.'*

* Dow, vol. iii. p. 164.

On this superb work of art was seated the Emperor of all India. He was a man singularly handsome, of tall stature, and with a face of marked amiability and good humour. Mohammed was hardly darker than a Spaniard, had regular features, hazel eyes, and a beard of reddish tinge. His dress was of white satin, finely embroidered in gold. His turban was made of cloth of gold. He wore a collar of pearls of inestimable value, hanging in rows round his neck, as far as his breast. In his turban was a strange jewel, a bird like a heron, whose front was formed of diamonds of extraordinary size, and with a great Oriental topaz, which shone like the sun.

It was a fine *coup d'œil* that of Mohammed Shah, gorgeously attired, seated on his splendid throne, while below him were ranged the chief nobility of India, to the number of seventy princes—the Moslems on one side, the Hindoos on the other, standing according to their rank.

'The Moghul system of government admitted of no hereditary honours, except in the case of ruling princes. Every officer owed his preferment and rank to himself and the favour of the prince. High birth was much considered and favoured by the Kings of Delhi, who were inordinately proud of their own illustrious descent from the great conqueror Tamerlane; and for five hundred years Mohammed's ancestors had been great sovereigns in the Eastern world.'*

* Dow's 'History,' vol. iii. p. 17.

Much excitement and curiosity was in the hearts of those silken-robed courtiers. That the two most powerful subjects in the empire were disaffected was well-known, but what the result of such disaffection would be, who could tell? especially in the East, where the only divinity that hedges a king is chance and revolutions. However, the probabilities were that these ambitious and discontented chiefs would be trodden under the feet of an elephant, as traitors to the public weal. Mohammed was personally beloved: he had a kindness of heart and a courtesy that had endeared him to those around him. Even his failings, his love of pleasure and his indolence, were not those faults that make rulers unpopular. He was idle and pleasure-seeking, but the representative of an historic name. His ancestors had ruled for three hundred years in India, and they had ruled with splendour and justice. Under them the land had prospered and become great, and a halo of loyalty hung around him, such as royalists have felt for the Bourbons or Stuarts.

The old Nizam was making his way up to the throne between the line of nobles of rival creeds. He was followed by several servants carrying trays of money, pearls, and vessels of gold. It is an ancient custom in the East for an inferior to approach a superior with gifts. He had reached a distance of twenty yards from the throne when he was commanded by one of the macebearers to bow very low, raising each time his hand from the ground to his forehead, the macebearer calling out aloud,

'Cuttulich Khan, Viceroy of the Deccan, and regulator of the country, salutes the Emperor of the World.' He was then led up between the two lines of nobles to the foot of the steps of the throne, and there the same ceremony was again performed. The old Nizam then moved slowly up the steps, and, on account of his high rank, he was permitted to make his offerings to the emperor himself, who touched one of the gold pieces, and then laid it down. The Lord of the Privy Purse then received all the gifts. Saadat, Governor of Oude, was introduced and performed the same ceremonies.

The Nizam was small, thin, and aged. His face was lined and wrinkled. He had a snow-white beard, and, although he had reached the unusual age of ninety, there was still extraordinary life and fire in his eyes. The Nizam had been a man of mark some sixty years before. He represented safe and great traditions. He belonged to the school and period of Aurungzebe, Mohammed's great-grandfather.

Saadat, Governor of Oude, resembled the nobles of the time. He was of swarthy colour, and tall and strong. He had an aquiline nose, of the Jewish type, and an air of excessive arrogance and dignity. In his passionate visage and proud air was to be found not the cautious, almost mean and subservient, look to be seen in the old man's face. The Nizam's dress was to be remarked by its absence of ornaments, its severe simplicity. Saadat wore the usual Oriental dress—an outer robe, long and ample, of gold brocade, a beautiful fabric from the looms of Bengal. It was open in front, and showed a shorter coat of crimson satin, girt at the waist with a Cashmere shawl. Round his neck was a necklace of diamonds and emeralds, and his sword had a crimson velvet scabbard and a jewelled hilt.

Then Mohammed Shah, courteously and pleasantly, as it was his nature, asked the Nizam about his journey, 'so trying to a man of his age,' and complimented Saadat on his brilliant victory over the Mahrattas. But what took the savour out of the emperor's condescension was that, standing close to them at the Durbar, was the erect, tall figure, and stern, soldierly face of Dowran Khan, their implacable enemy. Mohammed made a speech. He had an agreeable-toned voice, and some natural eloquence. 'He gently reproved the two lords for their contumacy in not obeying his orders in various matters. He argued that the power of monarchs ceased if their commands are unregarded. "But," he continued, "I have made you what you are. Let not the hand which raised you so high repent of the work which it has made."'

This speech was well received by the audience. For that matter, all the words of the Fountain of Honour were received by the courtiers with adulation and flattery. They rent the air with cries of 'Karamat! Karamat!'—'Wonder! wonder!' and among their voices could be distinguished the thin, aged voice of the humble-looking and deferential Nizam. But Saadat, haughty and daring in his disposition, was piqued by the way the emperor had spoken about his martial achievements, to which he considered more credit was due. He looked scornfully upon Mohammed, and said, in an excited manner, 'The refractory and infidel Mahrattas kill the women and children of the Faithful, and seize their land, and burn their houses; and you, who are God's shadow upon earth, do nothing, and stay at home.' The eyes of the emperor kindled with rage. He seized his sword, which lay by his side on the throne. The courtiers were silent from astonishment, and no one dared to resent this insult offered to the imperial dignity. The emperor's fury faded away as suddenly as it had risen, and he continued calmly to carry on a conversation of no moment with the Nizam. 'The soul of Mohammed,' said a Moghul who knew him well, 'was like the water of a lake, easily agitated by any storm, but which settled immediately after the winds are laid.'

But at length the two great officials retired, keeping their faces towards the sovereign, and performing the same ceremonies at the same places as before.

That such scenes as the above happened at Mohammed's Durbar may seem strange. But even under Aurungzebe they occurred; and under Shah Jehan words ran so high that swords were drawn, and the council ended in an engagement.

To be an Eastern despot is no sinecure. To be an Eastern despot is to be sole Head of the State, and motive-power of an extended centralisation, and requires extraordinary powers of mind. Though the reception of the nobility was over in about two hours, Mohammed had many other royal functions to perform, or, in his case, to neglect to perform, before he could resign himself to that ease and pleasure which he loved.

In a square, opening out of the marble audience hall, some soldiers of fortune were waiting, who sought employment in the imperial service. They presented themselves, with their dependents, completely armed. The emperor reviewed them, and after they had exhibited some feats of arms, and showed off their horsemanship and dexterity, some were received into the army. Then the lower nobility presented themselves to Mohammed in another court. In another square were artisans, with curious inventions; in another square again were huntsmen, who presented specimens of rare animals found in the empire.

Soon Mohammed turned his steps to his private apartments, known, since the time of Aurungzebe, as the 'Gussal Khana'—bathing-chamber. To this house only the great officers of the State were admitted, and affairs of inferior concern transacted, such as the disposal of offices. As a matter of established custom, Dowran Khan, and Kimmer-ul-Dien, the vizier, followed the king into the 'Gussal Khana,' a strangely beautiful suite of white marble apartments, of the same style and period as the Hall of Audience, which they adjoined. The floor was formed of white marble flags, inlaid, in beautiful designs of flowers and leaves, in cornelian and bloodstone. The Saracenic buildings of India are most beautiful, and are worthy of the praise which has been lavished upon Granada—a mass of gilding and of colour.

The 'Gussal Khana,' or bathing-room, which gave its name to the building, was so called in consequence of a square tank, with marble steps, in the centre of a pillared marble hall, into which running water was conducted. The king, accompanied by Dowran, passed through numerous marble rooms, all decorated in the same style, until they reached a beautiful kiosque that overlooked the river Jumna. It was octagonal in shape, the walls formed of the most exquisite fretwork of white marble carving, that resembled lace, or carvings in ivory. When the officers of the army in India gave a ball to the Prince of Wales in 1875, it was given in the 'Marble Hall of Audience' of the Great Moghul. This kiosque, the private room of so many sovereigns of the house of Timour, was fitted up with green velvet, as a boudoir or private room for the Prince of Wales.

These stone lattices are peculiar to India. They are worked in the most beautiful arabesques. They let in the air so much needed in a hot climate, and keep out the glare, and cause a cool, subdued light, most pleasing to the eye. The floor of the kiosque, in the time of the Moghuls, was covered by a mattress of cotton, four inches thick. On this was spread a piece of tapestry of cloth of gold, on which were embroidered silk flowers. Divans with backs, placed against the wall, were the only furniture. They were covered with velvet and flowered satin, worked in gold. There were also niches in the walls, painted and illuminated in brilliant colours, and in them were placed porcelain vases of flowers.

The only signs of habitation were ink-horns, and pen-boxes, and rolls of manuscripts, and books. Dowran and the King Mohammed, the only occupants of this room, were soon in earnest conversation, their privacy guarded by African eunuchs, who were in waiting without.

Dowran Khan, 'the best-abused man of his day,' for public opinion was against him, was in appearance a spare, thin, high-featured man of Arab type, eager, resolute, reckless of consequences, noted for his personal bravery, for his dexterity in hand-to-hand fighting. He had a gifted mind, but he was fierce, restless, and ambitious. He was out of the spirit of his age, and had not an idea in common with Mohammed's silken-robed courtiers, who were effeminate both in mind and body. He wished to reform Mohammed Shah, but he was opposed by the eunuchs, the debauchees, and the favourite ladies.

'He is too powerful a subject; he must die. Either we fall to him, or he falls to us. This Nizam, O King! will despoil you of your kingdom, despite of God, honour, and ancient right.'

'Oh! Dowran Khan,' sighed the weak prince, 'thou

art a man of brave and resolute spirit, but thou knowest what the Persian poet saith, "He who will impatiently haste to lay his hand on the sword, will afterwards gnaw that hand with his teeth with regret."'

'It was not thus your illustrious ancestors gained dominion,' said Dowran. 'Buckle on two swords, and, like your great ancestor Baber, "place your foot in the stirrup of resolution, and your hand on the rein of confidence in God," and fear not the infidel Cuttulich Khan, and this Saadat. One word, one glance from you, and my own hand would have planted a dagger into his false heart, and the Mansions of the Faithful would have had one enemy the less.'

'By my own head and your death!' cried the gentle-hearted monarch, 'my soul belongs to God alone. Could I be guilty of such black treachery as to murder one of the Strength of the Kingdom' (*i.e.* one of the nobility) 'in my own hall of audience? A deed to render myself accursed of God, abhorred of men, and worthy of execration and shame until the final day of retribution!'

At this moment a most grateful sound broke on Mohammed Shah's ears. He was weary of hearing of wars, and invasions, and revolts; he who only asked to injure no man, and to live joyously and peacefully. The sound was that of the heavy metallic clang of the gong by which the time-strikers proclaimed the hour. It was two o'clock, the hour Mohammed retired habitually to the women's house, where he dined.

There was treachery among the nobles, indecision among the rulers, blind confidence and indifference among the people. It was thus India was all unprepared for its last invasion.

Since the time of Baber Afghanistan had always been a province of the Indian Empire. Balkh and Badakshan had also at one time been provinces of the empire, but they were lost in the time of Aurungzebe. Afghanistan was threatened by a new invader. Mohammed allowed his north-west frontier to be attacked, and left it undefended.

Dowran was keenly alive to the danger of such conduct. He was commander of the forces, but he dared not leave the Court of Delhi, for he knew that in his absence the rival faction of the Nizam and Saadat would gain the ear of the weak king, and that his official ruin would be brought about by them.

CHAPTER II.

THE BATTLE OF PANIPUT.

Rise of Nadir Shah—He becomes a bandit—Is made King of Persia—He conquers Central Asia—Passes the Khyber—Great Battle and Victory of Paniput.

NADIR SHAH had been seven months in the kingdom of Kabul, burning cities and murdering the inhabitants. He had first taken Herat, then Kandahar; and he marched to the city of Kabul *viâ* Ghizni. The governor of that city submitted without a blow; but at Kabul he met with serious resistance from the governor, an old man of seventy, named Shirza. The place fell by treachery; some of the lives of the leading defenders were preserved by an Afghan woman, in Nadir Shah's harem, who had influence enough to protect them.

In Kabul great booty was found by the Persians. 'Two million five hundred thousand of our money in specie, and effects to the value of two million more; in these were included four thousand complete suits of armour inlaid with gold, four thousand of polished steel,' and much else that Shah Jehan had deposited in Kabul.

Nadir Shah marched *viâ* the Khyber upon India. The spots where he rested are still shown in these terrific hill-passes. He met with a very determined resistance from the tribes in the Khyber, and had at length to buy a passage. They delayed him for six weeks.

Nadir Shah was born at Kelat in the mountains of Khorassan, a hilly and semi-independent province of Persia. His father was the hereditary chief of a tribe of Turcomans, the Asshars, who are divided into three clans, and he owned the small but strongly-placed fortress of Kelat. Nadir Shah, at an early age, lost his father. His mother lived to see his extraordinary prosperity and greatness ; and to her he was an affectionate and dutiful son all his life, and his love to her was the one soft spot in his fierce and cruel character.

The fatherless boy was left in charge of an uncle, who, in consequence of his youth, succeeded in depriving him of his whole patrimony, the fort and the chiefship of the tribe. Nadir Shah was driven to enter the Persian army as a private, but he rose rapidly to the command of a hundred horsemen.

In the year 1720, the Usbegs threatened to invade Khorassan. The local governor, the Governor of Mushed, was cowardly, and there was the greatest terror in the province. Nadir Shah, young and of no military rank, promised, if he were given the command of one thousand horse, to drive the dreaded Usbegs back into Turkestan. The offer was accepted.

In a mountain-pass, where his small numbers were counterbalanced by the difficult nature of the country, he completely defeated the invaders. He had been promised a high military command as a reward if he succeeded in driving back the Usbegs. The high command fell vacant; but it was given, not to Nadir Shah, but to a worthless and unsoldierly hanger-on of the court. The promise that had been made to him was broken; the service that he had rendered his country was ignored.

Nadir Shah's fiery spirit could ill brook these wrongs; he complained hotly to the Governor of Mushed, with more spirit than discretion. The Pasha ordered him to be bastinadoed 'until the nails fell out of his feet;' and further, that he should be turned out of the army with disgrace: this happened in 1720.

Nadir Shah returned to his uncle at Kelat, wronged, ruined, indignant. He was ill received by his relations, and was even in want of his daily bread. He tried to recover from his uncle some part of his patrimony, but without success. Desperate, he turned on the society that had refused him justice; and he became a bandit-chief in the mountains of Khorassan. At first he had but two followers; but these quickly increased to five hundred malcontents, mostly disbanded soldiers.

Persia at this time was in a deplorable condition of misgovernment. The king had been dethroned by the Ottoman Turks, who overran the whole country; and there was no authority strong enough to cope with the mountain banditti under so bold and able a leader as Nadir Shah. His first public exploit was in 1726, to take the strong castle of Kelat from his uncle, whom he killed with his own hands, and thus obtained a rude justice for many wrongs of long standing.

Then with his small following of well-trained but desperate soldiers, he defeated the Turks; after which success he replaced King Thamas, of the race of Sofi, on the throne. In gratitude for these great national services, he was given command of the whole Persian army. The Ottoman Turks were completely driven out of Persia, and Nadir Shah's successful arms even won a province from Russia.

In 1736, Nadir Shah was proclaimed King of Persia by fifteen thousand nobles, and King Thamas was deposed on the grounds of his 'effeminacy.'

Nadir Shah was a free-thinker; he believed in no religion; but one of his first acts was a proclamation changing the national creed of Persia from the Shiah sect of Mussulmans to that of the Sunni; this he did for reasons of statecraft only, and to save Persia from ever-recurring invasions.

Persia held the tenets of the Shiah sect, which differs only in trivial matters from the Sunni, in matters of form and ceremony. But the Turks, who are Sunnis—the Afghans, who also are Sunnis—continually made this difference a pretext to invade Persia, on the grounds of her heretical opinions. To this day the

Turks and Afghans hate the Persians most bitterly because they hold the Shiah belief; to this day they would join any Christian Power in an attack on Persia, such is the bitterness of their sectarian bigotry.

The Persian nation adhered to their changed creed, or at least its outward ceremonies, as long as Nadir Shah lived; but they returned to the Shiah ritual after his death, and thus the policy of religious union in the Moslem world died with this great conqueror.

Nadir Shah was the last great military dictator of the Eastern world, but there his greatness ended. This is the opinion of his character of one who knew him well: 'Though Nadir Shah was of extraordinary military genius, he was a monster of avarice, and, from his extreme barbarity, a disgrace to humanity. It was a common boast of his "that he would reduce five families to one single cooking-pot;" that is, render them so poor that they should borrow it one from another.

'Nadir Shah,' continues the Jesuit, 'had great genius. Labour did not deter him, nor danger frighten him. Obstacles and difficulties were in the order of his plans. He had no settled dwelling-place. His camp was his palace. Cold, heat, hunger and thirst excited his courage and his invincible resolution. He was brave to the pitch of rashness. He was the first to enter and the last to leave a field of battle. Sordid avarice and unheard-of cruelty were his vices.'

Thus writes Père Bazin, the Jesuit priest who accompanied him in many of his wars and attended him as a doctor :* 'Courage, which he possessed in common with the lion, was his only virtue, and he owed his greatness to the defects of his mind. Had his eye melted at human misery, had his soul shuddered at human murder, had his breast glowed once with benevolence, or his heart revolted at injustice, he might have lived to an old age, but he would have died without the name of Nadir' (Wonderful).

Once, in India, in consequence of some unheard-of cruelty which Nadir had exercised, a 'dervish' had the courage to present a writing to him, conceived in these terms: 'If thou art a god, act as a god; if thou art a prophet, conduct us in the way of salvation; if thou art a king, render the people happy and do not destroy them.' To which Nadir Shah answered, 'he was neither a god nor a prophet, but he whom God sent to nations in His wrath.'

The evils we least fear are generally those that befall us. In vain Dowran had tried to move the lethargic monarch to march out against the maurauding Mahrattas and to act against the crafty Nizam. 'Masterly inactivity' kept Mohammed slothful within the walls of his citadel. The repeated calls of duty were neglected, and at last that easy, happy-tempered sensualist found himself face to face with an enemy whom it was impossible to evade. The treason of the Nizam and Saadat was bearing fruit. Nadir Shah, the terrible, the cruel conqueror of

* 'Lettres Édifiantes.'

all Central Asia, with his victorious Persians, had arrived within two days' march of Delhi itself. Like Sultan Baber he had reached Paniput unopposed.

The bulwarks of the Indian Empire had been given up without a struggle. Nasir, Governor of Peshawur, had applied for reinforcements from the Court of Delhi, but had received none, and was defeated. Zekirra, of Lahore, had met with the same treatment, and was also defeated. Nadir Shah might have been routed on the frontier, but the effeminate Court of Delhi had affected to the last to despise the King of Persia, and asserted 'that it was impossible he could meditate the conquest of Hindustan.'

What had made the conduct of the court the more infatuated was that Mohammed had received this warning from Nadir Shah himself five months before :

'A translation of a letter from Nadir Shah to Mohammed Shah, received the beginning of Jumadi al avul 1151, which is about the middle of August.

'"Be it clear to the enlightened mind of your high Majesty, that my coming to Kabul, and possessing myself thereof, was purely out of zeal for Islam, and friendship for you. I never could have imagined that the wretches of Deccan should impose a tribute on the dominions of the King of Mussulmans. My stay on this side the Attock is with a view that, when these infidels move towards Hindustan,* I may send an army of the victorious

* The province of Delhi was understood as Hindustan.

Kuzzlebash to drive them to the abyss of Hell. History is full of the friendship that has subsisted between our kings and your Majesty's predecessors. By Ali Mortisa, I swear, that (excepting friendship, and a concern for religion) I neither had, nor have any other views; if you suspect the contrary you may; I always was, and will be a friend to your illustrious House."

'About the latter end of August an ambassador came with another letter, demanding four crore of rupees (£5,000,000) and four soubahs or provinces.'

Nadir Shah took possession of the frontier city of Peshawur on the 3rd December, 1738. 'When this news arrived at the Court of Delhi,' says the secretary, Mirza Zuman, 'the king sent Khandoran Nizam and Kimmir-o'din-Khan against Nadir Shah, and, besides their own Jaguirs, advanced them one crore of rupees (£1,250,000) out of the Treasury to enlist men, Saadat being sent for from his province to join them. These Amirs pitched their tents in a place close by the city, and began to enlist men.

'The Omrahs have been divided in opinion and interest a long time; for which reason several unbecoming messages now passed between them. The emperor, who consulted Khandoran's ease and pleasure, ordered Nizam al Muluck and the vizier to leave him at court, whilst they were to go on with the expedition; but they excused themselves. In the meantime news was brought, that Nadir Shah (by Nasir Khan's advice) had put on the Indian dress, and sat on the throne in the manner of the Indian emperors, and that his forces had crossed the Attock, and were on their march to Lahore. On this news the emperor was quite confounded, and, sending for the Superintendent of the Boats, asked him how many days it would take to go by water to Patna or Kassi Benaris.* It being told the vizier and Nizam al Muluck that the emperor had such a design, they petitioned him that these slaves (meaning themselves) might not go upon the èxpedition.'

Nothing could exceed the supineness of the Turkish rulers. They were warned by Rajah Jessing. The Hindoos were anxious to defend their country from a new invasion from Central Asia. 'As Rajah Jessing was more attached to Khan Dowran than any other Omrah, he repeatedly wrote him to this purport: Nadir Shah's coming is a concerted thing. You must be watchful of the Moghul Omrah.' By this he meant all those Persian or Turkish nobles, whom the Indians, without distinction, call Moghuls. 'If Zekirra Khan, Governor of Lahore, makes any opposition, it will give the king's army time to advance pretty far, in order to check this invader. *As for us Rajpoots,* we are ready to join the royal ensign.'

The king, the vizier, and Dowran continued to trust the Nizam and Saadat; or, possibly, as the latter commanded large bodies of troops, they were too powerful to be attacked at that critical time. The enmity and disunion

* A city in the province of Bengal.

at the court were fatal to any united action among the Turks of Delhi, as they have been to the Turks of Constantinople. On the 17th of February, 1739, Nadir Shah had arrived within two days' march of Delhi. The army of Mohammed Shah that at length opposed him was composed of one million of men. 'There were four hundred thousand horsemen, four hundred thousand musketeers, three hundred thousand infantry, armed with lances and arrows, ten thousand pieces of cannon, thirty thousand camels, two thousand war elephants, armed and accoutred. Nadir Shah had only sixty thousand men to oppose this multitude.' These are the numbers given by the Jesuit.*

This immense host was a hoard of undisciplined rabble, most of them peasants drawn from the plough—the feudal retainers of the nobles. Mohammed nominally commanded them himself. The Indian army took up a position in a fortified and entrenched camp at Paniput, forty miles from Delhi. It was, rather, a number of small encampments, for each nabob fortified himself with his own troops. 'It was an army,' says the Jesuit, 'in which general, captain, and private soldier only acted according to the impulses of their own minds.'* The Indian entrenchments and redoubts had been hastily thrown up and mounted with five thousand pieces of cannon; for the Indian forces had only reached Kurnaul two days before Nadir Shah arrived there. The canal that supplies Delhi

* 'Lettres Édifiantes.'

with water divided the two armies. Nadir Shah's handful of sixty thousand men were of very different stamp and material from Mohammed Shah's myriads. They were men of all nations of Central Asia—Kurds, Georgians, Kuzzlebashes, Afghans, Turcomans. They were troops flushed with a hundred fights, 'who looked on the day of battle as the day of victory.' They were under the strictest discipline, and, above all, were commanded by a man of genius. 'Nadir Shah was severe to excess. He pardoned no neglect or disobedience in his soldiers,' says the Jesuit.

However, Nadir Shah's position was most critical. He had no open line of communications; he was without a base of operations; he had no reserves to fall back upon, He was thousands of miles from his own country, and he had a hundred nations of enemies in his rear. Defeat to him would be destruction. Between these two armies, the one superior by overwhelming numbers, the other by discipline, an engagement took place. The description of this battle I give from Dow, the Indian historian.

'Saadat, Governor of Oude, had joined Mohammed Shah's camp. He no sooner arrived than he made a pretended attack upon the Persians, in which he permitted himself to be taken prisoner. Saadat's design was to get the start of his partner in treason, the Nizam, in ingratiating himself with Nadir Shah, and engaging that monarch to his intents.

'During this mock engagement, he sent repeated messages from the field to Mohammed Shah, asking for more troops, and saying he would drive the enemy back to Persia. Dowran, who knew nothing of his being in league with the enemy, and was commander-in-chief, prevailed on the king to permit him to support Saadat with fifteen thousand men. When Dowran arrived, Saadat had given himself up as a prisoner; but the troops of Saadat, being strangers to the treachery of their commander, joined Dowran, and continued the attack. Dowran was immediately attacked on all sides by the bulk of the Persian army. He, however, for some time maintained his ground with great firmness and resolution, and was at length unwillingly drawn from the field (he had received a wound, which soon afterwards proved mortal) by three repeated messages from the king, commanding his immediate attendance. Mohammed was, with good reason, apprehensive that the Nizam, who was then in camp, was preparing to seize him, which made him anxious for the presence of Dowran. When the wounded general appeared before the king, he told him the situation of affairs, and earnestly entreated Mohammed to permit him to return to the field with the troops which were under his immediate command as captain-general, amounting to thirty-six thousand men. "Grant my request," said Dowran, "and you will never see me return but in triumph."

'The King Mohammed was now perplexed beyond measure. He dreaded the designs of the Nizam, should Dowran be absent, and at the same time he durst not permit the traitor to march out of the lines, for fear he should join the Persians. He therefore fell into the error of weak minds, and hesitated; in hopes that delay would give birth to a more favourable concurrence of events. He was deceived. The happy moment for the preservation of himself and his empire was now upon the wing. Mohammed's troops maintained their ground, under Muzziffer, the gallant brother of Dowran, and a reinforcement would have turned the scale of victory in their favour.

'When Dowran quitted the field, the command of the imperial troops who were engaged devolved upon his brother Muzziffer. That brave noble made a violent charge upon the Persian army, and penetrated to the very door of Nadir Shah's tent. There, from want of being supported from the camp, Muzziffer Ali, Dowran's son, and twenty-seven officers of distinction, covered one small spot of ground with their bodies. Ten thousand Indian soldiers were slain in this desperate action, which proved almost fatal to Nadir Shah, for his whole army was upon the point of giving way, several great detachments having fled back forty miles from the field of battle. After this engagement, the few that remained of the Indians retired within their entrenchments. Dowran, though wounded, had an interview that night with the Nizam. It was agreed that the whole army should next morning march out of the lines and attack the Persian camp. But when the morning came, Dowran's wound was so much inflamed that he could not act, therefore the meditated attack was delayed. In the evening of the 18th of February mortification ensued, which was attributed to something applied to the wound by a surgeon bribed by the Nizam, and many in India still continue in the same belief. Be that as it may, Dowran expired that night, amid the tears of his sovereign, who had a great friendship for him. When this brave nobleman, on whom alone the hopes of the emperor rested, was dead, the Nizam stood unrivalled in the management of affairs. The whole authority devolved upon him, and the king became a cipher in the midst of his own camp.'*

This is an account of the same battle, given by the secretary, but others have thought more troops of Nadir Shah were engaged: 'Nadir Shah, who had just then arrived from Tillauvri, being apprised of the attack, advanced towards that quarter, and detached 1000 Courds, 1000 Kajirs†, 1000 Backhtiaris, and 1000 harquebusers, in all 4000 horse—3000 of whom he planted in three different places in ambush, 500 harquebusers he sent towards Saadat Khan, and the other 500 towards Khandoran to draw them into the field; in which having succeeded, the horsemen who lay in ambush poured in upon them in three different places, and engaged them in a most obstinate manner. Besides these 4000 none else

* Dow's 'History,' vol. ii., pp. 338—340.

† Kajirs are a tribe of Turcomans, and the Backhtiaris, or Bactrians, are so called from Bakhtir, or Bactria, the place they come from.

of Nadir Shah's men joined in that action, excepting that he himself, attended by 1000 Asshar horse, rode to and from all quarters to encourage and direct these men. The rest of the army (according to his order) stood drawn up at a distance, each nation separate, ready at a signal to come to his assistance; but, as it happened, there was no occasion for them, these 4000 or 5000 having fought obstinately until near the evening, when the emperor's forces gave ground, Saadat Khan, Sheerjing, and Khandoran's youngest son were taken prisoners, Khandoran having received several mortal wounds.'

The secretary, Zuman, gives also a graphic description of the troops from Central Asia, and it shows how little they had changed since the time of Baber. 'On the 14th, Nadir Shah having left one Boungah* at Shahabad (which is one stage from Serhind) and a second at Taniseer, he advanced with 40,000 horse, partly lancemen, archers, and musqueteers, to the village Tillauvri, each horseman having two and some three attendants, grooms, and camel-drivers, all robust young men, completely armed and mounted, some on camels, some on mules, and others on yabous, not one in his whole army being on foot, even those who followed the camp, and trafficked for necessaries with the men, were completely armed and mounted, the number of all amounting to near 160,000. In the time of action the master could not be distinguished from the servant, nor the tradesmen and

* Boungah, a camp.

traffickers belonging to the camp from the common soldiers, all in general being bold and resolute, and well qualified to execute the most desperate attempt they could be employed in. There were also about 6000 or 7000 women, who had been taken captives from the Turks and in Kandahar, who on a march could not be distinguished from the soldiers, having a barranni* over their own clothes, girt round with a girdle, their faces veiled with a fine cloth, a shawl folded round their heads in form of a turban, and booted and armed as the men.'

One account of the battle of Paniput states that 'Saadat Khan's and Sherjing's elephants getting foul of each other, the Kuzzlebashes surrounded and took them prisoners.' The Kuzzlebashes are an order of soldiers of Persia, resembling the Janissaries of Turkey, and are so called from wearing red caps, the word 'kuzzlebash' meaning 'red cap.' Mirza Khan Dakbunda, grandson of the great Mohabit Khan, was killed in the engagement. On Nadir Shah's side were killed seven principal officers and 2500 men, and about 5000 were wounded.

Mohammed had lost his only true friend. The crafty old Nizam was made Amir-ûl-Omrah, or Commander-in-Chief, in the place of Dowran. On the day after the battle, on the 18th, he was despatched by Mohammed to negotiate a treaty with the invader. The Jesuit writes:

'The Nizam went to Nadir Shah with only ten officers. Nadir Shah rose to receive him, and remarked, "See how

* Barranni, an overcoat.

much I esteem you, that I rise to receive you." The Nizam made three obeisances, and seated himself. Nadir Shah's complaints against India were these: 'He required, first, the throne of Tamerlane, which had cost Persia nine hundred thousand pounds; the second, that Persia had lent ten thousand men to the grandfather of Mohammed Shah, uncle of Jehangire, to assist him to ascend the throne. Persia must be repaid for these expenses; that Mohammed had not assisted him in his war against the Turks; that he had attacked his ambassador; and, lastly and finally, that Mohammed had given him the trouble of coming so far for redress; also, Mohammed was required to come and see him.'*

So little hope had Nadir Shah at that time of overthrowing the most powerful kingdom of the East, that he agreed with the Nizam for the pitiful sum of six hundred thousand pounds to evacuate Hindustan. 'Then Saadat pointed out to the Persian conqueror that, with all the countless wealth of the Indies at his mercy, he might demand and would receive fifty times that sum. Saadat offered him a bribe of two million sterling out of his own private fortune, on condition that Nadir Shah would reduce the Nizam and place him—Saadat—at the head of the administration.'

Mohammed, finding his kingdom and crown being bargained for by these enemies of his household, made the resolution of visiting Nadir Shah and throwing him-

* Lettres Édifiantes.

self on his clemency. 'A declared enemy,' said Mohammed, 'is by no means so much to be dreaded as secret foes under the specious character of friends.'*

By this time famine raged in the Indian encampment. No means had been organised to feed the immense hosts of men and horses; and to feed an army well in war is the pivot on which all else turns. Besides, the Persians had possessed themselves of several strong forts round the Indian encampment, and had totally cut off the supplies and provisions.

Mohammed started on the morning of the 20th of February on his travelling throne, with a small retinue of the few friends who still adhered to him, to visit Nadir Shah. Around the King of Delhi were starving, desperate men, raw peasants drawn from the plough; the air was foul with the smell of the unburied dead. Mohammed might have seen misery painted in the countenances of his followers —a few of whom sadly 'salaamed' to this leader—who was a leader but in name. Perhaps Mohammed was too absorbed in his own sufferings to feel for those of others.

He had not far to go; the splendid tents of his adversary glittered before him; he could see Nadir Shah's coloured standard dancing joyfully against the azure sky. 'Nature was all unmoved with his unrest,' as Mahommed moved slowly to his unknown doom.

Mohammed reached Nadir Shah's camp, a city of canvas that covered six miles. 'Canvas was the home

* Dow, vol. ii. p. 340.

of Nadir Shah,' writes the Jesuit. 'He moved over many lands with a splendid city, which in a few minutes, with mushroom-like rapidity, rose as if by enchantment on some desert plain. This city was divided into long streets of tents; each official had a spot provided for him. Each corps, each regiment, had its appointed street. Tradesmen were arranged according to their trades. The Royal Diwan, or Tent of Justice, stood in the centre, in a large open space. Beyond this were the tents of the Royal Harem, the tents of the singing and dancing men and women and of their instructors. The tent of the chief physician (the Jesuit); the tents of the cooks and confectioners; the tent of the treasurers, of the law officers, of the priests; the tents of the executioners, of the numerous royal guard.'*

Mohammed and his scanty followers moved down the broad principal street of this canvas city; they reached a square, round which were pitched the tents of Nadir Shah's guard. There they were met by Nasir Alla, one of Nadir Shah's sixteen sons, and he was deputed to conduct them to the Royal Tent. This tent was splendid and gigantic. It was made of 'cloth of gold and worked with flowers, and covered with precious stones and pearls,' says the Jesuit. In front of it the great conqueror administered justice, a terrible justice. The square of justice was flanked on both sides by the tents of the executioners. Before Nadir Shah's tent,

* Lettres Édifiantes.

men were publicly strangled, bastinadoed, or burnt alive. Mohammed Shah had passed the grim place of execution; he was ushered into the great silken pavilion. Nadir Shah advanced a few steps from his throne and embraced Mohammed, and, sitting down, placed him on his right hand.

The letter from a soldier at Jellalabad to a friend in Delhi, in 1738, gives a picture of Nadir Shah's state and justice: 'After Morning Prayers, he sits on a Throne, the Canopy of which is in the Form of a Dome, and of Gold; 1000 Young Men with Royal Standards of Red Silk, and the Lance Tops and Tassels of Silver, are disposed regularly, and at a proper Distance; 500 beautiful Slaves, from 12 to 20 Years old, stand one half on his right Hand, and the other on his left; all the great Men stand fronting him, and the *Arrizbegi** stands between in Readiness to represent whatever he is desired, and every Body has his Cause decided at once; Bribery is not so much as known here. He has particular information given him of every Thing that passes; all Criminals, Great and Small, Rich and Poor, meet with immediate Death. He sits till Noon, after which he dines, and then reposes a little; when Afternoon-Prayers are over, he sits till the evening Prayers.'

The undecided and irresolute Mohammed was now with his enemy face to face. This was the appearance of the stranger at whose mercy he found himself: 'Nadir Shah was upwards of six feet high, and stout in

* The lord who presents petitions.

proportion. He was burnt brown from campaigns and exposure to all weathers. His nose was straight, delicate, and well formed; his mouth small and firm looking; his face more round than long; the under-lip was more protruding than the upper; and his glance was keen and piercing; his voice rough and rude, but which he could soften at pleasure. It was a face of power, on which was stamped courage and resolution; but his slightly projecting under-lip gave an air of sinister firmness, even cruelty, to this great captain.'*

These two men, of such different natures and antecedents, met each other for the first time. One was the Napoleon, the other a Bourbon, of Eastern history. They talked together for six hours. Nadir Shah taunted Mohammed for paying Chouth (tribute) to the Mahrattas; taunted him with having allowed himself to be invested in the centre of his dominions without one single effort to repel the invaders.

'It is not my intention,' said the great conqueror, 'to deprive you of your kingdom; but the expenses of this expedition must be paid; and during the time of collecting the money, my fatigued army must be allowed to refresh themselves within the walls of Delhi.'†

Mohammed was allowed to return to his own camp. The terms offered were much better than he had dared to hope for. He was happy and contented, and, with his natural buoyancy, he hoped now all would end well.

* Lettres Édifiantes. † Ibid.

This interview terminated in a feast, at which the finest of music, dancing women, and wine were not wanting. Mohammed was delighted by this hospitable entertainment; he gave a return festival to Nadir Shah, at which all the dishes were of pure gold; and he sent him a present of six perfect Turcoman horses and two elephants, one loaded with jewels and one with money. A few days after these feastings, Mohammed received a demand from the Persian, asking to be paid four millions sterling, 'to pay for his war in Turkey and his return home,' the Jesuit physician says. 'Mohammed sent him twenty cart-loads of gold pieces, each piece worth six pounds, and one hundred camels loaded with silver pieces (rupees) of the value of florins, and then he sent the old Nizam to try and negotiate to get better terms than the payment of the four millions.'*

Nadir Shah's real motive in allowing Mohammed to return to his army when he was completely in his power was that he feared, if he detained Mohammed, the Nizam would act with vigour, and declare his independence of both Mohammed and Nadir Shah. The Nizam was an able man and a good soldier. He commanded all the Indian forces since his rival Dowran's death, and there were still sufficient Indian troops in the encampment, if they were well led, to cause Nadir Shah's utter discomfiture, a disaster which in his position, far away from his reserves and base of operation, meant destruction.

Nadir Shah now began to lay schemes to seize the

* Lettres Édifiantes.

Nizam. This he succeeded in doing on the 24th February. 'The Nizam was taken in the Persian camp, where he had gone to conduct some negotiations. He was thrown into prison, and allowed no food during the first days.'

The Jesuit, who enters at length into all the phases of the negotiations, says that before he was seized, the Nizam tried to negotiate with Nadir Shah. The terms Nadir proposed and agreed to take were twelve millions, to be paid in five years, five million to be received at once, and the famous Peacock Throne. Mohammed, the king, refused. 'He said he would sooner live all his life as a dervish in Bengal' than agree to such terms. The Nizam and many nobles then wished Mohammed to fight. Nadir broke off the negotiations, and sent this message to Mohammed: 'That he had no more good faith than an infidel; that he would sack the city, reduce it to cinders, and seize him, his wives, children, and all his race, and cut them to pieces.' Many of the nobles, when they heard this threat, including even the Nizam, sent a message to Mohammed, 'begging him to defend his life and his throne.' Mohammed prepared to poison himself and his family. He sent to the Nizam a message to the effect that he agreed to the terms first mentioned.

The Nizam asked for an interview, at which he agreed finally to Nadir's terms. But Nadir Shah then said he would only come to terms 'If Mohammed placed himself in his power, and he would let him live or die as he thought proper.'

While these negotiations were carried on by the officers, the state of the army was deplorable. 'Famine increased within the doomed Indian encampment,' writes the Jesuit. 'A small measure of rice cost one pound. They ate their camels and horses; 60,000 men died from hunger. Parties of four or five thousand men, driven by hunger, used to issue out of the encampment to get provisions; they were quickly cut in pieces by the Persians. Three hundred thousand men disbanded themselves and fled, but of these also few escaped the swords of the Persians. Mohammed's mighty host of soldiers were defeated without one battle, and melted away like snow in the sun.'*

Then Nadir Shah quietly entered the Indian encampment; not a blow was struck. He seized upon Mohammed Shah's artillery, the jewel office—and the armoury—even Mohammed's clothing of cloth of gold, of velvet embroidered in gold and worked in jewels, was no mean booty; much of the armour was of beautiful workmanship, of steel inlaid with gold. Nadir Shah ordered three months' pay to be immediately advanced to his soldiers. The finest of the guns taken he despatched to Persia. The principal officers of the Indian army were placed in a sort of honourable confinement, and among those so placed were the old Nizam and Saadat.

On the unfortunate Mohammed giving himself up to the Persians, Saadat tried to rouse Nadir Shah's noted ferocity against this captive monarch. He recommended that Mohammed Shah's eyes should be put out, because,

* Lettres Édifiantes.

according to the Mohammedan law, a blind man could not be king; that he should be bricked-up alive; that he ought to be beheaded, and that Nadir Shah should mount the throne of Delhi; but his vindictive suggestions were not attended to.

A small supply of provision was thrown into what remained of the Indian encampment by the Persians, but at extravagant prices. Men and horses died by hundreds, and many officers of the Indian army, and many of the Indian Court officials, were beheaded in the square before the conqueror's tent.

No opposition was now to be feared. Nadir Shah entered the virgin city of Delhi on the 8th of March, with a triumphant procession, in which Mohammed was a prominent figure. Nadir Shah was to inhabit the palace, the Aesh Mahal, in the citadel, and Mohammed was taken to a part of the palace called 'the Tower of Solomon.'

Mohammed bore his reverses with equanimity. He ate very heartily, and betrayed no sign of being afflicted by his unhappy situation. Nadir Shah was surprised when he heard of Mohammed's behaviour. 'What kind of man must this be who can with so much indifference give his freedom and his empire to the winds? We are told by the wise that greatness of mind consists of two extremes—to suffer patiently, or to act boldly; to despise the world, or to exert all the powers of the mind to command it. This man has chosen the former, but the latter is the choice of Nadir Shah.'

CHAPTER III.

THE SACKING OF DELHI.

Nadir Shah enters Delhi—Mohammed, a Prisoner—The fate of Saadat—Rapacity of the Persians—A rising of the Townspeople—Terrible Massacre—Nadir Shah returns to Persia—His Death.

On the 8th of March the 'Silver Street' was breathless and excited to see the grim conqueror from northern lands march in and take the great city without a blow. The same crowd of harmless citizens were there who six weeks before had looked on the pageant of 'the Strength of the Kingdom,' the nobility going to the king's court. But the flower of that nobility were now dead, having fallen in battle or by the executioner's axe. The splendour of that pageant had passed from the world for ever, never to be revived.

A stipulation had been made that the city of Delhi was to be spared. The crowd breathlessly and silently watched the Persians march in; Nadir Shah rode at their head, with twelve thousand of his best troops. The Jesuit describes these troops thus: 'The Persian horses were large; their men big and powerful, their head-dress black skin caps, a foot and a half high, surmounted by an iron spike, with which they could, with certain movements of their heads, ward off the stroke of a sabre; their long, full robes were of brilliant colour, green, yellow, or red. They wore cotton trousers and long leather boots. Each man was armed with a matchlock and battle-axe, a sword and a shield.'* The hapless Mohammed, on an elephant, followed in the pageant of his conqueror's triumph. He was permitted to have all his domestics about him; they amounted in number to three thousand. Ten thousand Persians, however, mounted guard over him.

Nadir Shah entered the Red Castle, or citadel. Mohammed's palace filled him with astonishment. His war-trained eyes had never seen such luxuries, such elegance and splendour. Nadir Shah occupied Mohammed's marble palace, while Mohammed was conducted to a prison.

A strange scene a few days after took place in the beautiful marble Hall of Audience, in the same hall where the Nizam and Saadat had but lately been received by Mohammed with all the forms and splendour of that long-established court etiquette.

Nadir Shah was seated on the gorgeous Peacock Throne. Round him were his sons and his Persian lords, who trembled at his least word or glance; around him, too, were those who remained of the Indian Amirs,

* Lettres Édifiantes.

Turki and Rajpoot, sad and dejected. They were sick at heart. The two traitors who had deluged the land with blood—the Nizam and Saadat—had been summoned to Nadir Shah's presence. The once haughty Saadat and the feeble octogenarian stood below the throne of Nadir, a sombre sovereign, whose will was 'cruel, merci less, and irrevocable as the decrees of Fate.'

Nadir Shah's face, fierce and ominously moody, was terrible to look on when angry; few men could stand the glance of his eye. His cruelty was fiendish; his voice, which he could modulate at his pleasure, was loud and insulting when he addressed the two traitors in these words:

'"Are you not ungrateful villains who, possessing such wealth and dignities, have called me from my own dominions to ruin your king and country? But I will scourge you with all my wrath, which is the instrument of the vengeance of God." He then spat on their beards, the highest affront possible to Mussulmans, and, amid the taunts, jeers, and ridicule of the assembled court, they were driven with every mark of indignity from his presence. After the traitors found themselves beyond the precincts of the palace, the Nizam addressed himself to Saadat, and swore by the holy Prophet he would not survive this indignity. They agreed to poison themselves, and retired to their respective houses, determined upon death. Saadat, in the meantime, sent a trusty spy to bring intelligence when the Nizam should take his draught. The Nizam being come home, appeared in deep affliction; but having privately intimated his plot to a servant, he ordered them to bring him the poison; the servant acted the part well. He brought him an innocent draught, with great reluctance. The Nizam, after some hesitation, and having formally said his prayers, drank it off in the presence of Saadat's spy, and soon pretended to fall down dead. Saadat, ashamed of being outdone in point of honour, swallowed a real draught of poison, and became the just victim of his own villainy. The Nizam was not ashamed to live, though none had greater reason of shame; he even prided himself on his wicked trick, by which he had rid himself of his rival, and afterwards actually enjoyed the intended fruits of all his villainies.'*

Thus wrote Dow, the English historian, thirty years after the event, from the authority of eye-witnesses at Delhi, and the authority of Oriental manuscripts. Later historians seem to have doubted the truth of this tragedy; but so much is certainly true, that Saadat laid violent hands on himself on account of Nadir Shah's treatment of him; and the crafty old Nizam gained all he had played for, independence, sovereignty, honour, power, and wealth.

Nadir Shah had issued commands that no person in the city of Delhi should be molested; but he demanded thirty millions of our money as a contribution for sparing

* Dow, vol. ii. p. 345.

the city. The day after his entry into Delhi, he formed his army into two divisions; one was quartered in the citadel, the second at the eight gates of the town and the country outside. No one was allowed to enter Delhi without Nadir Shah's permission. Every commodity—food, fodder, and merchandise—as it entered the gates, was seized for his troops. Famine began to rage in the city, as it had done in the encampment; the inhabitants were only allowed to buy a few necessaries of life, and those at a very dear rate.

The Persian troops were allowed to commit every injustice with impunity. 'Nadir Shah, hearing,' says the Jesuit, 'of these excesses, tried to guard against this oppression, by not permitting a private or officer of his army to own more than ten pounds, under pain of being disembowelled; and this punishment was even put into practice.'

Nadir Shah himself appropriated all the riches of Mohammed's palaces—golden services and golden beds, beautiful china, and gold inlaid armour, and his immense store of silks and satins and gold brocade. Nadir Shah took the Peacock Throne, valued at twelve millions sterling, and he took all the pearls of the ladies in the seraglio; these alone were valued at two millions. In gold and silver in the seraglio were found coins to the amount of one million. Nadir Shah was delighted at gaining these treasures, and gaining them all with no losses to his army. Everything had taken place quietly so far, when an unforeseen accident happened.

The townspeople naturally were sullen and exasperated at the enormous ransom of thirty millions which had been demanded from their city. But how could the undisciplined, unwarlike citizens of Delhi oppose the invincible Persians?

The sentiments of freedom, of courage, of patriotism, had never burned hotly in the hearts of the traders of Delhi. Their little gains in trade had till then been the first thought in their minds. It seemed incredible to them that their peace and independence had passed away like a dream. Delhi had known no private or foreign invader for two hundred years. Men's hearts were hot within them; and a spark soon set this mass of smouldering indignation into a flame.

The magistrates were contriving ways and means of raising the enormous sum of thirty millions by a tax in proportion to the wealth of individuals, when the following event took place.

The Persians had made all the Indian generals prisoners of war. Four of these became drunk; they were guarded in a private palace, and waited on by their own servants; they killed the guards to the number of twenty Persian troopers. The riot became general; a report arose, and was willingly believed, that Mohammed had, with his own hand, assassinated Nadir Shah with a dagger. On every side the townspeople fell on the Persians, two thousand of them were killed, from eight o'clock at night until twelve all was tumult and confusion within the city.

But the hour of retribution was at hand. About twelve o'clock at night the King of Persia in the citadel was informed of these transactions. He turned the guns of the citadel upon the town. He immediately ordered what men he had with him under arms, and, putting himself at their head, marched down the broad boulevard of the 'Silver Street' to a small marble mosque with three gilded domes, called the mosque of Roshan-ul-Dowlat, and waited there until daybreak. Nadir Shah had his men drawn up, inactive, in the street. There was then no fighting going on; the *émeute* had subsided.

The next day at dawn he divided the city among his troops. Each division was given a quarter of the city. Every commander started through the sleeping town to the quarter assigned to him. Nadir Shah gave orders in words much like those the Maréchal de Luxembourg used on a similar occasion: 'Allez, camarades! Pillez—tuez—saccagez et violez! et si il y a des crimes plus abominables, ne manquez pas de les commettre.'

Nadir Shah's share, and the share of the troops under his command, was to be the 'Chandni Chouk' (the Silver Street), the richest quarter of the town. He himself entered the mosque of Roshan-ul-Dowlat, from the high minarets of which he could see all around. The sun had scarcely risen when, with a drawn sword, Nadir Shah took up his position in the beautiful little marble mosque with its three gilded domes.

There was no cruelty or abomination spared. From

every quarter of the city, amid smoke and flame, rose the groans of men, the screams of women and children. Neither age, nor sex, nor condition was spared. Those who escaped the flames expired by the sword. And not only the Persians, but the *canaille*, the scum of the bazaars, pillaged and murdered everywhere.

'Such was the panic, terror, and confusion of these poor wretches, that, instead of bravely opposing death, the men threw down their arms, and, with their wives and children, submitted themselves like sheep to the slaughter. One Persian soldier often butchered a whole family without meeting with any resistance. The Hindoos, according to their barbarous custom, shut up their wives and daughters, and set fire to their apartments, and then threw themselves into the flames. Thousands plunged headlong into wells, and were drowned. Death was seen in every horrid shape, and at last seemed rather sought after than avoided. Before two o'clock, one hundred thousand of the unfortunate inhabitants had been massacred.'

During this dreadful scene, Nadir Shah sat in the mosque of Roshan-ul-Dowlat, which commanded an extended view, and ate preserves from a golden dish.

At length the unfortunate Mohammed, attended by some of his chief nobles, among them the old Nizam, appeared before Nadir Shah, and they bowed down their foreheads to the ground. Nadir Shah sternly asked them what they wanted. They cried, with one voice, 'Spare the city.' Mohammed said not a word, but the tears flowed fast from his eyes. The old Nizam, who, at great personal risk, had made his way through the tumult, is reported to have said:

'Are you not afraid of the vengeance of Heaven? Give me leave to discover those who are guilty of the murder of your Persians, and they shall die by the most cruel tortures; but do not give up a whole innocent city to fire and sword.'

The tyrant, for once touched with pity, sheathed his sword, and said, 'For the sake of Prince Mohammed, I forgive.'

The Jesuit states that Nadir Shah ordered the recall of his troops. The massacre continued until nine o'clock that night. It was only stopped completely by the provost-marshal and his guard killing those he found still marauding. Three quarters of Delhi were ruined. The fire continued for eight days, without means of extinguishing it. The palaces of the courtiers and the lords were those that suffered most, as they were the special objects of the avarice of the soldiery.

This catastrophe was followed by another nearly as awful. Those of the inhabitants who had escaped the fire and massacre were ordered to bring all their silver utensils, coins, and jewellery to the citadel. Those who were suspected of hiding their treasures were stretched upon a species of cross, like the cross of St. Andrew, and were cruelly beaten, and either expired or had to give up all they possessed. Under an arbitrary government like that of India, individuals find it necessary to conceal their wealth. Some Amirs, therefore, who had very little were taxed very highly, whilst others who were rich came off with a moderate sum. In consequence, many of the nobles, under the supposition that they had more wealth, were tortured to death, after they had given all they were worth in the world. During all these transactions the gates of the city were kept shut, escape into the open country was impossible, and famine began to rage every day more and more. Among those who suffered thus unjustly was the Vaqueel of Bengal. He was cruelly beaten with sticks. When the vizier Kimmer pleaded his inability to pay the enormous sum of two and a half millions sterling, he had all his effects sold. Nadir seized three of his daughters and seven of his most beautiful women, and forced them into his own harem.

To Sirbullind Khan was given the hateful task by Nadir Shah of collecting the effects of all the courtiers and officials, from the simple foot soldier of the guard to the highest lord of the court. The effects also of the jewellers, and of the bankers and leading traders, were seized. Many persons, finding themselves reduced from great wealth to total poverty, poisoned themselves.

All day and night immense and countless wealth was brought into the citadel and to the court of the Nizam's palace. In these two places all the wealth of this great city was collected and carefully sorted. On one side rose a perfect mountain of gold pieces, each worth six pounds; other mountains of silver coin (rupees), each worth a florin; a mountain of gold or silver utensils; others of pieces of cloth of gold, rich silks, damasks, and worked tapestries. In this way eight millions were collected. In the public treasury was found specie worth nearly four millions sterling; in private vaults were two millions five hundred thousand. The jewel office was estimated at thirty millions; the royal wardrobe and armoury were reckoned worth seven millions. In all about sixty-two millions five hundred pounds of our money.

'Hundreds of workmen,' the Jesuit says, 'day and night, during fifteen days were employed in melting down gold and silver plate into rude ingots. Two ingots, pierced in the middle and tied by a strong cord, formed the load of one camel. They filled five thousand chests with gold pieces, and eight thousand with silver, and an inconceivable quantity of chests were filled with diamonds, pearls, and other jewels. The horses, camels, and elephants which carried the booty were taken from the city.*

'This account,' continues the priest, 'may seem inconceivable to English ideas, but it must be remembered that the diamonds of Golconda and the pearl-fisheries of the coasts had been for centuries both royal monopolies, and that for centuries these treasures had been accumulated at the court of the Great Moghul. It was besides

Lettres Édifiantes.

the custom for viceroys, tributaries, and the nobles on all State occasions to present gems to the king. Then from thirty-four provinces, hundreds of oxen, laden with gold and silver coins, arrived yearly, in the payment of taxes. Many of these provinces were larger in extent of territory than England.

'The whole greatness and splendour of the Moghul Empire was centred in Delhi. Many kings, nobles, and princes made it their residence. A powerful noble often maintained an army of from twenty to thirty thousand men. The feudal system was in full force. A lord, noble, or prince of the blood received a fief on condition of maintaining a certain number of men. For instance, the Nawab of Moorshedabad, in Bengal, by no means a premier noble, maintained at the time sixty elephants seven thousand cavalry, and four thousand infantry.*

'Delhi is so large a city,' writes the Jesuit, 'a hundred thousand men might leave it and never be missed.'

The last act of Nadir Shah was that he publicly strangled the four nobles who had caused the revolt. They were relations of the Nizam's, and one was his son-in-law, but he had to give them up. He dared not ask grace for them.

Nadir Shah having now raised all the money he could in Delhi, on the 3rd June reinstated Mohammed in the empire with a ceremony of great solemnity and pomp. He placed a crown upon his head with his own hands, and presented him with a rich dress. At the same time

* Lettres Édifiantes.

dresses were presented to forty of the leading Indian nobles. The bestowal of a dress is considered an honour in the East. Nadir Shah also gave Mohammed much good advice, and warned him against the Nizam, who, he perceived, aspired at being more than a subject. 'Had I not,' said Nadir, 'passed my word to that old traitor for his safety, he should not live to disturb Mohammed.'

On the 7th of June, Nadir Shah left Delhi laden with at least eighty millions of our money. His soldiers were not allowed to carry away any Indian women or slaves. He retired in perfect safety and order to Persia. The Mahrattas followed him in the hopes of plunder, but none mustered courage to attack him.

The provinces of Kabul, Ghuzni, and Kandahar, Peshawur, Scinde, and all the Trans Indus, were ceded to Nadir Shah.

They were never regained by the throne of Delhi. Exactly one hundred years afterwards, in 1839, Lord Auckland retook Afghanistan, and the English occupied it for three years. Nadir Shah's son, Prince Nasir Ali, was married at Delhi to a princess of the house of Timour, a cousin of Mohammed's. Mohammed, who was inordinately proud of his pedigree, wished that Nadir Shah should show his male pedigree, extending through seven generations, before he would allow him to marry a daughter of the race of Timour. The conqueror answered, 'Go tell your master my son is the son of Nadir Shah, the son of the sword, the grandson of the sword, and so on until he has a descent of seventy generations instead of seven.'

Soon after Nadir Shah left, Mohammed feasted and amused himself as much as ever, the whole authority fell into the hands of the Nizam, who occupied the place held by Dowran previously, and which he had envied. But, as he was a good soldier and administrator, under his wise government the country in part re-established itself.

While the Nizam engrossed the whole power at Delhi, his own viceroyalty of the Deccan fell into confusion. The Mahrattas attacked it. In consequence, the Nizam marched from the capital to the Deccan, upwards of a thousand miles. He drove away the Mahrattas, he re-established order, and then declared himself independent of the crown of Delhi. Thus the Deccan, one of the greatest limbs of the empire, was cut off. Mohammed was not in a position to resent this rebellion. The troops of the empire at Delhi were commanded by Ghazi-ud-deen, a talented young man, the Nizam's son, in whose charge the weak Mohammed had been left.

Cutturlich Khan died in the Deccan in 1747, in the hundred and fourth year of his age. His descendants rule the Deccan, at Hyderabad to this day.

In 1747, ten years after the sacking of Delhi, after a reign of ten years, Mohammed died suddenly in the hall of public audience at Delhi, seated on his throne. His death occurred in this manner :

'The emperor had inviolable friendship for his vizier,

Kimmer-ul-Deen. Through the whole thirty years of Mohammed's troubled reign, Kimmer had been a faithful servant and attached friend. He was killed in battle against a new invader, Abdalla, a Persian. Kimmer was much esteemed by the Indian army; it was necessary to conceal his death, lest the troops, who depended upon his courage and capacity, should be affected by that accident. It was resolved that the body of Kimmer should be mounted upon his own elephant, in the howdah, supported by pillows, and that in the morning they should issue out of the camp and engage the enemy. Abdalla was one of Nadir Shah's treasurers; on his master's death he managed to fly to Herat with three hundred camels loaded with treasure. This treasure enabled him to raise an army among the people of Khorassan, and, as he was a native of Herat, he easily persuaded his fellow-countrymen to join him. He there proposed to follow the example of his late terrible master, and advanced on Delhi with fifty thousand horsemen, in 1747. The unfortunate Delhians were struck with universal panic at the dread of the horrors of another Persian invasion. Mohammed shared in the universal terror.

The new invader was driven back when he had reached Sirhind, by the heroism and good generalship of Munnu, the vizier Kimmer's son.

The historic Koh-i-noor diamond fell into the hands of Abdalla.

'In the tottering state of the regal authority, all

Mohammed's confidence was reposed in Kimmer. When, therefore, the news of his death reached Delhi, the king considered his own affairs as desperate. He naturally feared a second invasion, and its accompanying horrors. He retired to a private apartment, and wept bitterly all night. In the morning he mounted the throne, as usual, to give public audiences, and, whilst every flattering courtier was running out in praise of the deceased, the emperor seemed much affected. He at last exclaimed: "O cruel fate! thus to break the staff of my old age! Where now shall I find so faithful a servant?" With these words he fell into a fit, to which he was sometimes subject, and expired sitting upon his throne.'*

Nadir Shah's career, after leaving India, had not been one of unbroken success. In 1741, with an army said to number one hundred and fifty thousand men, of Indians, Usbegs, and Afghans, he attacked some mountainous tribes near Derbent, on the Caspian Sea, and met with a heavy reverse.

In the same year that Mohammed died, 1747, Nadir Shah was murdered, at the age of sixty: he was very much broken in health by dropsy.

The circumstances of his death are thus reported by the Jesuit. He had put all his Indian treasure in a fortress which he had built at Kelat in Khorassan, his birth-place, where he lived as a poor boy in his childhood. 'In 1746, Nadir Shah became very suspicious of all who approached him. This occasioned him to commit many acts of

* Dow, vol. ii., p. 367.

cruelty. He ordered the death of his own son, and had his eyes put out in his own presence, and then executed fifty of his nobles for not having prevented his orders being carried out. His tyranny and cruelty made him universally hated and feared; this, in the year 1747, led his nephew, Ali Kouli Khan, to revolt. Nadir Shah was very much alarmed at this rebellion of his nephew. He lived in a state of perpetual fear and suspicion; he kept a horse always saddled and bridled in the harem to fly at any moment. He dared trust no man. He wished to fly to his strong fortress of Kelat, surrounded by mountains, but could not find the means. He knew there was a plot against his life; he particularly dreaded his own relations, and his own Persian guard. This well-grounded secret fear caused him to order some Afghan soldiers, in whom he had great confidence, suddenly to arrest and kill his whole Persian guard; this order transpired, though secretly given.'

The chief of this Persian guard was Mohammed Kouli Khan, Nadir Shah's own relation. The intendant of the household, Sala Khan, was also disaffected. These two determined to assassinate Nadir Shah, on hearing that he intended to sacrifice them with the whole Persian guard. Time was precious; they determined to kill the tyrant that very night. Fifteen or sixteen of these conspirators arrived at Nadir Shah's tent. It was in the seraglio, and protected first by a high net and then by a screen of cloth, which formed a private inclosure; the noise they made in getting through these obstacles woke up Nadir Shah. They heard the dreaded voice, before which so many men had trembled for so many years, call out, 'Who are they?—where is my sword?' This so affected the nerves of the conspirators that they fled. However, the two chiefs, Mohammed Kouli Khan and Sala Khan, made their return, and got through with what they had undertaken. Mohammed Kouli Khan was the first to cut down Nadir Shah with his sword. The tyrant was undressed and unarmed; he fell, he tried to raise himself—he was swimming in his blood. He showed a great want of fortitude on the approach of death, that he had so often wantonly inflicted on thousands of his fellow-creatures. He begged, he prayed for his life. 'Why do you kill me?' he cried. 'Save my life!' he shrieked despairingly, 'and all I possess is yours.' But as he spoke, Sala Khan detached his head from his body. The head of this remarkable man was despatched to his revolted nephew, Ali Kouli Khan, and it took a fortnight to reach him.*

The remains of Nadir Shah's palaces and fort of Kelat, of burnt brick, stand uninhabited and deserted. They were visited by Valentine Baker Pasha not many years ago, probably the only Englishman who has made his way to so remote a spot, in a country so disturbed by roving and robber Turcomans. General Baker describes the place as one of wonderful natural strength. It still retains its reputation for unhealthiness.

* Lettres Édifiantes.

Eighteen years after Nadir Shah's invasion, Clive founded the British Empire in India. What probably made the conquest so easy to the English was, that Moslem rule in India never recovered from the injuries Nadir Shah's invasion had inflicted. All the provinces soon after delared their independence; first the Deccan, then Oude, Bengal, Rohilcund, and the Punjaub, until the house of Timour ruled only within the walls of their city. Even this they lost; Delhi and its king fell into the hands of the Mahrattas. We freed the King of Delhi from them in 1805. The mutiny of 1857 saw the end of the house of Timour; for the King of Delhi of the day headed the rebels and our revolted soldiery. He was transported, and died a prisoner in Rangoon soon afterwards, leaving two sons.

For twelve years the heroic Munnu Khan, son of the vizier Kimmer-ul-dien, stood, as it were, a sentinel on the Indian frontier at Lahore. As long as he lived, he kept the dreaded Afghans at bay; but in 1761 he was killed by a fall from his horse; his mantle fell upon no other man; courage and enterprise seemed to have died with him; and quickly following his death, the Afghan King of Kabul, Abdalla (the Douranee) appeared before the walls of Delhi.

The terror of the citizens was extreme. Their leaders, the king, the nobles and army, were incapable of defending them. There were again, at this time, two Amirs fighting for place, power, and party. The one was Nigit ul

Dowla, a Rohilla; the other, Gazi, the young grandson of the wicked old Nizam, who was commander-in-chief. They again repeated the game of treason perpetrated thirty years before, and invited the Afghans to attack Delhi, so that in the confusions that would follow their fortunes might rise.

Abdalla, the Afghan, marched into Delhi unopposed. The awful scenes of thirty years before were again repeated. The citizens, with unavailing courage, again rose; the city was again sacked and burnt; the townspeople, without regard to age or sex, were again massacred. The city was burning for seven days. It was said still to contain two millions of inhabitants, and to cover seventeen miles; but it was reduced to those ruins, splendid in their overthrow, which are still to be seen.

But the city had not even yet reached its acme of misery. The Mahrattas heard that the Afghans were sacking the imperial city. They determined to share in the spoil, and to re-establish the ancient Hindoo Empire of Indraput, which had been overthrown centuries before; for they feared the possibility of a new and vigorous Mohammedan Empire being founded on the ruins of the old, by the hardy northern invaders.

The smell arising from the immense number of unburied dead had obliged the Afghans to abandon Delhi. The Mahrattas from the Deccan marched, therefore, unopposed, into the ruins of the city. They were numbered at two hundred thousand horsemen, under great leaders.

When they arrived at the capital, the Mahrattas were more barbarously cruel than even the Persians or Afghans had been. Finding little else to rob, they stripped the Delhians of their clothes, and whipped them naked through the streets. At length, after two hundred and fifty years of servitude, the Rajpoot had conquered the Turk, and was master of the imperial city, though in ruins. The state of horror was indescribable. Famine set in; women ate their children, men devoured each other, human beings fled from their own race in terror. The object of the Mahrattas was not merely plunder. They felt they had centuries of Moslem oppression to avenge.

This unexpected Pagan invasion of the Hindoos of the Deccan struck terror into the Moslems. They all united in the face of the common enemy. The inspiring rallying-cry of 'The Faith!' was raised. The Afghan and Persian invaders, under Abdalla; the Turkish troops of Delhi, under Gazi Amir-ul-Omrah; the Rohilla Afghans, under Nigib ul Dowla—Turk, Persian, Afghan, Pathan, Moghul—made common cause, and met as brothers. In the bond of brotherhood of the creed all former wrongs were forgotten, and those who were lately deadly enemies joined with one accord to fight the Pagan.

A decisive battle took place between the Moslems and the Hindoos again at Paniput. The Mahrattas occupied the place of Mohammed's ill-starred encampment, the Mohammedan allies that of Nadir Shah. This battle was fought February 7th, 1761.

Among the Mohammedan leaders was Saadat Ali, King of Oude (a grandson of the Saadat of the time of Mohammed). This man turned the tide of battle by a charge on the Mahratta flank, when Abdalla's Persians had been thrown into confusion by the fiery impetuosity of the Mahratta attack. Among the Mahratta leaders was Scindiah (second of his race) and his three brothers. Three were killed on the field of Paniput, and Scindiah himself, though he survived, was so desperately wounded that he was maimed for life.

The crescent was still victorious, as it had been for one thousand years, over the Hindoos. The carnage was terrific. It is said to have amounted to one hundred thousand men. The Mohammedans pursued the flying Mahrattas for three days. All the Hindoo generals were slain, except Scindiah. The overthrow of the Mahrattas was complete.

Abdalla, the Afghan commander, was recalled by affairs of importance to Kabul. Nigit ul Dowla was left in command of the city of Delhi, nominally, in the name of the king. Gazi returned to the Deccan, where his brother had usurped his throne; and there he met his fate by being poisoned by his aunt, at his brother's instigation.

Two kings of the house of Timour had been murdered in quick succession: Ahmed, the son of Mohammed, in 1753, and, secondly, Alumgire, in 1760, who was succeeded by Shah Allum, from whom we took Delhi forty years afterwards.

Shah Allum's life was a long romance of war and adventure. In his youth, with French assistance, he fought, though unsuccessfully, the rising British power in Bengal. He was restored to his throne at Delhi by Mahratta assistance, under Scindiah.

This alliance of the house of Timour, the head of the Moslems, with the Mahrattas was hateful to the Amirs, and caused ceaseless rebellions and civil wars. In one of these risings Shah Alum was deposed, and blinded by his own slave, Gholam Kadir; but reinstated soon after by Scindiah, he ruled nominally in Delhi until 1805, when the English took the city. As we have stated before, the mutiny of 1857 saw the end of the house of Timour, for the King of Delhi of the day headed our revolted soldiery. He was transported, and died a prisoner in Rangoon soon afterwards.

CHAPTER IV.

THE RISE OF THE BRITISH POWER IN INDIA.—1756.

The East India Company—Their servants and trade—Surajah Dowlah declares war and attacks Calcutta—The Black Hole—Revenge of the English—The Battle of Plassey.

In 1756 the English in Bengal were simply traders. They had not a thought beyond their counting-houses and their ledgers, their profit and loss. They were the servants of the East India Company, and were styled 'senior' and 'junior' factors. These factors were gentlemen. Their hair was powdered, they wore rapiers and ruffles, diamond buckles and silk stockings. Some were members of impoverished county families; some were Scotch Jacobites, whom the troubles of ''15' and ''45' had driven from their homes; some were the sons and nephews of East India directors, prosperous city people received at court and struggling into society.

Nothing is more curious to contemplate than the spirit of adventure and enterprise that drove these English gentlemen across such weary wastes of water in ships that we should consider little better than yachts in size. It took at least nine months in those days to reach India.

In India we were never agricultural colonists; we were simply dwellers in a foreign land. We found ourselves face to face with an ancient Mohammedan civilisation, and we submitted to its laws and customs. The English factors in Calcutta led uneventful lives. They spent the hot, sultry days over ledgers and accounts, in giving orders to the Bengalee weavers, ordering and receiving produce and manufactures. At night they retired to their homes, large, airy, and luxurious houses, standing in detached grounds.

Their duty was to collect for the Company piece goods, gold and silk brocades, or the muslin, fine as gossamer, which was so prized by the ladies of the courts of George II. and Louis XV. The spinning jenny had not then been invented, and no fabrics of Europe could rival the fairy webs which came from the Indian hand-looms. These manufactures, with raw silk, pepper, and drugs, were despatched to England in the three-decked and three-masted vessels which lay at anchor in the river Hooghly, before the windows of the English merchants, whose homes were situated on its banks. This was the factors' work; but for amusement they shot tigers, they hunted the wild boar, they rode the small thoroughbred horses of Nejid or the large sixteen-hand horses of Turkestan. The great event of their lives was the arrival of 'the fleet' from England. It came every winter, bringing with it home letters. It brought also articles of iron and wool for traffic, and took back the Company's muslins, silks, and drugs.

As early as the year 1640, in the reign of Shah Jehan, some 'factors' and merchants' clerks settled at the spot now called Calcutta.

By the year 1756 this trading settlement had grown into a town. The richer merchants had built themselves large houses, not unlike the manorhouses of the day in England—houses with large airy rooms, with long rows of high, narrow windows, and surrounded by enclosed parks and gardens. The English had also a church, a mayor's court, and, following their national love of green trees and grass, had made for themselves a public park. Around some of their warehouses they had raised small and contemptible defences.

On one side of the English town rose an Indian city, mostly of straw huts, with a few more substantial buildings. This was inhabited by the hundreds of subordinates whom the English trade and fair-dealing had collected. The English merchants rented from the Moslem rulers about ten miles of land. On this Calcutta was built, and on their estate were many villages of weavers. Like all other great Indian landlords, they were allowed a certain amount of jurisdiction over their Indian underlings.

Eastern writers speak of Bengal as the Paradise of India. It was one of the richest countries in the world; it was perennially green as England in May.

Its soil is a rich mould, lying upon sand, and through its level plains a hundred rivers run to the sea, forming natural highways for its merchandise.* It is watered besides by daily rains from May until August. Rice, ginger, turmeric, and red pepper grow almost without cultivation; sugar requires only a little more care. The cattle are numerous, the rivers abound in fish, and in the islands at the mouth of the Ganges are found deer in abundance. The area of Bengal was 600 miles, its population at the time fifteen millions, whilst its revenue was calculated at five millions. 'Few countries,' says an eye-witness and English factor, 'exhibited a higher degree of populousness, wealth, and civilisation than were to be found there on the banks of the Hooghly, one of the principal rivers of Bengal.† Ghauts occurred at short intervals, with their wide flights of steps from the banks into the water. The towers of a hundred Hindoo temples rose from among its groves of cocoanut trees, or the slim minarets of a mosque, where the imaum prayed with his face towards Mecca.'

On the banks of the Hooghly was to be found the civilisation of Europe, as well as that of Asia. Six miles up the river from Calcutta stood the Danish town of Serampore. Fifty miles higher up the river were the towns of Hooghly and Chandernagore; both were thriving fortified European towns, where the sound of church bells could be heard from the churches built by the Portuguese

* Orme, vol. i. p. 4.

† Dow, 'An Inquiry into the State of Bengal,' vol. i. p. 47.

colonists. Hooghly belonged to the Dutch, and Chandernagore to the French. On the great river sailed fleets of ships that had come round the Cape of Good Hope, carrying the flags of all nations.

This rich, green, and fertile kingdom of Bengal was governed in 1756 by a young Usbeg Turk, called Surajah Dowlah. He was nephew of Aliverdy Khan, a soldier of fortune, who had seized Bengal from the weak Mohammed.

'Surajah Dowlah, a youth of nineteen, reigned under the title of viceroy. He discovered,' writes an Asiatic, 'vicious propensities at an age when only follies are expected from princes. He ordered boats to be filled with men, who were then drowned in his very sight, while he sat in his palace and enjoyed their dying struggles. He bricked up one of his wives alive between four walls. He kept in his seraglio a guard composed of Tartar, Georgian, and Abyssinian women, armed with sabres and targets, who murdered people in open day in the streets of Moorshedabad, his capital.'* This amiable youth no sooner mounted the throne than he determined to attack the English merchants in Calcutta. He hated the English, for no reason at the time, only it was his whim to do so, therefore a *casus belli* was found. A native named Kassindas had been received in Calcutta, though at the time the English were not aware that this would give offence to Surajah Dowlah; they had also slightly increased,

* 'Travels of a Hindoo,' vol. i. p. 77.

without his consent, the mean fortifications round their city, as they feared the possibility of the French at Chandernagore attacking them. There had long been hostilities between the English and French at Madras. At length, without a word of warning, Surajah Dowlah threatened to attack Calcutta.

The English were seriously alarmed at this sudden danger. Their fortifications consisted of a low wall three feet high, and some small bastions. There was no ditch, nothing to prevent the approach of an enemy to the very foot of their walls. In some places warehouses and buildings even overlooked these poor defences.

None of the cannon were above nine-pounders; they were mostly honeycombed, and their carriages decayed. The garrison of the fort consisted of twenty-two privates, mostly Dutchmen, and twenty Topasses (Portuguese born in India). The very powder was damp. 'Many of the defenders did not know the right from the wrong end of their muskets.'* To add to this force, the inhabitants, to the number of five hundred and fourteen, served as a militia; of these only one hundred and seventy-four were Englishmen. Surajah Dowlah, on the other hand, was at the head of a splendid army; he had fifty thousand infantry, strong fine men, from the province of Bheerboom (the land of heroes), a northern part of Bengal. He had eighteen thousand cavalry, who in spirit and equipment were equal to any of the vaunted cavalry

* Orme, vol. i. p. 20.

of Asia, the Janissaries of Turkey or the Mamelukes of Egypt. They were mostly Turks, Afghans, and Persians, dressed in chain-armour; splendid horsemen, riding the fine horses of Central Asia. They were no raw levies either; they had been raised and trained by the late viceroy, Aleverdy Khan, a military adventurer, who with these men had gained many victories, and kept at bay the whole noted Mahratta forces for ten years.

The English could not believe that they were to be driven from a spot where they had lived unmolested for upwards of one hundred years. The most submissive messages were sent to Surajah Dowlah, with the offers of large sums of money—money which had settled so many difficulties with the Moslem viceroys on other occasions. But the self-willed youth would not be turned from his purpose; he had an increasing hatred of the English, who had never injured him; besides this, he imagined that Calcutta was one of the richest places in the world, and he expected to get immense sums from pillaging it.

In this dark hour the English looked around for allies. They sent to Madras; but help could not come from thence or from Bombay for many months, and the danger was imminent. They sent to the French at Chandernagore, to the Dutch at Hooghly; but these allies also failed them. The Dutch simply refused all assistance; the French said they would protect such English as chose to come to Chandernagore. It seems wonderful to us that when the English knew they would be attacked by such overwhelming numbers, they did not abandon a place where they could make no defence; but they seemed to have had the truly English dislike to deserting a post of danger.

Meanwhile, Surajah Dowlah marched from Moorshedabad, a distance of about three hundred miles, with such rapidity that many of his men died from fatigue and sunstroke, for it was in June, the hottest time of the year. He crossed the river Hooghly, at the town of Hooghly, in an immense fleet of small boats. Here he ordered the French and the Dutch to assist him in taking Calcutta. But they refused, pleading the treaties subsisting between their nations and the English in Europe. These refusals highly irritated Surajah Dowlah, who was little used to contradiction; but he dared not show his resentment then, as he feared that they might make common cause with the English.

The Moslem viceroy's army arrived in Calcutta on the 16th June. The English had thrown up some hasty defences of earthworks. There was two days' fighting in the principal streets, and for this time the English gallantly held out against overwhelming numbers.

On the 18th June, all the women were sent on board the ships. Mr. Manningham and Frankland, two 'senior factors,' volunteered to see to their embarkation; and having on this pretence quitted the scene of danger, they refused to return. The ships, eight in number, were much galled by the enemy's fire-arrows; they dropped in consequence three miles down the river, with the women and Messrs. Manningham and Frankland on board; this was the first desertion. Mr. Drake, the governor, and Captain Minchin, the military commandant, next fled in a boat. 'The astonishment of those who remained in the fort was not greater than their indignation at this desertion,' says an eye-witness.* Mr. Drake had behaved with great courage at first, but finding the defence hopeless, which it was from the outset, he was completely panic-stricken at the idea of being exposed to Surajah Dowlah's well-known barbarity, for the viceroy had been often heard to express the greatest indignation at Mr. Drake's having attempted the defence of Calcutta, and his fixed resolve of putting him to death. After Mr. Drake had left, Mr. Pearkes, the next senior merchant, refused command. Mr. Holwell, to whom it was next offered, and who had been the soul of the defence from the first, took the lead, and, to prevent any more desertions, he locked the western gate leading to the river. There was still one ship in which the garrison hoped to escape, but that ran aground, and then all hope of rescue was lost. For two days they defended themselves, but at length they were driven to surrender. Surajah Dowlah promised, 'on the word of a soldier, that their lives should be spared.' This put all the brave defenders into high spirits.

Immediately on this there followed one of the strangest

* Orme, vol. i. p. 71.

and darkest tragedies in history, a tragedy which, even after the lapse of one hundred years and more, can neither be read nor related without horror. Surajah Dowlah, seated in regal pomp, had Mr. Holwell brought before him—he and all the principal English officials in Calcutta. All the English prisoners were then made over to an Indian guard. There was a prison in the fort called the Black Hole, which had never been intended for more than one or two prisoners at most. 'The size of this cell was eighteen feet by fourteen, and the ceiling was low. Into it were driven one hundred and forty-six human beings, mostly Englishmen, some of whom were wounded. It was dimly lighted by two small windows, and secured by iron bars. The weather was intolerably stifling. It was a hot night at the hottest time of the year, in a tropical climate, where Englishmen, reared in a cold country, find it impossible to exist without every luxury of lofty, airy rooms, and the constant waving of punkahs. They were so crowded in this cell that there was barely standing room, so that when the last man entered the door could scarcely be closed. One of the survivors declared they would sooner have rushed on the swords of the guards, and have met death at once; but they were confused and taken by surprise, for none of them knew the place. When the door was closed, the truth flashed upon them in all its bitter reality that few, or none of them, could live through the night. They tried to break open the door, but that was impossible. Mr. Holwell, who retained his usual presence of mind, offered a bribe to the guard of £100 if they would divide them into two rooms. The sum was doubled, quadrupled. They answered always, they dared do nothing without Surajah Dowlah's orders; that he was asleep, and that no man dared to wake him. Various means were tried to obtain more air and more room. Every one stripped off his clothes, every hat was put into motion, yet even in the first hour many had fallen to rise no more. Their thirst became intolerable, and, at their request, the guard brought them skins of water to the window; but the sight of water nearly drove the prisoners mad. They fought, they struggled, they raved.'* 'They took care, said Holwell, one of the survivors, 'to keep us well supplied with water, that they might have the satisfaction of seeing us fight for it, as they phrased it, and held up lights to the bars, that they might lose no part of their inhuman diversion.'†

Then the half-maddened prisoners endeavoured to obtain air by trying to scramble over the heads of those who stood between them and the window. They fought, they trampled each other down. By twelve o'clock at night all were raving, or in a lethargic stupor. By two o'clock not more than fifty were alive. When dawn broke, Mr. Holwell was lying among the dying and the dead. The survivors hunted for him, thinking he would have more influence than they with the guard. He was insensible, but a Captain Mills, with rare generosity, when

* Thornton, ch. iv. p. 196. † Holwell's 'Tracts,' p. 398.

all the others refused, gave up his place at the window to him, and he in some degree recovered. When morning broke, at length an order came from Surajah Dowlah to let out the English prisoners. Out of the hundred and forty-six who went in the night before, no more than twenty-three came out alive—such ghastly spectres that their own mothers would not have known them. The weak survivors inside the cell had great difficulty in clearing away the heap of corpses that closed the door of the prison. A ditch was dug on the outside of the fort, and the naked bodies were thrown in quickly ; for the smell was so intolerable that even the Indians feared a pestilence. A Mrs. Carey, the wife of a sea officer, was one of the survivors. Her husband had died that night in the Black Hole. She was young and handsome, and was sent away to Moorshedabad, to the harem of Meer Jaffer, the viceroy's principal general.

Mr. Holwell, in a nearly speechless state, was conveyed before Surajah Dowlah, who showed no compassion at his deplorable condition, and no indignation at the inhumanity of the guard. He only immediately demanded where the treasures of the English were concealed. Surajah Dowlah was extremely disappointed at the small amount of booty he had found in Calcutta, only £200,000. In June Calcutta was nearly empty of merchandise, the only wealth of the English. The winter fleet had left, laden with the investments, and the merchandise that had come from England had been sold in the country and removed from Calcutta.

Mr. Holwell, Mr. Court, and Mr. Walcot, who, Surajah Dowlah fancied, knew more about the hidden treasures than they chose to tell, were sent to Moorshedabad in fetters, confined in a cowshed, and fed on rice. The other survivors made their way on foot to the English ships, three miles down the river. 'Their appearance,' says Orme, an eye-witness, 'and the dreadful tale they had to tell, were the severest of reproaches to those on board, who, intent only on their own preservation, had made no effort to facilitate the escape of the rest of the garrison. A single sloop, with fifteen brave men on board, might, in spite of all the efforts of the enemy, have come up and anchored under the fort, and have carried away all who suffered in the dungeon.'

The English ships, with the fugitives on board, moved farther down the river towards the sea. They anchored at a small village, called Fulta, with the usual ghaut, or landing-place of broad steps, leading down to the river. There they remained for five months, from June to October, sleeping on their ships, and exposed to every hardship. They were so overcrowded that men, women, and children slept on the decks, without shelter from the heavy rain of the tropics, many without even one change of clothing. The supply of food was very scanty, because the country people hardly dared to bring in provisions;

they so greatly feared the Moslem viceroy's anger. Most of the fugitives had been used to lives of ease and luxury in their large houses, surrounded by troops of servants. The climate of the mouth of the Ganges is perhaps the most unhealthy in the world. The fugitives were decimated by dysentery and fever. A long line of newly-dug graves on the low, melancholy shore showed the many that had fallen victims to the climate.

Meanwhile Surajah Dowlah's army were employed in pillaging Calcutta; they burnt the English houses, and they then built a mosque inside what had been the British fort. Surajah Dowlah then returned to Moorshedabad. He never contemplated any retribution; he was too ignorant to reason on the subject. He believed 'there were only ten thousand men in the whole of Europe,' and it is probable he did not even know the name of the island from which the English came. He was planning another expedition, to take place as soon as the tropical rains had subsided, to punish the Foujdar of Purneah, a refractory lord, one of his own relations.

Moorshedabad was a large city. The town proper was five miles long and two-and-a-half broad; but, including the suburbs, it had a circumference of thirty miles. On one of its banks stood the palace of the General Meer Jaffier, strongly fortified, and 'large enough to hold three European monarchs.' Surajah Dowlah's palace was on a sheet of water, called the Pearl Lake; it was built of black marble brought from the ancient city of Gaur.

The river Ganges divided the city, and for about two miles it was crowded with crafts. To speak of its greatness in the words of Clive, 'The city of Moorshedabad is as extensive, populous, and rich as the city of London, with this difference—that there are individuals in the first possessing infinitely greater property than in the last city.'

But to return to the English at Fulta, at the mouth of the Hooghly. Their numbers had been increased by various ships that arrived from sea. 'All was lost,' writes Orme, 'before the presidency of Madras even received intelligence of their danger.' They no sooner knew of the peril than a detachment of two hundred and fifty men were despatched, under Major Kilpatrick. They were mostly of the 39th Regiment, which still bears the motto of 'Primus in Indis.' This force was too small to do anything. They arrived at Fulta on the 2nd August. By the middle of December half the soldiers were dead, and of the remainder not more than thirty were fit for duty, in consequence of the deadly climate.

On the 2nd of December, 1756, hope breathed again among the wretched fugitives at Fulta. 'Clive arrived with 1500 men, after a stormy passage of two months from Madras. It was not a large force to attack a sovereign who had as many subjects as Louis the Fifteenth or the Empress Marie Therese.'* But Clive's name was

* Macaulay's Essay on Clive.

a talisman which gave confidence to his countrymen and brought confusion to the enemy. Clive had been fighting ceaselessly for ten years against the French, who were in alliance with the Moslem governors at Madras. Some ten years before, the united forces of the French and the Mohammedans had taken and sacked Madras, and ruined our trade; much as Surajah Dowlah had taken Calcutta. In our dark hour of distress and difficulty a 'heaven-born general,' as Pitt called him, arose. This was Clive. He was only a 'factor,' a young man twenty-five years of age, but he turned the tide of battle and rescued all our possessions from the French. Clive was the son of a poor Shropshire squire—poor, but of ancient lineage. Since his victories in Madras he had returned to England, enriched his family, and had been presented at Court to George the Second, and had received from him a colonel's commission in the regular army.

On the 27th December, 1756, the English fleet left Fulta. It consisted of upwards of twenty vessels, of which only six or eight had troops on board. There were nine hundred English soldiers; two hundred and fifty of these were regulars belonging to the 39th Regiment, and were commanded by Colonel Aldercron, and were known as 'king's troops.' The rest were Company's troops, 'the Madras Regiment,' paid and enlisted by the East India Company. These men had gained most of Clive's victories in Madras. There were also 1500 Sepoys, Indian infantry soldiers, trained and drilled by the English. They also were veterans of Clive, raised and drilled by him, and sharers of his many victories.

The ships of the royal navy were the *Kent*, 69 ; the *Tiger*, 60 ; the *Salisbury*, 50 ; the *Bridgewater*, 20 guns. Admiral Watson commanded the squadron, Clive was on board the *Kent*.

Two other ships—the *Cumberland*, 70 guns ; and the *Marlborough*, a Company's vessel—had not reached Fulta. It was feared they were lost, for the whole fleet had met with adverse winds and heavy weather in the Bay of Bengal. The *Cumberland* had on board two hundred and fifty men of the 39th Regiment, and the *Marlborough* nearly all the field artillery. It was a serious loss, but in spite of the missing ships, it was decided to push on. A small addition of forces was gained by seventy of the fugitives at Fulta joining the army as volunteers. Among these volunteers was a young man of the name of Warren Hastings, a factor who had escaped from Moorshedabad.

On the 28th December, 1756, the first English success in Bengal took place. The enemy made a stand under a Hindoo general called Monichchund, at Budge-Budge, where there was a fort. They were driven back, and retreated on Calcutta. This success was gained by Clive and the Madras regiment.

On the 2nd of January, 1757, the English re-entered Calcutta, from which they had been driven so miserably six months before. They found it abandoned. The fleet arrived first. Clive, after driving the enemy from Budge-Budge, marched up along the river bank. On reaching Calcutta he was informed 'that none of the Company's officers or troops should be admitted into the fort.' He had been placed in supreme command of the expedition by the Council at Madras. Clive found the fort in possession of Captain Eyre Coote, of the 39th Regiment, who showed him a commission from Admiral Watson, appointing him governor of the fort. Clive was not a spirit to submit tamely to such an assumption of his just authority. He declared if Captain Coote did not immediately evacuate the fort he would fire on it. At length the dispute was settled by Clive receiving the keys of the fort from Admiral Watson, 'in the king's name, as the Company's representative.'

Surajah Dowlah was advancing on Calcutta with a large army. This prevented the country people from supplying the English with provisions. *Viâ* Aleppo the news had arrived that war had been declared between France and England. It was feared the French at Chandernagore would be sure to join Surajah Dowlah. There was at Chandernagore a disciplined force of Frenchmen almost equal to the English in numbers. The odds against Clive's little army were overwhelming if the Asiatic hordes of Surajah Dowlah were joined by the well-disciplined French, under French officers. Surajah Dowlah arrived at Calcutta on the 2nd of February, and encamped in the direction of the Salt Lake, but without the French. His arrival was announced by the plunderers that followed his army, armed with great clubs, attacking the native part of the town and plundering it.

Clive started on the night of the 2nd, at midnight, to attack Surajah Dowlah with 600 sailors, armed with firelocks. The English forces were in all 650 infantry, 100 artillerymen, and 800 Sepoys, with only six six-pounder guns. At dawn the rival armies met. There was a dense white fog, common at that time of year, which hid assailants and defenders from each other's view. The English were first attacked by a body of Usbeg cavalry, who were excellently mounted. The result of this engagement was that 500 of the enemy were killed, but on the English side also a rather large number of privates and some officers. This engagement, however, had one very important effect, though the success in the field had been doubtful. The fighting was close to Surajah Dowlah's tents; he was so alarmed at the din of battle and at seeing the English force so near him that he opened negotiations, and offered to restore Calcutta to the English, and also to restore the trading rights that had been granted them by various Emperors of India.

This was exactly what Clive wished. Even his intrepid spirit doubted the expediency of continuing hostilities if they could make peace. He knew that one defeat under the existing circumstances would be certain ruin to the English in Bengal—not but that he and every other Englishman wished for retribution, swift, sure, and terrible, to fall on the tyrant who had inflicted such uncalled-for injuries on their nation.

There was war between France and England; Chandernagore was temptingly near. It was fifty miles up the river; the English fleet could reach it and bombard it with ease. Surajah Dowlah gave a sort of half consent to this attack on the French. He took no active measures to defend it, and therefore Chandernagore fell. In it was found booty to the amount of £100,000. Surajah Dowlah addressed a letter of congratulation to Clive on its fall, but he protected all the Frenchmen who escaped from the city.

He addressed, however, the following letter to M. Bussy, a French general at Madras: 'These disturbers, the admiral and Sabut Jung' (Colonel Clive—Sabut Jung means 'the daring in war,' by which name Clive is still known in India)—'whom bad fortune attend, without reason whatever, are warring against M. Renault'—the Governor of Chandernagore. 'This you will learn from his letters. I, who in all things seek the good of mankind, assist you in every respect. I hope in God: those English, who are unfortunate, will be punished for the disturbances they have raised.' Hooghly we had taken also.

Our rivals from Europe had all fallen, and the following circumstance placed Surajah Dowlah in our power. He was hated, feared, and despised by his subjects—by his warlike fellow-countrymen for his cowardice and ignorance of war, by the subject Hindoos for his capriciousness and tyranny. A plot was formed against him by some of the leading men of Moorshedabad.

These men were Meer Jaffier, his own kinsman, the principal leader of his army; the Juggit Setts brothers, enormously rich bankers; and Roydullub, the Minister of Finance. These discontented courtiers of Moorshedabad opened communications with Clive and the Council at Calcutta. They wished, with the assistance of the English, to depose Surajah Dowlah and place Meer Jaffier on the throne of Bengal. The negotiations had been carried on by a native merchant named Omichund and an English factor, Mr. Watts, at Moorshedabad itself. Omichund threatened to reveal the whole secret to Surajah Dowlah unless he was given a bribe of £300,000. Clive promised the bribe, but intended to evade his promise. The lives of Mr. Watts, Meer Jaffier, and others were at stake, so that he dared not refuse this extortionate demand. But Omichund would not be satisfied by Clive's bare word.

The English had drawn up a treaty with Meer Jaffier. Omichund insisted that the sum he was to receive should be entered in this treaty, and that it should be signed by the English members of the Council at Calcutta. Clive had two treaties drawn up—a real one and a fictitious one.

In the real treaty Omichund's name was not mentioned; in the fictitious one it was stated he should receive the £300,000. Admiral Watson refused to sign the fictitious one, or to be any party to the deception of Omichund. Clive knew Omichund was as keen-witted as he was grasping. The absence of the name of a man of such mark as Admiral Watson would have revealed the whole fraud to him. Clive's expedient was this—he forged Admiral Watson's name.

During this time Clive wrote Surajah Dowlah many of what he himself called 'soothing' letters. Mr. Watts, Meer Jaffier, and Omichund were not less active in 'soothing' the fated prince. At length everything was ready for action. Mr. Watts and Omichund fled from Moorshedabad. This first awoke Surajah Dowlah from the false security into which he had been lulled by the conspirators. The next thing that confirmed his suspicions was, that Clive wrote him a letter very different from the 'soothing' ones that he had so lately penned. He taxed him with all the unmerited injuries that he had heaped on the English, and asked that Meer Jaffier should decide the differences between them, adding that he would receive the answer to his letter in person at Moorshedabad.

Rumour soon asserted that Meer Jaffier had joined the English. But Surajah Dowlah at first could not, would not, believe that his kinsman, a pious Moslem and distinguished soldier, could have joined his enemies and those of the true Faith. He visited him at his palace in

Moorshedabad. He reminded him of his indebtedness to, and years of friendship with, Aliverdy Khan. The Koran was brought in, and Meer Jaffier swore on it to abandon the English.

Surajah Dowlah immediately assembled his whole forces and marched down to meet the English, and the principal command was given to Meer Jaffier. Clive was in a terribly critical position. He was encamped near Plassey, awaiting Meer Jaffier, who had promised to join him with all the divisions under his command. But instead of appearing with the flower of the Moslem army, he only sent evasive answers to the English general's remonstrances. Clive knew that his small body of picked troops would do all that men could do, but it was a terrible responsibility to have to decide upon pitting 3000 men against 70,000. In his perplexity he called a council of war. He gave his opinion first, and it was in favour of remaining where they were, near the Fort of Cutwah, which the English had taken. They had found in it great stores of grain, and were waiting until they were joined by the Mahrattas.

The river Hooghly was before them; it rolled between them and Moorshedabad. 'It was very easy to cross it,' said Clive; 'but in case of defeat not one man would return alive.' Out of the council of war, composed of twenty officers, seven were for fighting at once, twelve were for delay. Clive spent an hour in solitary thought under the shade of a tree, and there he made up his mind to risk all on the single throw of a die, and determined to go on, let the consequences be what they would.

On the 22nd of June the British force crossed the Hooghly in the evening. After a toilsome march, up to the soldiers' middle in mud, at one o'clock they arrived at Plassey, and took up their position in a grove. All night they could hear the drums and cymbals which marked the night-watches of the enemy. Until then they had no idea they were so near. The next day was to decide the fate of India.

The grove at Plassey was called the Lakka Bagh, or garden of ten thousand trees. It was eight hundred yards long, and three hundred broad. The trees grew in straight rows, as in an orchard, and were planted so close that they cast a dense shade, under which neither grass nor brushwood grew. The grove was surrounded by a bank and ditch, the ditch choked with coarse weeds and brambles. A little to the north of the grove, and on the banks of the river, stood a small hunting-lodge of Surajah Dowlah, also surrounded by a wall.

At daybreak on the morning of the 23rd the English observed the enemy marching out of their encampment towards the grove of Plassey, with the intention apparently of surrounding it. Clive drew up his 1200 Englishmen and his 2,100 Sepoys outside the grove, their left resting on Plassey House and the river, and their right on the grove. The small band of English observed with wonder the enemy's imposing hosts. They had

50,000 infantry, 18,000 horse, and fifty guns on the field. Their infantry were armed with matchlocks, pikes, swords, bows and arrows. Their cavalry were mounted on large, powerful horses, each man carrying a small circular shield, and armed with a scimitar, and many of them clothed in chain armour. The guns were 18, 24 and 32-pounders, dispersed into brigades of not more than two or three guns between the divisions of the troops. Each of the guns was dragged by a train of white oxen, and behind each gun was an elephant, trained to assist it by pushing it on from behind with its head if required.

The engagement began. Fifty Frenchmen, under an officer of the name of Sinfray, were the most advanced of the enemy. They had taken up a position on a mound with four light guns. In the same line with these were two large guns, and behind them 5000 horse and 7000 infantry. The English were exposed to a galling fire. In a few minutes they lost twenty Englishmen and thirty Sepoys, killed by this cannonade. Clive ordered them to retire behind the bank that enclosed the grove. The enemy were much elated by their retreat.

But then the English field-pieces moved forward and poured a well-directed fire into the dense masses of the enemy collected before them. The enemy suffered cruel losses from our guns, while the English were protected by the high earth-bank of the grove, and the thickly planted trees. Both armies remained in this position until twelve o'clock in the day. Then the flower of the horsemen of Islam, in all their panoply of shining armour, charged down; but they broke and fled before they reached the grove, unable to face the fire of our infantry and artillery. In this charge their leader was killed, Meer Moodeen, an apostate Hindoo of high rank. He was, perhaps, Surajah Dowlah's only devoted general. Surajah Dowlah was in his tent, out of the reach of danger, when he was informed that Meer Moodeen was killed; and when he knew he had lost his most loyal commander, he sent for Meer Jaffier. As soon as the latter entered the tent, he flung his turban on the ground, saying, 'Jaffier, that turban you must defend.' Jaffier promised his utmost services.

At three o'clock in the day, the enemy retired to their entrenchment. It was about three miles in extent, on a peninsula formed by the winding of the river. The Frenchmen were the last to leave the field. On their retiring, Major Kilpatrick pushed forward and took the mound they had occupied. This mound commanded the enemy's encampment; all the English artillery were brought up to it. They poured ceaseless cannon-shot into the crowded camp, which caused extreme confusion, wounding and killing men, bullocks, and elephants.

At this juncture a large corps of the enemy were seen separating from the main body. The English did not know for what purpose, and fired on them. It was the long-expected division of Meer Jaffier coming at length to join the English, as their cause seemed triumphant. Then the line of British infantry, only two deep, with a loud and ringing cheer, bayonet in hand, charged straight into the encampment. All the enemy fled in a confused mass, and the English pursued them for six miles.

Surajah Dowlah had been the first to flee, on a fleet dromedary, escorted by 2000 horsemen. He entered Moorshedabad the same evening. That night he fled from his palace in disguise, accompanied by an eunuch and one of his wives. He carried in his hand a small casket of jewels. The fugitives embarked in a boat, in hopes of being able to reach M. Law, who commanded some Frenchmen at Patna.

Meer Jaffier had given the English no assistance during the battle; he was in great uneasiness as to how he should be received by them. He visited Clive the day after the engagement, who received him with the greatest cordiality, and saluted him as 'Viceroy of the three provinces of Bengal, Behar, and Orissa.' A few days after this visit Clive entered the great city of Moorshedabad, guarded by 200 English troops and 500 Sepoys. 'The inhabitants,' wrote Clive, 'if inclined to destroy the Europeans, might have done it with sticks and stones.'

Without any delay, in Surajah Dowlah's palace of black marble on the banks of the Pearl Lake, and in his pillared Hall of Audience, was performed the ceremony of the installation of Meer Jaffier. Clive led the new viceroy to the throne, and presented him with pieces of gold on a golden plate, as tribute, the time-immemorial custom in the East. The leading courtiers also presented tribute.

A meeting was held at the house of the Setts, the rich bankers, to carry out the stipulations of the treaty made between Meer Jaffier and the English. 'Omichund came thither, believing himself to stand high in the favour of Clive; for Clive, with a dissimulation surpassing even the dissimulation of Bengal, had up to that day treated him with undiminished kindness.'* 'It is time,' said Clive, carelessly, 'to undeceive Omichund.' Clive never acquired the Hindustanee language, and therefore Mr. Scrafton, a factor present, addressed Omichund in his own tongue. 'Omichund, the treaty you saw was a trick. You have nothing.' He fell back insensible into the arms of his attendants. He revived, but his mind was irreparably ruined.

Clive, who was not inhuman, was much touched at his state. He visited him and spoke kindly to him, but from the moment of that great shock the unhappy man sank gradually into idiotcy. He languished for a few months, and then died.

The next victim of the revolution was Surajah Dowlah. In need of food and shelter, he sought refuge in the hut of a devotee. It chanced that in the days of his power he had ordered the nose and ears of this man to be cut off. The devotee betrayed him to Meer Cossim, a relation of Meer Jaffier's, who commanded in the neigh-

* Macaulay's Essay on Clive.

bourhood of Rajmahal. Surajah Dowlah was carried back to Moorshedabad. He was brought before Meer Jaffier in what but a few days before had been his own palace. He threw himself on his knees before Meer Jaffier, and, with sobs and abject cries, 'implored the mercy he had never shown.' Meer Jaffier was touched. He had owed all his prosperity to the generosity of Aliverdy Khan—he could not bring himself to injure his former prince. Meer Jaffier's son, Meeran, a cruel youth, in character not unlike Surajah Dowlah himself, had no such scruples. Surajah Dowlah was privately assassinated by his orders the same night, and his remains the next morning paraded about the streets of Moorshedabad on an elephant. He was buried near his grandfather, Aliverdy Khan.

Meer Jaffier paid the English the money stipulated in the treaty, two millions. The English received at first £800,000 sterling. 'This treasure was packed up in 700 chests and laden in 100 boats. As it neared Calcutta, all the boats of the squadron and many others preceded it, with banners displayed and music sounding. A committee in Calcutta distributed the money for the restitution of the losses of individuals, and executed the office with much discretion and equity.' The sum total the English received from the treasury of Surajah Dowlah was two millions of money, but, besides this, large sums were given as gifts to private individuals. Clive received £100,000; Mr. Drake, £24,000; Mr. Watts, £80,000;

Major Kilpatrick, £30,000; Mr. Walsh, £50,000; Mr. Scrafton, £20,000; many junior factors, £10,000 a piece.*

When the English took Moorshedabad, in Surajah Dowlah's treasury 'were vaults piled with heaps of silver and gold, and these crowned with rubies and diamonds. Sixteen years afterwards, when Clive had to defend his conduct before the House of Commons, for having received his share of Meer Jaffier's money, he declared, 'By God, Mr. Chairman, at this moment I stand astonished at my own moderation.' Meer Jaffier, in a few years, was in his turn deposed by the English, and Meer Cossim placed on the throne of Moorshedabad.

The Setts, the rich bankers, two brothers, were drowned in the river Ganges, by the order of Meer Cossim, and their enormous wealth confiscated.

Meeran was killed instantaneously by lightning, while in a tent. The vulgar believed that it was a judgment on his bloodthirsty cruelty.

Admiral Watson died of a malarious fever, almost immediately after the fall of Moorshedabad, and Clive returned to England, and was made a peer, after having acquired a fortune of £60,000 a year. He died by his own hand in London, about 1774. His latter days were embittered by a parliamentary inquiry into his conduct in India. 'A great mind, ruined by satiety, by the pangs of wounded honour, by fatal diseases, and more fatal remedies.'

* Thornton, chap. iv. p. 248.

Meer Cossim died in poverty at Delhi. His last shawl was sold to pay his funeral expenses. Roydullub, another of the conspirators, fell into disgrace with the English, and into poverty and obscurity.

Moorshedabad exists in the present day, but as a ruined, third-rate provincial town. It is nearly depopulated; barely a trading-boat floats on the Ganges near it. The river has changed its course, and flows some distance from the city. The art of the hundreds of looms in Bengal has been killed by the spinning jennies of Manchester. A few arches remain only of the palace of Surajah Dowlah.

The descendants of Meer Jaffier live at Moorshedabad, in a new large white stucco palace, of Italian architecture. They receive £300,000 a year. They live in much state and luxury, but have less power in the government of Bengal than the youngest English ensign or boy civil officer.

The representatives of the Setts live in their former large palace at Moorshedabad. It is half-ruined, and they have been rescued from absolute want by a pension granted by the English Government to them of twelve hundred a year.

The field of Plassey itself has ceased to exist; the river has swept it away. Of the grove of mango-trees, all are gone except one, under which one of the Moslem generals who fell is buried; and the spot is held sacred to the present day by the Mohammedans in India.

Thus India was gained. It is a received axiom that it is easier to conquer than to rule a conquered country. That we kept India was due to one man alone, Warren Hastings, and to his ability, industry, and statecraft.

The next great crisis in the history of India was the war of 1785. This storm, perhaps the greatest the British Empire in India has ever been called on to weather, was met by Warren Hastings.

A great Mohammedan leader, Hyder Ali, a man of genius, from the hilly and difficult country of Mysore, defeated the English, and overran the whole province of Madras. What made this attack so peculiarly dangerous was that Hyder Ali had in his pay three thousand French soldiers, and, besides, a large number of officers, notably Bernadotte, who afterwards became King of Sweden. Not only did the French cause this attack from Mysore, but they were also in league with the Mahrattas to overrun Bengal also from the north. So long, tedious, and difficult was the war with Mysore that it was not until eighteen years afterwards, in 1793, that the quarrel was ended by the fall of Seringapatam. The Mahrattas were not subdued until 1805, in the battle of Assaye, when they were defeated by Wellington. The city of Delhi fell into our hands during this campaign.

These decisive wars were followed by a comparative peace of thirty years. The English had nothing to fear from any Asiatic power; but at length Russia threatened our Indian Empire, and this caused the war of 1837.

THE

ENGLISH INVASION OF KABUL,

IN 1839.

CHAPTER I.

Activity of Capt. Burnes—He visits Kabul—Returns to India—Is sent back on a commercial mission—A Russian rival—Dost Mohammed is driven into the arms of Russia—England declares war—Passage of the Bolan.

On one more occasion the question of the invasion of India from Central Asia arose. India had been for many a long year under the control of England, when the fears of Russian encroachments led to many fierce fights in the old frontier passes. But this time Delhi invaded Kabul, and not Kabul Delhi.

A young Scotch officer of ability, named Alexander Burnes, was the prime mover in these complications.

In 1831 Kabul, Peshawur, Lahore, the Kheiber—places that had played so great a part in Indian history—were hardly known even by name to the English in India.

Central Asia was an almost unknown land. A few Englishmen had penetrated into these unsettled and dangerous countries in the pursuit of geographical knowledge and from curiosity to see the homes of once great empires and civilisations. Among these early travellers were Elphinstone, Forster, Moorcroft, Sterling, and Fraser. Burnes was seized with an irresistible longing to explore these unknown lands. He had been sent on an embassy to Runjeet Singh, at Lahore. From then he went to Simla, where he gained the consent of the English Governor-General, Lord William Bentinck, to be allowed to travel in Central Asia. He was given no political power; he was simply to gain geographical knowledge, and, if possible, increase English commerce.

In 1831 Burnes started on his venturesome journey from Delhi. A Dr. Gerrard accompanied him; Mohan Lal, a Hindoo who had acquired some knowledge of English at the English college at Delhi, and another servant, formed the party. Burnes reached Lahore, where he was most cordially welcomed by Runjeet Singh, the head of the Sikhs, who ruled the Punjaub. Burnes at length reached Kabul, *viâ* Peshawur, the Kheiber, and Jellalabad. By Dost Mohammed, the then King of Kabul, he was received with every courtesy and attention. Hospitality to strangers is a cardinal virtue among Moslems, and to entertain any stranger of note devolves upon the king. Dost Mohammed was a man who had risen by his own abilities. He was like Baber, a good specimen of the Oriental ruler. He did not oppress the people of Kabul, and it is certain they were not of a temper to submit to oppression. The active-minded, enlightened young English traveller took the fancy of

Dost Mohammed, and the attraction was mutual. They were kindred spirits, and Burnes always retained the highest opinion of his host in all the after events that arose from this first visit. After a pleasant sojourn of some months in the sociable Court of Kabul, Burnes made his way across the mountains of the Hindoo Koosh to Bokhara. There he stayed two months. It was in the mountains of the Hindoo Koosh that the hapless Moorcroft had died, far from his native land. From Bokhara, through many dangers and difficulties, Burnes reached Persia safely, though his party had many times been in great peril of being carried away into hopeless slavery among the Turcomans. Burnes returned to Calcutta after a year's wanderings, and was warmly received by Lord William Bentinck, who recommended him to the Court of Directors. He then returned to England, and wrote a book on his adventurous travels in these semi-civilised lands. The book was well received by the public. 'Bokhara Burnes' became the hero of the hour; he had made his mark, though he was only twenty-six.

While in London, Burnes had tried to persuade the Court of Directors to send him on a commercial mission to Kabul. They refused, 'feeling perfectly assured that it would soon degenerate into a political agency, and that we should, as a necessary consequence, be involved in all the entanglements of Afghan politics.'

Burnes returned to an insignificant appointment in India, 'Assistant to the Resident of Cutch.' From this place, in 1835, he was ordered by Lord Auckland to proceed on a 'commercial mission' to Kabul, and also to explore and navigate the Scinde or Indus river. Nothing could have pleased Burnes more than to fly from the heat and *ennui* of Scinde to the cool mountains of Kabul, where he had many personal friends. Burnes's orders were to sail up the Indus; and by this route he arrived at Peshawur, to find the Kheiber Pass filled with unburied corpses. There had been a battle between the Sikhs and Afghans, which had resulted in the loss of Peshawur to Dost Mohammed. It was to him what the loss of Calais was to Queen Mary.

Burnes encamped the first night among the beetling crags of Ali Musjid, and was shown the very spot where Nadir Shah had rested.

He was received most hospitably by Ackbar Khan at Jellalabad, who was governor of that place, and was Dost Mohammed's favourite son. At Kabul Burnes was again welcomed with every courtesy and attention. The delight of the Afghans at Burnes' return was great and sincere. Before he had only been a traveller, now he was an accredited agent of the English Government on a 'commercial mission.' Dost Mohammed saw him daily, and talked and consulted with Burnes in the most free and unrestrained manner. The loss of Peshawur to the Sikhs rankled in his heart, and he was beset with difficulties in the government of Kabul. The King of Persia, aided by Russian officers, had attacked Herat, in Khorassan, and was believed to be on his way to attack India through Kabul.

Dost Mohammed trusted in the Englishman as a brother. He had travelled so far, knew so much; he could speak their language with grace and facility; he represented a great and powerful people. In the midst of the complication of dangers that threatened Kabul, Dost Mohammed turned eagerly to his foreign friend for advice and help. And 'Sekunder Burnes' was a power behind the throne, stronger than the throne itself.'

At this time a stranger appeared at Kabul, whose appearance caused as much surprise as dismay—a man called Vichovich, who was no less than a Russian agent, also on a 'commercial mission.' He was a young man of slight make, very fair complexion, with bright eyes and a look of great animation. He wore a Cossack uniform.

On the 19th June, 1835, from Kabul Burnes wrote to a private friend; 'We are in a mess here. Herat is besieged and may fall, and the Emperor of Russia has sent an envoy to Kabul to offer Dost Mohammed Khan money to fight Runjeet Singh! I could not believe my eyes and ears; but Captain Vichovich—for that is the agent's name—arrived with a blazing letter, three feet long, and sent immediately to pay his respects to myself. I, of course, received him and asked him to dinner. This is not the best of it. The Ameer (Dost Mohammed) came over to me sharp, and offered to do as I liked—kick him out, or anything; but I should be too much in fear of

Vattel to do any such thing; and since he was so friendly to us, said I, give me the letters the agent has brought—all of which he surrendered sharp; and I sent an express at once to my Lord A. with a confidential letter to the Governor-General himself, bidding him look what his predecessors had brought upon him, and telling him that after this I knew not what might happen, and it was now a neck-and-neck race between Russia and us; and, if his lordship would hear reason, he would forthwith send agents to Bokhara, Herat, Kandahar, and Koondooz, not forgetting Scinde. How this pill will go down I know not, but I know my duty too well to be silent.'

Dost Mohammed wanted to know what the English were prepared to do for him. Would they help him to recover Peshawur? Would they assist him against the King of Persia, who was near at hand, besieging Herat? Would they secure him against treason and treachery in Kabul itself? Burnes had no authority to promise any assistance. The only thing he insisted on was that the Ameer of Kabul was not to join the Persian and Russian alliance.

The handsome Vichovich promised all that Dost Mohammed wanted. He had brought presents and a letter from the Czar. Then was it any wonder that Dost Mohammed went over to the Russians, dazzled with their brilliant offers? Vichovich was received daily, and paraded in public with Dost Mohammed, while Burnes was given the cold shoulder. Finding he could do no good he returned to India, and, going down (as King Baber had done) the Kabul river in a raft, he arrived at Peshawur. At Peshawur Burnes received letters from Mr. W. Macnaghten, the Foreign Secretary, recalling him to Lahore. On rejoining his countrymen he found that Lord Auckland had decided upon a policy which was, at least, vigorous. As Dost Mohammed had joined the Perso-Russian alliance, the Governor-General intended to dethrone him and place a worthier king on the throne of Kabul. The name of the man chosen as the new monarch was Shah Soujah. Burnes remonstrated. He pointed out that Shah Soujah was an incapable ruler, while Dost Mohammed was much valued by the Afghans, and was a man of more than ordinary abilities; that Dost Mohammed was well affected to the English, that he had only joined our enemies from utter necessity, as the English had refused him assistance and the Russians had promised him much help; that one-third of the men and treasure that would be required and expended to place Shah Soujah on the throne of Kabul would serve to make Dost Mohammed the faithful ally of the English. All that Lord Auckland had offered Dost Mohammed, though he had sent repeated offers of friendship, and said he 'valued the friendship of England more than that of Russia or Persia,' was that he would restrain Runjeet from attacking Kabul. This message was laughed at by the Afghans. When had the Hindoo ever dared to attack Kabul? Jubbar Khan, Dost Mohammed's brother, and a warm friend of the English, said 'that such an offer indicated very little knowledge of the state of Afghanistan, for that, so far from the proffered protection from Runjeet being of the value stated, that the Maharajah never sought to attack Kabul, and that hitherto all the aggression had been on the part of the Afghans. It appeared that the English valued their offer at a high rate, since they expected in return that the Afghans would desist from all intercourse with Persia, Russia, and Turkestan. Were the Afghans to make all these powers hostile and receive no protection against the enmity raised for their adhering to the British?' But the policy had been decided upon, and was a *fait accompli*. Burnes' remonstrances were not listened to. Mr. Macnaghten, the Foreign Secretary, by Lord Auckland's orders, was at Lahore arranging with Runjeet Singh, the head of the Sikhs, to allow British troops to pass through his territory. As a Hindoo, Runjeet was delighted to join in a scheme against the hated Afghans. The Sikhs were to be secured in the possession of Peshawur; they even asked for Jellalabad, in the heart of the Afghan mountains; but instead of that city, they were to receive a tribute of twenty thousand pounds a year from the new ruler of Kabul, Shah Soujah.

After being present at several State pageants at Lahore, the grotesque Oriental splendour of Runjeet's camp losing all charm to the English from the intolerable burning heat and scorching winds of June in the Punjaub, Burnes and all the English officials, as soon as the preliminaries of the treaty were settled, left the Punjaub with pleasure for Simla.

The very thought of Simla in June to the exiled English in India gives new life, new hope. It is only in these mountain retreats of the Himalayas in India that we northern races are ever 'at home.' At Simla there are forests of pine trees, rhododendrons in flower, blooming roses and honeysuckle, cream and strawberries, and English fruits, and, above all, the blessing of cool air. Modest little villas, embosomed in green woods and covered with creepers, are dotted on the well-wooded hill-sides. Leaving behind him the heat, the dust, the glare, the sickening splendour of cloudless skies, the languor born of heat and malaria in the Punjaub, Burnes found himself at Lord Auckland's pleasant English vice-regal court in June, in green, shady Simla. At Simla Lord Auckland, the Governor-General, on whom had fallen the mantle of the power of the kings of Delhi, was living with but little more state than an English gentleman of moderate fortune.

Auckland House, which he rented, was but a moderate-sized villa residence, standing in small private grounds on Elysium Hill, a hill which is justly so called. The charms of the unrivalled position of the house made up for its very modest architectural pretensions. From its windows could be seen far ranges of wooded hills, lying in delicious stillness, and beyond them the great range of perpetual snow which divides India from Chinese Tartary.

The interior of Auckland House was not more impressive than the exterior. There were some good-sized reception-rooms, but all was most poorly furnished. Miss Eden, Lord Auckland's sister, records with what ingenuity they made for themselves curtains and furniture covers for the drawing-room, by joining alternate strips of white and red cotton stuff, as furniture chintz was not procurable. The well-known artistic taste of the Misses Eden soon converted the bare walls of Auckland House into an in-habitable English home.

The vice-regal party were charmed with the beautiful scenery, with their English surroundings and climate. Lord Auckland had marched from Calcutta, *viâ* Delhi, a journey which had taken him six months; and Miss Eden, in her letters, gives a lively description of the splendour and discomfort of the march. It retained much of the magnificence and pageantry of the camps of Nadir and the kings of Delhi; for Lord Auckland's camp consisted of ten thousand followers—secretaries, clerks, guards and troops, and domestic servants.

Simla resembles Torquay or Ventnor, in the way its villa residences are dotted about amongst wooded hills. Living in these pleasant homes were the secretaries, members of Civil Service, aides-de-camp—the English Amirs of the new order of things, upon whom had fallen the mantle of the old Turcoman Amirs. This was, perhaps, the happiest time in Burnes's life. Courted, flattered, successful, happy in the present, full of buoyant hopes for the future, his budding honours thick upon him, he wandered under the pine trees and joined in all the pleasant life of the place. He was the only Englishman at Simla who had seen the country and knew the road to the distant unknown land. Lord Auckland had settled to invade. Burnes was again, therefore, as he had been in London, the hero of the hour. Sir Henry Fane, the commander-in-chief, had a high opinion of him and so had Lord Auckland.

The invasion of Afghanistan had been settled before Burnes reached Simla. 'When he arrived there, Torrens and Colvin came running to him, and prayed him to say nothing to unsettle his lordship; that they had all the trouble in the world to get him into the business; and that even now he would be glad of any pretext to retire from it.'

'What!' Lord William Bentinck had exclaimed, 'Auckland and Macnaghten gone to war! The last men in the world I should have suspected of such folly.'

Lord Auckland was quiet and unobtrusive in manner, reserved and retiring in disposition. He had never been considered a man of mark or an able man in England; but he had been considered a good man of business, safe and practical, and he had the most philanthropic intentions of benefiting India. He was a Whig, and had been appointed by the Whigs. His father had been given a peerage for ratting in the time of Pitt. Lord Auckland held all the traditions of the Liberal party—the virtues of economy and retrenchment, the blessings of peace, and the folly of prestige. He had announced publicly that his policy was not to interfere in the affairs of other independent states. 'The wish I have had,' wrote Lord Auckland to Sir Charles Metcalfe, 'to confine my administration to objects of commerce, finance, and improved institutions, and domestic policy, will be far indeed from being accomplished. But, as you say, we must fulfil our destiny.' With the most peaceable intentions, when he found an invading force at Herat, led by Russian officers, Lord Auckland felt under the dire necessity of doing something. After the teaching of one thousand years, and of the fatal nature of Afghan invasions, the bare mention of such a catastrophe sent a thrill of horror through Northern India.

Mr. John Bright himself could not have stood with folded hands to see Peshawur and Lahore taken, and Delhi sacked. It was better to take the war beyond our frontier into the enemy's country.

Herat was besieged by our enemies. It must be relieved if it held out; it must be avenged if it fell. Herat has been called the key of India; for it is only in the rich wheat-bearing plains around it that an army bent on attacking India could assemble and be fed. Lord Auckland's council had remained at Calcutta. The people who advised him at Simla were Mr. William Macnaghten, Mr. John Colvin, Mr. Henry Torrens, and Alexander Burnes.

Mr. William Macnaghten had been twenty-five years in Bengal, and had spent many years of his official life as 'Registrar of the High Court of Appeal,' an office of a purely legal character. Such experience as he had of India was solely in Bengal, the 'Italy of India;' and among the slavish, effeminate race of Bengalese he had heard nothing for thirty years but the fawning flatteries of a conquered people. Misled by these flatteries, he proposed lightly enough to legislate for the manly, brave, fanatical Afghans, with the same ease as if they were Bengalese. A superstitious man might have marked the day and the hour that Burnes met with Macnaghten. The latter was to cross his path fatally, and dash all his high hopes to the ground.

Mr. Henry Torrens was a much younger man than Mr. Macnaghten. He was an under-secretary in the Foreign Office. He was clever and well-read, and had all the accomplishments that make a man shine in society. He could act, dance, sing to perfection. He was most agreeable and companionable, and his social gifts had made him very popular among the English. The Misses Eden found him invaluable. These ladies had the place of the Rochenaras and Jehanaras of the old *régime*, and were supposed to influence their brother greatly. Mr. Torrens was always well received at Auckland House. Mr. John Colvin was Lord Auckland's private secretary.

All three of these gentlemen belonged to the Bengal Civil Service; they were supposed to have Indian experience—'experienced,' as Sir Charles Napier puts it in his bitter way, 'experienced! yes, but in doing things wrong.' They formed the head of an official circle on whom the destinies of India and Kabul rested. Of these self-constituted advisers to Lord Auckland, undoubtedly the most mischievous was Mr. Torrens, who used to boast 'he had made the Afghan war.' He was the son of an officer, and, with his universal cleverness, had studied military affairs. He was the only man about Lord Auckland who had any knowledge of how a campaign should be undertaken. Full of the rash confidence of youth and success, he was as ready to plan a campaign as to lead a cotillon, to fill a throne as to whisper a well-turned compliment into a lady's ear. Sir Henry Fane, the commander-in-chief, a Tory of the old school, disliked the idea of this Whig campaign. He disliked the plan on its own merits, or defects; he still more disliked the men who were engaged in carrying it out, all except Burnes.

The fiat for the campaign had gone forth in a manifesto from merry Simla, dated October 1st, with a notification that Sir W. Macnaghten was to be head Envoy minister from the Government of India to the court of Shah Soujah. Burnes was to be an assistant 'political-officer to the Khan of Kelat.' Not exactly what Burnes had expected, but on the road to it he still hoped. That he was to be under Macnaghten was a reverse he never dreamt of, as he painted a bright future for himself. That a Calcutta lawyer should be sent to Kabul, the place he had earned by so much labour and enterprise, he never anticipated.

On the 23rd of July, Burnes wrote to a private friend: 'We are now planning a grand campaign to restore Shah Soujah to the throne of Kabul, Russia having come down upon us. What exact part I am to play I know not; but if full confidence and hourly consultation be any pledge, I am to be chief. I can plainly tell them that it is *aut Cæsar, aut nullus;* and if I do not get what I have a right to, you will see me soon *en route* to England.' He wrote later, when he heard that Macnaghten was appointed: 'I plainly told Lord Auckland that this does not please me, and I am disappointed.' However, Lord Auckland persuaded him to go to Kabul, with the promise 'that I should succeed to the permanent employ after all is over;' the 'permanent employ' being resident-king in all but in name of Kabul. Another reason Burnes consoled himself with: 'I am not sorry to see Dost Mohammed ousted by another hand than mine.'

Burnes had given his opinion against Shah Soujah's restoration: he was only a subordinate, and he could do no more; but he was glad to escape the unpleasing task of injuring Dost Mohammed, a man who had always treated him well and most kindly. Sir Henry Fane, the commander-in-chief, had been asked to go in joint commission with Macnaghten, but he refused.

The distance to Kabul was great; it was at least one thousand miles from our frontier at Ferozepore to that unknown land the gay world of Simla was going to invade. The troops were to collect at Ferozepore, on the borders of the Punjaub, and they were to be called the 'Army of the Indus.' They were to reach Kabul by the Bolan. Lord Auckland himself went to Lahore to meet our ally, Runjeet Singh. Then, on the part of the Sikhs, there was a picturesque display of the Oriental magnificence of the old Eastern world; tents of crimson and yellow silk, warriors in chain armour, with gaily-caparisoned horses. Still Runjeet would not allow the English to go through his dominions *viâ* the Kheiber. His Sikh forces, accompanied by Shah Soujah's son, Prince Timour, were to attack Kabul by that difficult route. The Ghilzies and mountain tribes of the Kheiber were in favour of Shah Soujah, and would not, it was believed, attack his friends.

The Kabul campaign, though rash and ill considered, was exceedingly popular with the army. There had been peace for thirty years in Northern India, ever since Wellington broke the power of the Mahrattas in 1805. 'The commander-in-chief was Sir Henry Fane, a fine old soldier of the Tory school, with a great contempt for Whig shabbiness.' Though he admired and liked Burnes personally, he disapproved of Lord Auckland's policy. He wrote to a friend: 'Every advance you might make beyond the Sutlej to the westward, in my opinion adds to your military weakness. . . . If you want your empire to expand, expand it over Oude or over Gwalior and the remains of the Mahratta empire. Make yourself complete sovereigns of all within your bounds. Leave the far west alone.'

When Lord Auckland was at Lahore with the Army of the Indus, surprising and unexpected news arrived—news surprising to both English and Sikhs; this was, that the siege of Herat had been raised. It startled every one. The city had been saved by one of those unexpected *coups de théâtre* in which Indian history abounds. Herat, the lordly city, standing in rich level land of field and orchard, and which in Baber's time had been full of pleasure-houses, gardens, mosques, and palaces, had, like Delhi, been a battle-field ever since; it was in a state of ruin, but still of some strength. Kamran, Shah Soujah's brother, was Khan of Herat; 'it was his last of eighty cities.'

The city of Herat was ruled by Kamran and his vizier Yar Mohammed, an able man but of fiendish inhumanity, of the Gholam Kadir type. When the King of Persia invested Herat, a young English officer happened to be living in that city of ruined splendour. His name was Eldred Pottinger; he had gone into Khorassan for amusement and love of adventure, and was in the disguise of a horse-merchant. He had attracted little notice in his disguise; he was there for amusement, and not by any order of the English Government Herat, as we have said before, has been called the key of India; it is only in the rich, level, wheat-bearing country around that an army invading India could be fed for any time. Mohammed Shah, King of Persia, proposed following the career of Nadir Shah, and taking Herat and Kabul on his way to India. In whose brain this brilliant scheme of invasion originated it is difficult to say, probably in that of his Russian advisers, General Simonich and other Russians who accompanied the King of Persia. The Perso-Russians expected that Herat would have fallen without a struggle, but the Persians were detained eight months before its crumbling walls, to their extreme bewilderment. The courage and heroism of the garrison were extraordinary. Eldred Pottinger was the soul of the defence; he gave the most valuable advice. Day and night he was at every post of danger, mending breaches in the walls, heading sorties. The Persians insisted on the Heratees giving up the Englishman. The Afghans of Herat refused. Famine raged in the city, and the position of the besieged was most desperate, when at length the King of Persia had to raise the siege. Lord Auckland had sent a force and some men-of-war to the Persian Gulf, and the King of Persia, finding his capital threatened, had to retire. He mounted his horse 'Armeej' and returned to Teheran, his capital, baffled and foiled.

The English Government asked Russia why they encouraged Persia in these aggressive designs, to which

Count Nesselrode answered, that Vickovich had been despatched to Kabul on a 'commercial mission,' and that Simonich had exceeded his instructions, which had been to discourage the King of Persia.

Under these circumstances, Simonich acted with wonderful boldness; for before Herat he directed the whole of the Persian army.

Now that Herat had been relieved, and the Persians had retreated, the prime motive of the English invasion of Afghanistan had ceased to exist. It was no affair of the English if Dost Mohammed, a capable man, or Shah Soujah, an incapable one, filled the throne of Kabul.

But the army of the Indus had been assembled; Mr. Macnaghten was ambitious of being Resident of Kabul; Burnes hoped to gain that post by-and-by; the Whigs had planned a policy, and it might bring discredit on their party if it was abandoned. Sir Henry Fane resigned the command of the army. His health was failing; he never cared very much for the enterprise. Sir John Keane, from Bombay, succeeded him, and it was resolved to carry on the campaign to its bitter end.

The quarrel between Dost Mohammed and Shah Soujah was this: Shah Soujah was a grandson of Abdalla, the fraudulent treasurer of Nadir Shah. He belonged, therefore, to the Douranee tribe. Dost Mohammed was the son of the late vizier. The vizier's office was hereditary in this family, and his brother, Futeh Khan, became vizier on his father's death. From the low birth of his mother, a Persian, in his early days Dost Mohammed had been looked down on as almost illegitimate; but, from his daring character, he soon gained his elder brother's admiration and affection, and they became deeply attached to each other. As long as Futeh Khan was vizier, Dost Mohammed lived with him, and shared in his wealth, power, and prosperity.

Futeh Khan met his death under the following tragic circumstances, by the order of Shah Soujah's brother. 'Futeh Khan was brought into a tent, in which sat a circle of his mortal foes. They each in turn accused him of injuries received at his hands, and heaped on him insulting epithets. One Amir rose, and seizing one of his ears, cut it off with a knife, saying, "This is such and such an injury done to such an one of my relations." In this way his nose, his hands, and his feet were cut off by different Amirs in revenge for various offences. Summurdar Khan cut off his beard, saying, "This is for dishonouring my wife." Hitherto the high-spirited chief had borne his sufferings without either weakness or any ebullition of his excitable temper. He only once condescended in a calm voice to beg them to hasten his death. The mutilation of ears and nose, a punishment reserved for the meanest offences of slaves, had not been able to shake his fortitude; but the beard of a Moslem is a member so sacred that honour itself becomes confounded with it, and he who had borne, with the constancy of a hero, the taunts and tortures heaped upon him, seemed to lose his manhood with his beard, and burst into a passion of tears.'

After Futeh Khan's inhuman death Dost Mohammed and his brother devoted their lives to revenge him. Revenge is considered a virtue among the Afghans. The vizier, Futeh Khan, had twenty brothers, and Dost Mohammed was one of the younger ones. In his father's lifetime, as we have seen, he had been little thought of. His education had been much neglected, and he was given to drink and dissipation. His favourite brother's awful death changed his character. With the assistance of his numerous brothers, and his own courage and enterprise, he drove away Shah Soujah, and gained the throne of Kabul. Dost Mohammed not only overcame his enemies, but he gained a harder victory over himself. Like Baber, he publicly renounced the vice of drinking. He devoted himself to acquire that difficult language, Arabic. He read and studied the Koran in the original. He became a wise and good ruler of Kabul, and was much beloved by the people of that country for his equity.

Shah Zemaim and his brother, Shah Soujah, after the successful rebellion of Dost Mohammed, fled from Kabul, and took refuge in India, at Loodianah. For thirty years the English Government had protected these *ci-devant* kings, and even allowed them a pension of four thousand pounds a year.

They had not a shadow of claim on the English;

what they received was from compassion. Shah Soujah had made five unsuccessful attempts from India to recover his crown. He proved wanting in courage on several occasions, when a little daring on the battle-field would have saved him.

Shah Soujah had gone through many adventures. He once for weeks had wandered through the Himalayas, starving and in misery, but with the Koh-i-Noor diamond in his possession. He had at length reached Runjeet Singh's court at Lahore. There that crafty Hindoo had imprisoned and starved him until he consented to give up that valuable jewel. Shah Soujah managed ultimately to escape to the English at Loodianah, but never recovered the Koh-i-Noor. This was the man we proposed to replace on the throne of Kabul, with the aid of English bayonets. Shah Soujah was a tall, handsome man with a long black beard. He, like most Oriental princes, has written his own autobiography. He was courteous and agreeable, rather inclined to be haughty to all except his English vizier, Mr. Macnaghten.

On the 10th of December, 1837, the long march of the English to Kabul was begun. Many leading men, both in India and England, were opposed to this invasion. The Duke of Wellington said that 'the consequence of crossing the Indus once to settle a government in Afghanistan, will be a perennial march into that country.' The Marquis of Wellesley also talked of 'the folly of occupying a land of rock, sand, desert, ice and snow.'

Runjeet Singh had objected to the English army passing through his territory to reach the Kheiber; they were accordingly to go by Shikarpore and the Bolan Pass. This was through the territories of the Amirs of Scinde. They also objected.

The project of putting Shah Soujah on the throne of Kabul was particularly distasteful to them. Scinde had once been one of the richest provinces of the kings of Kabul. They thought Shah Soujah had designs against them. It was a direct violation of existing treaties to use the river Indus for military purposes or to march through Scinde. But the Amirs were weak and disunited, and not in a position to dispute the English passage by force of arms.

The beginning of the march was through the territories of the Khan of Bhawulpore, a Mohammedan chief loyal to the English. The weather was beautiful, provisions were abundant, every one was in good spirits. The army marched along the banks of the Scinde, or Indus, river. Sir Willoughby Cotton, the general commanding, floated down the splendid river in a boat. The Indus or Scinde river is to Western India what the Ganges is to the eastern provinces. Scinde is the Egypt of India. The great river, like the Nile, inundates the land to a distance of twenty miles on either side, and keeps it always green and fertile. The Scinde river is from four hundred to sixteen hundred yards broad. It runs for nine hundred miles from Attock to its mouth at Kurrachee, and is navigable the whole way.

Alexander Burnes knew every inch of the river, for when on his way to Kabul three years before he had made charts and carefully studied the navigation, by Lord Auckland's orders.

The English crossed the river at Bukkur, on a bridge of boats. This passage was a great distress to the Amir Meer Roostum of Scinde. Alexander Burnes, who was personally known to him, used every argument and persuasion to reconcile him to what he considered an injury and insult.

By the 20th February the English reached Shikarpore. It is called 'the gates of Khorassan' by the Indians. It is a city of Hindoo traders and bankers, and a wealthy place. There is hardly a city of Central Asia that has not Hindoo or Shikarpore traders, but they bring back their wealth, when they have made money, to their native country.

Burnes, by his personal influence, had gained a pacific passage of the river Indus at Bukkur, but the force coming up the Indus, from Bombay, under Sir J. Keane, was not so fortunate. The Amir of Hyderabad, in Scinde, refused to allow the English to pass. It was necessary that he should be coerced. Sir J. Keane marched at once upon Hyderabad. The troops under his command were charmed at the expedition.

It was a very wealthy place; there would be plenty of prize money and other rewards.

Mr. Macnaghten had arrived at Shikarpore, and so had Shah Soujah. They were in despair on hearing that half this army was starting on a campaign of its own. Mr. Macnaghten wrote to Lord Auckland to complain of Burnes, 'whose letters were most unsatisfactory.' Then, with Lord Auckland's sanction, he wrote to the general commanding, Sir Willoughby Cotton; 'In my opinion it would be infinitely better that we should let loose fifteen or twenty thousand of Runjeet Singh's troops (Sikhs), who would march down upon Hyderabad in a very short space of time, than that the *grand enterprise* of restoring Shah Soujah to the throne of Kabul and Kandahar should be postponed for an entire season. By such postponement it might be frustrated altogether.'

The attack on Hyderabad was abandoned, but not in consequence of Mr. Macnaghten's letter. The mere advance of English troops was sufficient to bring the Amir to his senses. This, however, was but a foretaste of further troubles. From the first the envoy and generals of the army quarrelled.

Now the difficulties of the undertaking really commenced. From Shikarpore to Dadur was one hundred and forty miles; it was a barren desert, the soil a mixture of sand and salt. On the 10th March, at Dadur, the troops entered the Bolan Pass. This pass is a rugged, un even mountain road, sixty miles in length. The draught cattle were lamed by sharp pebbles, Beloochee robbers came down from the mountains and cut off all stragglers. A resolute defence in this pass would have been difficult to withstand. The English were encumbered with an immense quantity of baggage, as the cattle became lame or died; this was all abandoned, and much was carried away by the Beloochees. Even his majesty Shah Soujah had been left behind for want of carriage. When the English arrived at Quettah, on the 26th March, they had only one month's provisions with them, and no prospect of receiving any more, for none were to be obtained in the country.

Quettah was a wretched little town, defended by mud walls and a small castle. The English were now in the territories of the Khan of Khelat.

Burnes had been sent on ahead to persuade this ruler to supply the English with food, but there was no food in the country. They obtained, however, some sheep. The ration of bread to the English soldiers was reduced; the native soldiers were given only one pound of flour a day to bake bread themselves; the camp followers only one quarter of a pound daily.

As English troops are again stationed at Quettah and Khelat, it may be interesting to enter into details concerning the Bolan Pass.

From Shikarpore to Dadur is distant one hundred and forty-six miles, the road passing through twenty-three miles of desert called Rajghan, which is pestilential in summer and becomes an impassable swamp during the rains of autumn.

For the first march of ten miles up the Bolan the road is the dry bed of a mountain torrent, full of stones and boulders, and it passes through the water seven times.

The second march is to a place called Kurlat, and very much resembles the former.

The third march is through a narrow defile ; on one side of the road there is a rapid river, on the other precipitous mountain.

The fourth march.—Nine miles through the dry bed of a torrent to a place called Beeber Manee. Here, when the English invaded Kabul, many camels succumbed to the severity of the march through such a country.

The fifth march.—A distance of nine miles to Abeyjoon. The road became so difficult that the baggage had to be abandoned. The infantry soldiers had to assist the guns into camp, the horses and cattle being exhausted.

The sixth march.—Ten miles to the top of the Pass Sir-i-Bolan, five thousand feet above the level of the sea.

The seventh march.—Descent by a narrow zigzag road, covered with boulders, and with high, precipitous rocks on either side.

The eighth march.—Through a fine grassy valley for twenty miles to Quettah, a miserable little town.

The road from Quettah to Kandahar presented even more difficulties than the Bolan Pass.

First march, to Koochlak, ten miles.

Second, to Hykalzie, twenty miles; a difficult river, the Lora, to be crossed. Many horses died from exhaustion on the march when the English invaded Kabul.

Third.—A long march.

Fourth.—Through the Pisheen valley to the mouth of the Kojuk Pass; a defile for four miles so narrow that with difficulty one camel could advance at a time, to Dand-i-Golai, a hot pestilential place; thermometer rising to 100°.

Fifth.—To Killah Abdullah.

Sixth.—To Killah Quazee. To both of these the heat is intense, and the Afghans can cut off the supply of water; the English underwent dreadful suffering from thirst in 1837.

Seventh.—On the banks of Doree river.

Eighth.—Dilkazee.

Ninth.—Kandahar.

When the English reached Quettah, all the troops, both English and Indian, began to look sick and famine-stricken. Sir W. Macnaghten was exceedingly angry with the Khan of Kelat. During the whole of his thirty years in Bengal, he had never received such treatment; he proposed a remedy in the annexation of Kelat. Macnaghten writes on the 6th April, 1839, to Colvin: 'The fact is the troops and the followers are nearly in a state of mutiny for food; and the notion of waiting for such a person as Mehrab Khan, who has done his best to starve us, seems utterly preposterous. I trust the

Governor-General will see fit to annex the provinces of Shawl, Moostung, and Cutchee.' He says in another letter, 'There never was such treatment inflicted upon human beings as we have been subjected to on our progress through the Khan of Kelat's country.' The only thing to do, in consequence of the want of food, was to push on to Kandahar, which the English accordingly did. They found that city a mean place, of no importance architecturally. It was in the Dowranee country; here Shah Soujah would be welcomed by his own clan, who had found Dost Mohammed's hand heavy on it. Dost Mohammed's brother, the governor, had fled from the city on the approach of the English. About fifteen hundred of the inhabitants, well dressed and well mounted, had welcomed the exiled king's return. Some neighbouring ruling nobles also gave in their allegiance; but the Khan of Kelat made excuses and did not come in. Among those who came to pay speedy allegiance was an Amir called Hadjee Khan Khankur. Mehrab Khan on a former occasion, in 1835, had loyally assisted Shah Soujah, but it was the presence of the infidel English which hindered him from joining heartily in the ex-king's cause.

Burnes writes to Macnaghten on March 30th: 'The Khan of Kelat with a good deal of earnestness enlarged upon the undertaking the British had embarked in, declaring it to be one of vast magnitude and difficult accomplishment; that instead of relying on the Afghan nation, our government had cast them aside and inundated the country with troops; that if it was our end to establish ourselves in Afghanistan, and give Shah Soujah the nominal sovereignty of Kabul and Kandahar, we were pursuing an erroneous course; that all the Afghans were discontented with the Shah, and all Mohammedans alarmed and excited at what was passing; that day by day men returned discontented, and we might find ourselves awkwardly situated if we did not point out to Shah Soujah his errors, if the fault originated with him, and alter them if they sprung from ourselves; that Dost Mohammed was a man of ability and resource, and though we could easily put him down by Shah Soujah, in our present mode of procedure we could never win the Afghan nation by it.'

Was it to be endured that the 'British minister and envoy' should be criticised by a paltry Beloochee chief and a young military officer? This was calling in question the Macnaghten policy—the advice he and his friends had given Lord Auckland at Simla, the people who alone could entertain opinions of any value or weight. A black mark was put against the name of Mehrab Khan by the envoy for his unpalatable advice; and when circumstances permitted, fifteen months after, his fort was taken and he was killed fighting gallantly in its defence.

Mehrab Khan had never injured us. If he had attacked the English in the Bolan Pass, they would have fared badly when in his country. Macnaghten wrote, on the 19th March: 'Camp Bagh—This very day, had they been inimically inclined, they might with the greatest ease have turned an inundation into our camp, which would have swept away our entire camp.' The hardships and want of food were put down by the soldiers to the Khan of Kelat; but this was unjust; there was no food in the country that he could give.

For three months the famine-stricken and worn-out English army rested at Kandahar, waiting for the crops to ripen. The want of food and of carriage was an insuperable difficulty to a further advance. An Afghan merchant conducted a large convoy of grain from India through the Bolan Pass with great fidelity, though tampered with by Dost Mohammed, but he refused to advance further than Kandahar.

It is clear that if the Khan of Kelat and the Governor of Kandahar had made any stand against the invaders, the English, exhausted and famine-stricken, would have been in a most difficult position. But the jealousies and rivalries of the Afghans prevented them acting in unison. Dost Mohammed imagined the English intended to attack Herat. On the 21st July the English left Kandahar; on the 27th June our ally, the great Sikh, Runjeet Singh, died at Lahore.

Sir William Macnaghten soon found that invading Afghanistan was not so easy as registering deeds in Bengal; he was already heartily weary of the enterprise.

He writes, April 25th, to Lord Auckland: 'I really have no leisure. Of this your lordship may judge when I state that for the last three days I have been out in the sun, and have not been able to get breakfast before three in the afternoon. I think it would be in every way advantageous to the public interests if, after Shah Soujah gains possession of Kabul, I were to proceed across the Punjaub to Simla, having an interview with Runjeet Singh. His Majesty's new adherents are all hungry for place, he tells me; he has informed them, in answer to their premature solicitations, since it took God Almighty six days to make heaven and earth, it is very hard they will not allow a poor mortal even the same time to settle the affairs of a kingdom.'

CHAPTER II.

The march to Ghuznee—Storm and capture of the fort—Flight of Dost Mohammed from Kabul—Entry of the English troops—Injudicious measures of the Envoy—Disturbance and British reverses—The murder of Burnes.

On the 21st of July the English marched forward to Ghuznee. The town was two hundred and forty miles from Kandahar, and ninety from Kabul. Ghuznee was a strong place, strongly defended, and was considered by the Afghans altogether impregnable. Hyder Khan, one of Dost Mohammed's sons, commanded in the castle. Afzul Khan, another of the Dost's sons, commanded a large force outside the walls. He was considered a very good soldier, and had made a brilliant reputation in defeating the Sikhs at Jumrood four years before, at the mouth of the Kheiber.

Sir J. Keane, for want of carriage, had been obliged to leave his heavy guns at Kandahar. He had been told that Ghuznee was not a strong place. The English reached the city unopposed. They were surprised to find a fortress of much greater strength than they had expected.

'It burst suddenly on the view, with its fortifications, rising up as it were on the side of the hill which seemed to form its background.' The massive, medieval walls were not to be breached by six-pounder guns, which was all the cannon the invaders had.

Mohan Lal, the Hindoo, Burnes's *ci-devant* servant, came to their assistance. On the occasion of the 'commercial mission' from India he had made the acquaintance of Abdool Reshed Khan, Dost Mohammed's nephew. He brought this man over to the English interest, and the traitor informed Sir J. Keane that all the gates of the fortress were bricked up, except the Kabul Gate. This was the very information they required. They could not breach the walls; to take the fort by escalade was pronounced equally impossible; but with gunpowder it was possible to blow in the gate. On the 22nd of July, on a dark, windy night, the English attacked Ghuznee. The Kabul Gate was blown in by Captain Peats, of the Engineers. There was not a sign of life from the walls of the fortress when the English fired their six-pounder guns on the impregnable walls; but this brought out the garrison, who returned the fire, manned their walls, and prepared for an escalade. This attack was but a feint. The English 13th Light Infantry, under Colonel Denny, rushed in at the Kabul Gate of the fortress. The Afghans hurried to defend it, but the English were in the heart of the place before the Afghans realised which was the point to defend.

Inside the fort, however, there was hard hand-to hand fighting, which is proved by the fact that afterwards five hundred Afghans were buried by the English, and many English officers and men were killed and wounded. The victory was complete. Sixteen hundred prisoners fell into our hands, and great stores of flour and grain. Hyder Khan, the commandant, was taken prisoner, and all his women. They were placed under the charge of Sir Alexander Burnes and Mohan Lal, who treated them with every kindness. That Kandahar should fall, that the English should march through the Bolan Pass, hardly disconcerted Dost Mohammed. He almost expected this. But that Ghuznee should be taken he could not believe, and he knew it must be due to treachery.

Afzul Khan, on knowing that the fort of Ghuznee was lost, fled to Kabul. His camp equipage and elephants fell into the hands of the English. When he arrived, his father, Dost Mohammed, refused to see him. He had expected greater things of the conqueror of the Sikhs.

Dost Mohammed, on the 24th of July, sent to capitulate. He despatched his brother, Jubbal Khan, to open negotiations. In the days of the 'commercial mission' Jubbal Khan had been hotly in favour of a British alliance, and even more friendly than his brother with Burnes. They met again under strangely altered circumstances. The only terms Jubbal Khan could obtain for Dost Mohammed were, 'An honourable asylum in British dominions.' Jubbal Khan said to Macnaghten, 'If Shah

Soujah is really king, and come to the kingdom of his ancestors, what is the use of your army and name? You have brought him by your money and arms into Afghanistan. Leave him now with us Afghans, and let him rule us if he can.

Dost Mohammed refused the English terms. He prepared to make a last stand at Maidan, on the Kabul river. There he placed all his guns into position. He knew there was treachery and disaffection in his ranks. He turned to his Amirs, and asked those who were false to him to leave him. Then, like Baber of old, he rode forth with the Koran in his hand, and called upon his followers to strike but one blow 'for the Faith, in the name of God and the Prophet.' 'You have eaten my salt,' he said, 'these thirteen years. If, as is too plain, you are resolved to seek a new master, grant me but one favour in requital for that long period of maintenance and kindness: enable me to die with honour. Stand by the brother of Futeh Khan, whilst he executes one last charge against the cavalry of these Feringhee dogs' (Franks). 'In the onset he will fall. Then go and make your terms with Shah Soujah.' This appeal was but feebly responded to. The Afghans would not stand by him, and Dost Mohammed, not being able to depend on his Amirs, fled from Kabul with a few followers towards the mountains of the Hindoo Koosh. The policy of Macnaghten, to all appearance, was working well. After the fall of Ghuznee he wrote to Lord Auckland 'that he felt sure Dost Mohammed would take himself off, as his brothers had done at Kandahar;' and his sanguine hopes had been realised. Dost Mohammed was accompanied by his son, Ackbar Khan, who had contracted a malarious fever while opposing the advance of the Sikhs and Prince Timour in the Kheiber. The Sikhs and Prince Timour, assisted by Colonel Claude Wade, had made their way successfully through the Kheiber, meeting with little opposition from the Ghilzies.

The sick prince had to be carried in a litter, which much delayed his father's flight. A body of English officers mounted in hot haste to pursue Dost Mohammed. They were Captains Wheeler, Troup, Laurence, Backhouse, Christie; Lieutenants Broadfoot, Hogg, Ryves—in all thirteen. But among them rode as guide a traitor, Hadju Khan Khaukar. This Amir had but lately offered his allegiance to Shah Soujah at Kandahar. He manœuvred so well that Dost Mohammed and his son escaped from their pursuers into the country of the Wallee of Kooloom. The English imprisoned Hadju Khan for his double dealing at Chunar, in far Bengal, where he died. But still, Dost Mohammed had escaped, and so had Ackbar Khan.

On the 6th of August the English troops reached Kabul. On the 7th Shah Soujah entered his capital in state. He wore royal robes, he was bedecked with jewels, and rode with a coronet on his head. His subjects, however, noticed that his most regal gem, the Koh-i-Noor, was absent. By his side, in uniform, rode Sir W. Macnaghten and Sir Alexander Burnes; and a conspicuous and gaudy object in the procession was Moonshee Mohun Lal, in very gay clothes, and wearing a gay turban.

The people of Kabul looked on unmoved; hardly a salaam was tendered to the returned king. The foreign English attendants and troops riveted all their attention.

The city of Kabul is well described by Lieutenant Rattray. It is well-built and handsome, and is one mass of bazaars. Every street has a double row of houses, of different height, flat-roofed, and composed of mud in wood frames. Here and there a porch of carved larch-wood intervenes, giving entrance to the courtyard of the residence of a noble, in the centre of which is a raised platform of mud, planted with fruit trees and spread with carpets. A fountain plays near, and here, during the heat of the day, loll the chiefs at ease, listening, as they smoke their pipes, to the sound of the saccringhi, or guitar, the falling water, or the wonderful tales of the Persian story-tellers. The houses overhang the narrow streets; their windows have no glass, but consist of lattice-work wooden shutters, which push up and down, and are often richly carved and otherwise ornamented. The shop windows are open to the sun, and the immense display of merchandise, fruit, game, armour, and cutlery defies description. These articles are arranged in prodigious piles from floor to ceiling. In the front of each sits the artificer, engaged in his calling, or from amidst the heaped-up profusion the trader peeps out at his visitor.

Shah Soujah wandered through the gardens and palaces of the Bala Hissar, or citadel, with almost childish delight. He had returned to the scenes of his youth, after an absence of thirty-five years. He wandered about, noticing changes and marks of disrepair and neglect. Burnes and Macnaghten, the king-makers, had reseated him on the throne of his ancestors, but he soon discovered that the throne of Kabul had almost lost its charms under its altered circumstances. His majesty Shah Soujah was king—a king, however, only in name. The English resident ruled, and in what Shah Soujah soon thought to be an unwise and impolitic fashion. Neither had the envoy a bed of roses; on every side difficulties and dangers cropped up.

Burnes also had some cause to be dissatisfied. He said that 'he was in a nondescript sort of situation'; he had said he would be *aut Cæsar, aut nullus,* and he was nothing. He drew a large salary—three thousand pounds a year; he wrote minutes and long State papers upon the position in Kabul, and what was best to be done, but these papers Macnaghten threw aside with a few contemptuous notes in pencil on the margins. His opinion even was not considered necessary. Burnes turned to his old pursuit of literature, and wrote a second book of travels, giving an account of his trip on the Indus and the commercial mission in 1839.

To the public the Afghan invasion had appeared a thorough success. Honours were conferred on the principal actors in this drama. Lord Auckland was made an earl, Mr. Macnaghten a baronet, and many C.B.'s and brevets were bestowed on the officers of the Army of the Indus. Sir J. Keane was made Lord Keane of Ghuznee.

In fifteen months there were dangers enough to disquiet a spirit even as buoyant as Sir W. Macnaghten's. Dost Mohammed had reappeared on the borders of Afghanistan, backed by forty thousand fanatical Usbegs. In fact, all Turkestan was up, and, worse than all, the Russians were still in the field with a force which rumour numbered at a hundred thousand men. The Ghilzie and Dowranee tribes were in open rebellion among their inaccessible mountains, as licentious as in the days of Baber, and troops could be ill-spared to put them down. The fact was patent that until Dost Mohammed was secured there was no prospect of peace in Kabul; he was a rallying-point for all the fanaticism and revolt, and the deadly hatred of the English. But how to secure him was the difficulty. He was in the mountains, often heard of but never seen by the English. For the last fifteen months the ex-ruler's life had been a bitter one. After the taking of Ghuznee, Dost Mohammed and his sons, Afzul Khan and Ackbar Khan, had made their way across the Hindoo Koosh to Bokhara. The ruler of that state was a hateful tyrant, the Oriental despot in his worst type, and who, from his cruel freaks of tyranny, was believed to be insane. He imprisoned the three luckless Afghan fugitives, and even attempted to poison them in prison. In consequence of the King of Persia's remonstrances, they were allowed greater freedom and better treatment, and, taking advantage of being again partially at large, Dost Mohammed and his sons joyfully effected their escape from Bokhara. They retraced their steps to Khooloom, a small Usbeg state in the Hindoo Koosh, where the Wallee, or ruler, had, with great fidelity, protected Jubbar Khan and the Dost's wife and children. Khooloom is a neighbouring state to Kabul, and on its borders the English had, at Bamean, a large force stationed. Dost Mohammed determined to attack the English, and marched on Bamean with six or eight thousand Usbeg horsemen.

It must be recorded that the English were as unsuccessful against these redoubtable Usbeg Turcoman cavalry as Baber had been. A regiment of Ghoorkas (our best Indian troops), under an officer of the name of Codrington, was completely cut up by the Usbegs. Another disaster took place—a whole regiment of Afghans, Shah Soujah's troops, who had been raised, paid, and armed by the English, went over and joined the Dost. Other reverses occurred, and every hour brought tidings of fresh disasters. On the 19th of September, 1840, Sir William Macnaghten wrote: 'At no period of my life do I remember having been so much harassed in body and mind as during the past month. Nor is my uneasiness yet much lessened. The Afghans are gunpowder, and the Dost is a lighted match. Of his whereabouts we are wonderfully ignorant. I have no hope he will attack Bamean, and I have a great fear he will throw himself into Kohistan, where it is said the whole country will rise in his favour. But I am weary of conjecture, and we must make the best preparation we can against every possible contingency.

The Dost did attack the English; and when warned of the danger of such a course, for his family had fallen into their hands, he replied sadly, 'I have no family. I have buried my women and children.' The one final cavalry charge on the Infidel the Dost had proposed to give at Maidan he made at length in the Hindoo Koosh, fifteen months afterwards, on the 2nd of November. The 12th Bengal Cavalry were opposed to him. He had a small body of Usbeg followers, badly mounted. He had his blue flag unfurled. The Indian cavalry all fled. Their English officers alone stood their ground. Dr. Lord, with Captains Broadfoot, Crispin, Fraser, and Ponsonby, were killed.

This reverse more than ever depressed the envoy. He wrote to Lord Auckland for more troops. He talked of hanging Dost Mohammed. 'He talked of showing no mercy to the man who was the author of all the evils that now distract the country.'

Broadfoot was a very able and distinguished man; but

in bitter anguish of mind Burnes lamented the loss of Dr. Lord. They were warm friends. They had travelled much together in Kabul, and had many tastes and pursuits in common.

Macnaghten had every reason for anxious fear. Of the thirty Afghan tribes, half were in open rebellion in their inaccessible mountains; and the small force of English troops in Kabul were cut off from India by thousands of miles of unfriendly states. Their position was most critical.

The envoy was taking his daily evening ride outside the walls of Kabul. He was absorbed in melancholy forebodings of the future, when an Afghan rode up to him, and said the Amir was at hand. 'What Amir?' asked the envoy. 'Dost Mohammed.' It was, in fact, the ex-king. Another Afghan rode up. He dismounted, and offered Macnaghten his sword. Having done enough to retrieve his honour, Dost Mohammed explained that he had come to give himself up. The Englishman and the ex-ruler rode into the town together. Macnaghten treated him with the greatest courtesy and attention; and he soon felt the same admiration and esteem for this man that Burnes had always entertained. Numbers of English officers called on him, and paid him every civility. Many of those who would not pay respect to Shah Soujah, who was very much disliked by the British army, visited the Dost.

He was put into a tent without an English guard or

sentry, and under the charge of Captain George Lawrence, who writes, 'I scarcely closed my eyes during the two nights he remained under my charge, every now and then getting up and looking into the tent to see that he was still there. It seemed all so much like a dream that at last we should have the Dost safe in our hands, that I could hardly credit it, except by frequent visits to the tent.'

In appearance the Dost was a robust, powerful man, with a sharp, aquiline nose, highly arched eyebrows, and a grey beard and moustache. He and the envoy were exactly the same age—fifty years. He was surprised to find the envoy so 'young-looking.' He had been told he was an old man.

Macnaghten could be generous to a fallen foe—pity disarms envy—although he could brook no rival in talent.

Macnaghten wrote to Lord Auckland: 'I trust that the Dost will be treated with liberality. His case has been compared to that of Shah Soujah. I have seen it argued that he should not be treated more handsomely than his majesty was; but surely the cases are not parallel. *The Shah had no claim upon us.* We had no hand in depriving *him of his kingdom, whereas we ejected the Dost, who never offended us, in support of our policy, of which he was the victim.*'

The victim of Lord Auckland's policy left for India on the 12th of November, accompanied by his son, Afzul

Khan. Ackbar Khan was still at large. At length, when the much-dreaded Dost was safe in India, Macnaghten began to breathe freely, and was allowed once more to feel the blessing of repose. Everything in Kabul was quiet. He accompanied Shah Soujah to Jellalabad, to escape the cold of Kabul; and in the pleasant semi-tropical climate of that valley he could wander with a light heart under the chequered shade of the beautiful plane-trees, in the garden Baber had planted three hundred years before.

It was wonderful how the lowering clouds had suddenly lifted. Everything succeeded beyond the envoy's wildest hopes. All his causes of anxiety were as suddenly removed, for the Russians had failed miserably at Khiva in a most unexpected manner. The fort of Khelat was taken by the English, and Mehrab Khan killed, so that he would trouble no more with unpalatable advice, or more real injuries; and his territory had been 'annexed.'

Herat, which Elred Pottinger had defended so gallantly, was, however, again giving trouble. Pottinger hated cruelty and the slave trade; Yar Mohammed, the vizier, delighted in both. The young Englishman had left the place in disgust, and Yar Mohammed had begun to intrigue with the Persians.

On this fact Macnaghten writes to Lord Auckland: 'Herat should now be taken possession of in the name of Shah Soujah. To leave it in the hands of its present possessors, after the fresh proofs of treachery and enmity towards us which they have displayed, would, in my humble opinion, be most dangerous. Herat may be said to be the pivot of all operations affecting the safety of our possessions and our interests in the East, and thence Balkh and Bokhara would be at all times accessible. The Sikhs should no longer be suffered to throw unreasonable obstacles in the way of our just and necessary objects; and if they really feel (as they are bound by treaty to do) an interest in the success of our operations, they should not object to the passage of our troops, or even to their location in the Punjaub, should such a measure be deemed conducive to the welfare of us both. Your lordship will, I feel assured, forgive the freedom of these remarks. I am convinced that one grand effort will place the safety of our interest on a firm and solid basis. . . . . I shall only add that, should offensive operations against Herat be undertaken, I should not entertain the smallest doubt of their complete and speedy success. . . . We have a beautiful game in our hands, if we have the means and the inclination to play it properly. Our advance upon Herat would go far to induce the Russian Government to attend to any reasonable overture on the part of the Khan of Khiva.'

One more 'annexation' was proposed by Macnaghten; and this was simply the whole of the Punjaub. The Sikhs had been false to the treaty with the English. While the envoy was indulging in these gigantic schemes, he was totally blind to what was near at hand: that everything in Kabul itself was in utter confusion; that the mountainous tribes were in rebellion; that the heads of the English military forces were indignant. The revenue of Kabul amounted only to £150,000 a year, and this was spent on Moslem priests, soldiers, and the court of Shah Soujah. The occupation of Kabul had cost one million and a quarter a year from the revenues of India. Lord Auckland complained of the expense. The Court of Directors, who were always opposed to the Afghan war, remonstrated. The new commander-in-chief, Sir Jasper Nicolls, pointed out to Lord Auckland that India was drained of troops, that there were more troops in Kabul than were required by Wellington to destroy the whole Mahratta power. Still Macnaghten clamoured for more money, more bayonets, for fresh conquests, to carry on 'the beautiful game.'

The Tories were coming into power. Lord Auckland foresaw that his conduct would be called in question by these, his political antagonists. He was heartily sick of the 'beautiful game.'

Macnaghten lived in a fool's paradise. He believed every one to be contented and everything tranquil. In June he wrote to Rawlinson: 'I don't like reverting to unpleasant discussions, but you know well that I have been frank with you from the beginning, and that I have invariably told you of what I thought I had reason to complain. This may be confined to one topic—your taking an unwarrantably gloomy view of our position, and entertaining and disseminating rumours favourable to that view. We have enough of difficulties and enough of croakers without adding to the number needlessly. I have just seen a letter from Mr. Dallas to Captain Johnson, in which he says the state of the country is becoming worse and worse every day. These idle statements may cause much mischief, and, often repeated as they are, they neutralise my protestations to the contrary. I know them to be utterly false as regards this part of the country, and I have no reason to believe them to be true as regards your portion of the kingdom, merely because the Tokhees are indulging in their accustomed habits of rebellion.'

Then the envoy goes on to tell Rawlinson how to act. 'Send for the Jambaz' (Afghan horse). 'Let them make a forced march by night, and come to the rear of Aktur' (the Douranee chief in rebellion). 'Seize the villain and hang him as high as Haman, and you will probably have no more disturbances. The Jambaz may remain out while the collection (of revenue) is going on, if necessary.'

The month of August finds the English envoy still cheerful and sanguine. He writes to Rawlinson:

'I must pen a few remarks, in the hope of inducing you to regard matters a little more *couleur de rose.* You say "the state of the country causes me many an anxious thought. We may thrash the Douranees over and over again, but this rather aggravates than obviates the difficulty of overcoming the national feeling against us; in fact, our tenure is positively that of military possession, and the French in Algiers and the Russians in Circassia afford us an example on a small scale of the difficulty of our position." Now upon what do you found your assertion that there is a national feeling against us, such as that against the French in Algiers or the Russians in Circassia? Solely, so far as I know, because the turbulent Douranees have risen in rebellion. *From Mookoor to the Kheiber Pass all is content and tranquillity, and wherever we Europeans go we are received with respect, and attention, and welcome.* But the insurrection of the Douranees is no new occurrence. In the time of Dost Mohammed they were always in arms,' and, as he could reduce them, the envoy thought they should occasion the English no anxiety.

Macnaghten then drew many historical parallels in India—how there had been local risings and rebellions, but they had come to nothing. He could not see that all Asiatics are not alike, that all his experience was drawn from Bengalese, and that he now had to deal with the Afghan.

Gifted with many good qualities, Sir W. Macnaghten could not brook the least contradiction; every individual, even every ruler, every country, must prostrate themselves before him or be humbled.

All the military men that he had under him he

quarrelled with. They were not subservient enough, they were as easy to crush as the Afghans. He wrote to Lord Auckland to request that Nott, an able man and good soldier, should be recalled because he had refused to visit Shah Soujah. Brigadier Roberts, the very stamp of man wanted in Kabul, had thrown up his post in utter disgust. Burnes, from the moment they were placed together, he sneered at and ignored. Sir Willoughby Cotton he had fallen out with even at Shikarpore. Major Todd, Captain Leach, and others, he had caused to be recalled and disgraced. Sale—'Fighting Bob'—Sale, the gallant and noble, was as insufferable to him as the rest. Mediocrity is always thus uneasy in the presence of talent. Keane, when he left Afghanistan, saw whither things were drifting. He said to an officer who left when he did, 'For the sake of the service I am sorry you are leaving, but for your own sake I am glad. Mark my words, there will be some great catastrophe.'

Lord Auckland had to choose a military commander for Kabul. The place fell by rights to Nott, but, in consequence of Macnaghten's representations he was superseded. It was necessary to find some one of a pliant and facile disposition, to pull with the envoy; all other considerations were waived. Lord Auckland's choice fell on General Elphinstone. The motive of this selection seems to have been the one Talleyrand gave for choosing his wife, *Il ne pouvait en trouver de plus bête.*

It seems inconceivable that such a man could have been selected for such a difficult position in a warlike and dangerous country. Elphinstone was crippled with rheumatic gout, to the extent that he could not mount a horse. His physical sufferings had so affected his intellect that he was virtually imbecile. There was at least no fear that he would oppose the envoy. Sir Jasper Nicolls and the Governor of Agra remonstrated with Lord Auckland; still Elphinstone went to Afghanistan, to do so much injury at the end of his obscure, though honourable and blameless life, as to render him notorious to all time. When he arrived, the envoy told him 'he would have nothing to do, for the country was perfectly quiet.'

Sir William Macnaghten was at length to leave Kabul, where, in his view, he had overcome all the difficulties of his position. He had received a reward for all the work and anxiety he had undergone. He had been made Governor of Bombay, a splendid appointment. Elphinstone, after having spent nine months in Kabul, was to accompany the envoy to India. He had sent in his resignation on account of his ill-health. All his property had been sold by auction, and such was the belief in peace that his effects had fetched good prices. The envoy's things were all packed, and he was ready to start. Captain George Lawrence was to accompany him as private secretary to Bombay. They all rejoiced at the prospect of leaving Kabul, where they had spent two such eventful years. All their bright hopes were dashed to the ground suddenly and unexpectedly. Burnes, after such long and humiliating waiting, was at length to succeed the envoy. Burnes was, however, a little anxious that he had heard nothing definite from Lord Auckland. There were rumours of a Colonel Sutherland being appointed, when the following wholly unforeseen circumstances happened.

The Englishman of all others that the Afghans hated was 'Sekunder Burnes,' as they always called him. He had come, they said, as a spy. They had twice received him with every hospitality and kindness, as a stranger; and he had requited this kindness by coming back with an army and taking their country, and depriving them of their liberty. The odium of all the envoy's unpopular acts fell upon 'Sekunder Burnes,' though Burnes had no voice in the matter. He disapproved strongly of most of the measures for which he was blamed. 'Sir William Macnaghten is an excellent man,' he often wrote to his private friends, 'but he is in the wrong place in Kabul.' Burnes had no authority, his suggestions were unnoticed; he had made himself disliked more than ever by the envoy by interfering. He lived little in the present and much in the future. When Macnaghten was gone he thought he should be first and sole, and act more wisely than the envoy. That time had at length arrived—the cup was at his lips.

But to the high-spirited Amirs of Kabul that 'Sekunder Burnes,' the traitor, the spy, the false friend, should rule paramount in their country was intolerable. He was a man who had deceived them with more than Asiatic duplicity, as they thought, and this was particularly hateful to the Afghans. There was an Afghan khan called Abdullah, who had been deprived of his chiefship. Burnes had sent him, it was said, an insulting message, 'that he was a dog, and that he should cut off his ears.' On the night of the 30th December thirty malcontents had met at the house of this man, and they vowed they would be revenged on the Englishman. Early in the morning, at dawn of the 1st November, these thirty men attacked Burnes' house, which was not in the English cantonments, but in the city of Kabul, next door to the English paymaster, Captain Johnson. Soon from the few men who had begun the riot, the whole narrow street was filled with an angry and excited crowd, screaming and howling. In Burnes' house were his brother, Dr. James Burnes, and Captain Broadfoot, who was to be secretary to Alexander Burnes when he became Resident. Burnes, who knew the Afghan language perfectly, from a balcony of his house tried to pacify the mob, though his brother and Captain Broadfoot were firing on the crowd. There was a small guard, but they were insufficient in numbers against the excited multitude. A Mohammedan, a Cashmeree, a race who among all Asiatics are noted for double-dealing and deceit, approached Burnes and told him that he would show him a private way out, through a garden, if they would cease firing on the crowd. Burnes trusted him, and hastily dressed himself in an Afghan disguise, and prepared to follow the Cashmeree. But the three Englishmen had no sooner descended the stairs than their guide called out to the furious mob, 'This is Sekunder Burnes.' The mob rushed on them. Burnes' brother was the first killed; the other two were soon hacked to pieces, and the dogs of the city eat their unburied bodies. Thus, at the early age of thirty-five, perished Burnes.

His house was sacked and robbed of all his property, and the English treasury adjoining was robbed to the extent of seventeen thousand pounds.

Burnes had been warned of the proposed attack several times; Mohun Lal, for one, told him. Burnes replied that he could do nothing until Macnaghten left. Mohun Lal says, 'He stood up from his chair, sighed, and said he knew nothing but that the time had arrived we should leave the country.' Burnes was not so infatuated as the envoy; he mixed more as an equal with the people. He foresaw the danger when Mohun Lal asked him to increase his guard. He would not. 'He replied that if he were to ask the envoy to send him a strong guard, it will show that he was fearing,' says the Hindoo, in his ungrammatical English. On the morning of this fatal 1st of November an Afghan came before dawn to warn Burnes, whose servants would not allow their master to be disturbed. Shah Soujah's vizier, Osman Khan, next came, and would not be refused, and he saw Burnes. Burnes on this sent to the envoy asking for assistance—a guard. Before any came the mob was before his house. He knew who had instigated the attack. He sent two messengers to Abdullah Khan, and promised that his case should be reconsidered ; but that chief killed one and wounded the other of his messengers. When the mob came to his house he offered a large sum if they would spare his life. At the beginning of the riot a general rising was not intended. At eight o'clock in the morning, long after Burnes had been sacrificed, Macnaghten and Elphinstone were still consulting what could be done. The envoy never made an effort to save him.

It had been necessary to find house-room for the seven thousand soldiers that the envoy had found himself obliged to retain in Kabul. For the purpose, the citadel, the Bala Hissar, with its strong mediæval walls, was the only suitable place. It was large, strong, well-defended, and built for the very purpose of lodging troops. But Shah Soujah objected strongly to this necessary measure. He said it would be unpopular in the city, and that the English troops would overlook his private palace. The envoy humoured the king, and began to build barracks, the extreme cold of the winter rendering it impossible for the soldiers to live in tents. Burnes had reported that there were three small deserted Afghan forts that might answer the purpose. They were declared unsuitable. Cantonments, or barracks on a gigantic scale, were then planned, and the execution of them was left to a young English engineer of the name of Sturt. They were to resemble Indian cantonments—those of Meerut or Cawnpore—which consist of broad, straight roads, and on each side a row of detached houses, standing in gardens, for the officers, while the men live in large roomy barracks near parade-grounds. The Kabul cantonments covered a mile. Brigadier Roberts, who commanded the Shah's troops, finding what had been arranged, remonstrated. He protested that it was ridiculous; that among a nation of thieves and assassins, like the Afghans, it was impossible to live without defences; that in a cold climate, where the men were dying of diseases of the lungs, these detached, airy barracks, open to every wind, were absurd; that something of the nature of a compact building, like a barrack-square, was wanted. A low wall and ditch were ultimately built round this straggling city, but so low that the officers could ride over them.

The envoy was on bad terms with Brigadier Roberts, 'an alarmist' as he always called him, and paid no attention to this remonstrance. Captain Sturt continued his work. The English officers built the houses at their own expense, and began to plant gardens, and to establish themselves, to furnish their houses, and make themselves comfortable in the way they were accustomed to do in India. Labour and materials were cheap, and the style of house was not costly. A palace, 'The Residency,' was begun, standing in a fine public garden, where the band played. Sir William Macnaghten had one hundred workmen building his house.

At first the occupation of Kabul was very unpopular among the English troops. Wine was thirty pounds a dozen, cheroots two shillings each; but the soldiers soon began to enjoy the cold, bracing mountain air, so refreshing after the wearisome heat of India, the beautiful scenery, and the curious, crowded Oriental town. The men and officers soon became reconciled to being detained in Afghanistan. They made excursions to the beautiful mountain glens of Istalif; they fished; they went shooting; they rode races; they held athletic sports. When the ice came in winter, they skated, much to the amusement of the Afghans, who had never before seen this pastime. The women of Kabul are fair and handsome, tall, and of graceful carriage. They lead freer lives, and live on terms of greater equality with the men, than among most Asiatics. They are witty, lively, and amusing. Noor Mahal and Jehanara were exceptional women, but among their race such women still existed. The shrewd Dost Mohammed, when he found one of his brothers acting unwisely, sent a sister, in whom he had much confidence, to keep him straight. The English officers and men soon had *liaisons* and intrigues with these attractive women, and this excited the bitterest hatred among the Afghans. They complained to the envoy, but no redress was obtainable; and this seemed to them the more unjust, as in Moslem states these matters are most rigorously punished if discovered.

Lady Macnaghten, Lady Sale, Mrs. Trevor, Mrs. Sturt,

Lady Sale's daughter, and many other officers' wives and children, had arrived, and established themselves in their new homes; and soon a kindly and hospitable English society had sprung up among the mountains of Kabul.

CHAPTER III.

THE ENGLISH INVASION OF KABUL.

Fatal inaction of Macnaghten and Elphinstone—Rapid progress of the Rebellion—Seizure of the British provisions—Terrible straits of the Defenders—Proposal to treat with the enemy—Murder of Macnaghten—Retreat decided upon—Massacre of the army in the Khoord Kabul Pass.

At the beginning of the rising, it was revenge on 'Sekunder Burnes,' and on Burnes alone, that was contemplated. When the envoy heard of the attack, he hastened to cantonments to see General Elphinstone. The incapacity of both soldier and civilian was so lamentable that, with six thousand good troops at their disposal, they allowed a mob to go on plundering the city within a mile of cantonments without stirring a sub-division. The mediocrity of officialism had preferred a 'safe' puppet to a General Nott; and once more in India it had to be shown that the functions of a military commander require other intellectual qualities besides servility. Shah Soujah did make an effort to quell the riot. He sent out a regiment and a couple of guns. By-and-by Elphinstone sent off Brigadier Shelton. He arrived only in time to cover the retreat of the king's troops back into the castle. He attempted nothing more. Three hundred men could have stopped the whole *émeute* in the morning; three thousand were powerless by night.

'Henceforward,' writes Eyre, who has chronicled the unspeakably terrible events of the following month, in which he himself was a sufferer, 'it becomes my weary task to relate a catalogue of *errors, disasters,* and *difficulties,* which, following close upon each other, disgusted our officers, disheartened our soldiers, and finally sunk us all into irretrievable ruin, as though Heaven itself by a combination of evil circumstances, for its own inscrutable purposes, had planned our downfall.'

'Against stupidity,' said Schiller, 'the gods themselves are powerless.' It was only with such leaders as Elphinstone and Macnaghten that all that followed was possible. The next day, the 2nd of November, though the Afghans were still pillaging the city, nothing was done. On the 3rd of November the English authorities were still inactive. On the 4th an appalling disaster befell the English. The food of the English army was in a small fort outside the defences of the cantonments. The Afghans succeeded in taking this fort. No assistance had been sent to Captain Warren, the officer who held it, with only eighty men, for three days. Reinforcements were written for in vain. Elphinstone could not make up his mind. Volunteers in plenty offered. They were not permitted to go. In this fort was all the grain, beer, spirits, medical stores. The fort was lost, without an effort to save it. In consequence, starvation now stared the English in the face; but, what was even worse still, it was an open proof to the Afghans of our utter imbecility. On the 6th of November the townspeople came by thousands to carry off the stores out of the fort. They were unmolested. Shah Soujah watched them from the heights of the Bala Hissar, hurrying backwards and forwards like ants. 'Surely the English are mad,' he exclaimed. They were worse than mad; they were stricken by an appalling and fatal imbecility.

Elphinstone, on account of his deplorable state of health, was to have left with the envoy. On the 2nd of November, to add to his already acute physical sufferings, he had had a heavy fall from his horse. He could never make up his mind; he always agreed with the last speaker. The officer next in command was Shelton. The army hoped to find in him a deliverer; but Elphinstone and Shelton could never act in concert. Shelton has left on record that every step he took 'Elphinstone soon corrected, by reminding me that he commanded, not I.' General Elphinstone has left on record: 'Brigadier Shelton appeared to be actuated by an ill-feeling towards me. I did everything in my power to remain on terms with him. I was unlucky also in not understanding the state of things, and being wholly dependent on the envoy and others for information.' Shelton in the field was the bravest and most daring of men, but he had no capability as a leader.

Nott and Roberts, the men of clear brain and resolute heart, had been disgraced and displaced because they had had the wisdom to see, and the courage to speak of, the difficulties and dangers that threatened them.

For this the blame lay with Macnaghten alone.

Still, how often, how generally, in English wars and difficulties it has happened that when the first rank failed, the second rank, the unknown men, have come forward to help their country at its need. But in Afghanistan fortune, luck, or fate was more cruel to us in this respect than the blind folly of Macnaghten or Auckland.

When Elphinstone, from ill-health, was forced to a great extent to give up the command, the promotion fell by seniority on Brigadier Shelton.

Never did chance more betray the fortunes of the English than when Shelton was placed at their head. Two eye-witnesses speak of him. George Lawrence says that after Burnes' murder 'Shelton seemed beside himself, not knowing how to act, and with incapacity stamped on every feature. Brigadier Shelton's conduct at this crisis astonished me beyond expression. I had always regarded him as an intelligent officer, and personally brave. I knew he was unpopular with his own corps, but I did not attach much weight to the fact, as popularity is no sure proof of merit. But he was apt to condemn all measures not emanating from himself, and call in question the merit of others. I confess to a doubt having crossed my mind before then as to whether, if tried, he would not be found a failure, but I as often dismissed it as unjust to the man.'*

Lady Sale, with a woman's keen insight, when he took command, wrote in her diary: 'The people in cantonments expect wonders from his prowess and military judgment. I am of a different opinion, knowing he is not a favourite with either his officers or men, and is most anxious to get back to India. I must, however, do him the justice to say that I believe he possesses much personal bravery; but, notwithstanding, I consider his arrival as a dark cloud overshadowing us. Most glad shall I be to find that by his energy the general (Elphinstone) is roused up to active measures. It is, perhaps, a part of his complaint, but, nevertheless, equally unfortunate for us, that General Elphinstone vacillates on every point. His own judgment appears good, but he is swayed by the last speaker, and Captain Grant's cold cautiousness and Captain Bellew's doubts on every subject induce our chief to alter his opinions and plans every moment.'† The military and civil authority, on which all hopes of safety rested, had sunk to this.

In the cantonments, added to constant attacks of the enemy, were cold, and famine, and sickness, despondency and gloom.

* Sir George Lawrence's 'Reminiscences,' p. 67.
† Lady Sale's 'Journal,' p. 83.

'A number of young men gave much gratuitous advice —in fact, the greater part of the night was spent in confusing the general's ideas, instead of allowing a sick man by rest to invigorate his powers. Brigadier Shelton was in the habit of taking his rezai (bed-quilt) with him, and lying on the floor during these discussions, when sleep, whether real or feigned, was a resource against replying to disagreeable questions. Major Thain, A.D.C., a sincere friend and good adviser of the general, withdrew in disgust from the council; and Sturt, who was ever ready to do anything, or give his opinion when asked, from the same feeling no longer profferred it.'*

The envoy also perpetually interfered, even in these desperate circumstances, and with his habitual imperiousness would say, 'This line of conduct was impolitic;' 'Such a proceeding would not be sanctioned by the Government of India.'

Even after this national outbreak, the English might have been saved if they had moved into the strong mediæval fortress, the Bala Hissar. They hoped that help would soon come from Sale at Jellalabad, and from Nott at Kandahar, to whom the envoy had sent for help. Sir William Macnaghten tried also to buy off their enemies, and, with his old constitutional sanguineness, he could not, he would not believe that the circumstances of the English were as hopeless and desperate as they seemed.

For six weeks the English held out against the

* Lady Sale's 'Journal,' p. 4.

Afghans. The open, unprotected cantonments, a mile round, were commanded by several Afghan forts, and from the shelter of their thick walls, the enemy could fire on the English with impunity. There were soon seven hundred English wounded; the cold was intense, the snow covered the ground. Food and fuel were very scarce. All the English had they had been able to buy in small quantities, and at famine prices, from the Afghans. Macnaghten would not move to the Bala Hissar. Both Elphinstone and Shelton also thought it too difficult and dangerous, but it was not so dangerous as what they proposed to do. The envoy writes as early as November 24th to Elphinstone:

'My dear General,—I reply to your note just received. I beg to state my opinion that the move into the Bala Hissar would be attended with the greatest difficulty, and I do not see what advantage would accrue therefrom, although the disadvantages, as pointed out by you, are apparent in the event of our ultimate retreat.'

The envoy wrote to Elphinstone on the same day, to inquire whether they could hold out any longer or should negotiate, to which General Elphinstone answered:

'Kabul, 24th Nov., 1841.

'Sir,—I have the honour to acknowledge the receipt of your letter of this day's date, calling for my opinion as to whether, in a military point of view, it is feasible any longer to maintain our position in this country.

'In reply, I beg to state that, after having held our position here for upwards of three weeks, in a state of siege, from the want of provisions and forage, the reduced state of our troops, the large number of wounded and sick, the difficulty of defending the extensive and ill-situated cantonment we occupy, the near approach of winter, our communications cut off, no prospect of relief, and the whole country in arms against us, I am of opinion that it is not feasible any longer to maintain our position in this country, and that you ought to avail yourself of the offer to negotiate which has been made to you.

W. K. ELPHINSTONE.'

But after the 24th November, when the English leaders had given up the defence as hopeless, the English defended themselves behind the low cantonment wall. The defence they had made for six weeks was heroic. The Ghilzies and half the mountain tribes were besieging them, the whole of the warlike citizens of the town of Kabul, nearly all the Afghan Amirs and their followers; and yet all Afghanistan had not dared to scale the paltry wall, not three feet high, behind which they held out.

A new actor arrived on the scene, Ackbar Khan, Dost Mohammed's son. He was rapturously welcomed by the people of Kabul. The envoy entered into negotiations for surrender with him, as all hope of further defence had been given up.

Ackbar Khan invited the envoy to a private conference to discuss the terms of negotiation. Ackbar Khan offered these terms: 'That Shah Soujah should re-remain king; that he, Ackbar Khan, should be vizier; that the English should remain unmolested until spring, and that they should then retire of their own free will. For these services Ackbar Khan was to receive a gift of three million and an annuity of thirty thousand a year.' These terms were far better than anything the envoy had expected, anything he had dared to hope, in their present desperate circumstances. When they were first mentioned, Macnaghten's wan, careworn face had lit up with a smile; it seemed a chance of escaping with honour from their present intolerable position—the long-hoped-for 'something' that he had always believed in had at length turned up.

A small party of Englishmen rode out of the cantonments at noon on the 23rd December—they had been besieged since November 2nd. It consisted of the envoy, and of Captains Trevor, G. Lawrence, and C. Mackenzie, who were his counsellors and friends. They only rode for about six hundred yards, when they found the Afghan Amirs assembled by appointment to discuss the negotiations. They had reached some low hillocks, on which the snow lay less thickly than on the surrounding country. There Ackbar Khan's servants spread some horse-cloths as carpets. The Englishmen and the Afghans dismounted. The envoy threw himself on the ground, Lawrence stood behind him, Trevor and Mackenzie near. A beautiful Arab horse had just been given to Ackbar Khan by the envoy, which he professed to admire very much. The Afghans had been crowding on the principal actors. The envoy had remarked, 'If this was to be a private interview, they had better move farther back.' Ackbar Khan said, 'It did not matter; they were all in the secret;' but some of his attendants made a feint of driving the crowd back with their whips. Ackbar Khan then asked Macnaughten if he agreed to the terms. The envoy answered, 'Why not?' The words had hardly been spoken when the four Englishmen were attacked and their arms pinioned from behind. A scene of great confusion ensued. Ackbar Khan himself tried to secure the envoy, who, with his habitual imperiousness, resisted. The young Afghan drew his pistol from his belt and shot him. He was then hacked to pieces by the Afghans with their knives. Captain Trevor was also killed; Mackenzie and Lawrence were put *en croupe* behind Afghan horsemen, and were carried away— Lawrence to Mohammed Ṣhah Khan's fort, where he was well treated. The three English officers with the envoy had been seized before they could help Macnaghten. Some Afghan troopers, his guard, never assisted him. A single Rajpoot chuprassi (servant), who had accompanied him, with the courage and chivalry of that race, flew to the envoy's assistance, and perished in the attempt.

The only words the envoy uttered were 'Aczil Khodi' (O God!), but his white, upturned face haunted those who saw it until their dying day.

Macnaghten had been warned by the Englishmen about him that treachery might be intended. Suspicion that there was treachery on foot had struck several people from the first. When the envoy told Elphinstone of the terms that had been offered him by Ackbar, which were better than those offered by the other chiefs, Elphinstone asked him 'if he did not think it was a plot?' But the envoy had so often of late heard the general's fears, that he answered hastily, 'I understand these things better than you.' Mackenzie, who was one of his friends, on the day they were started on the fatal expedition, also asked him if it was not a plot. 'A plot,' replied the envoy, hastily, 'Let me alone for that; trust me for that!' On the 23rd, when they left the cantonments, the officers who were with Macnaghten noticed many suspicious circumstances, such as the many ill-looking Afghans who were hanging about. The envoy knew that there was danger; he admitted it to George Lawrence, but added: 'A thousand deaths were preferable to the life I have of late been leading.'

Macnaghten's decapitated head was placed on a pole in one of the principal bazaars in the city of Kabul. His hands were also exhibited as trophies.

The miserable English in cantonments battled on for another fortnight against famine, cold, and the ceaseless attacks of their enemies. It seemed as if they had reached the lowest depths of suffering; but what they then endured was as nothing compared to what followed.

Negotiations were again opened with the Afghans. Shelton longed to get back to India; every man, indeed, wished it most ardently. 'Retreat! retreat!' became a cry and a daily clamour among the starving, miserable people within the cantonments. Shah Soujah sent them a warning notice on no account to leave the shelter of their walls; but Shelton and the other commanders, who considered it impossible to retreat one mile into the Bala Hissar, proposed to carry seven hundred wounded, and an endless number of camp followers, fifty miles, through the most inclement winter weather and heavy snow, over the stupendous mountain passes of Khoord Kabul, 7000 feet high; and this through a country of such treacherous robbers as the Ghilzies.

The retreat was decided on, under promise of a safe-conduct from Ackbar Khan. The first march was to the Kabul river. Even from the first march in the snow, without shelter, hundreds were frost-bitten, and were left as they fell, having lost the use of their feet. On the second day the same scene of horror was repeated. On the third, the fugitives began to toil up the Khoord Kabul Pass. Here they were attacked by the Ghilzies. Four thousand fell in the first attack, the snow meanwhile falling heavily. On the fourth day the loss was equally heavy. On the fifth day not a single Sepoy was left, every particle of baggage was gone, and only about five hundred men, mostly English soldiers, were still living.

Ackbar Khan had agreed to conduct the English in

safety to Jellalabad. It was only fifty miles off. It was this false promise that lured the English from the cantonments. At Jellalabad, behind the crumbling old walls of the fort, Sale was most gallantly holding out. The fifty miles were over a most rugged mountain-pass.

On the 6th of January the 'retreat' commenced. The English numbered 5000 fighting men, seven hundred only of which were English, 12,000 camp followers, and had seven small guns. Nothing in modern history is more horrible than the details of the retreat. Struggling up the snow-clad mountain-path was a long line of Indian servants—men, women, and children—without shelter, without food, for five days in the bitterest winter cold. The soldiers were worn out before they started, by two months of starvation and fighting; and it is said some of the Sepoy corps were not over-valiant from the first. The narrow path that ascends the Khoord Kabul Pass is hemmed in by high, rocky defiles. The camp followers were three times as numerous as the fighting men, and swayed backwards and forwards through their ranks. If the enemy attacked in front, these wretched people flew to the rear; if to the rear, they pushed forward with frantic efforts to the front, causing hopeless confusion. Hampered by them at every step, still the soldiers fought on and pushed on, and kept up some order and discipline. In every post of danger Shelton was to be seen.

On the sixth day seventy English men and officers

reached Jugdullick; but of the 16,000 who had started —men, women, and children—but one man reached Jellalabad, ten miles farther than Jugdullick, and this was Dr. Brydon. Ackbar Khan, it was said, had vowed that but one man should live to tell the tale of the British Invasion of Kabul. All this multitude who perished were mostly murdered with knives by the Ghilzie tribe, and were hacked to pieces when they fell wounded, and frost-bitten, and exhausted, in the snow.

Ackbar Khan held as prisoners gained by various expedients nine English ladies, fourteen officers' children, twenty officers, seventeen English soldiers, two soldiers' wives, and one soldier's child. Among the officers were Elphinstone, Shelton, G. Lawrence, and Mackenzie. Their lives were preserved probably as hostages, as Ackbar's four wives, children, and his father were in the hands of the English in India. The prisoners were well-treated. Ackbar Khan slept out in the open air, to give his tent to the English ladies, on several occasions. At one time the prisoners were taken to Bamean, *en route* to be sold as slaves in Bokhara, but were ultimately rescued, after eight months' captivity. Ackbar Khan affected that he could not control the Ghilzie tribe, although he was their chief. He was thought, before the invasion of Kabul by the English, a good-natured, light-hearted youth, and one unlikely to be prime mover in such bloody treachery.

It is the opinion of Vamberg, who travelled lately through Central Asia, and had unusual opportunities of gaining information on the spot, that the whole of these disasters were due to Russian intrigues. Ackbar Khan had been hiding in the direction of Bokhara, where Russian influence was paramount. There is a certainty, however, that our enemies could not have inflicted upon us the injuries that arose purely from our own imbecility, and from the vacillating and disunited counsels of the English commanders.

Lady Sale gives a curious story in her Journal: 'A very strange circumstance occurred last night. Some people were endeavouring to remove the barricade at the gate of the Mission Compound (*i.e.* Macnaghten's house). On being discovered, two Europeans galloped away who were not recognised. The third, ——, a clerk in Captain Johnson's office, was taken prisoner. He refused to name his companions. —— is a man of bad character. He has lately got himself into bad repute. He was also connected with a man of the name of O'Grady Gorman in a correspondence with the Russians, which was proved by letters found amongst the papers of the latter after he was murdered at Kandahar.'*

Lady Sale says also that they found it very difficult to communicate with the Bala Hissar because 'The Afghans, having persons who can read English, French, and Latin, were aware of all our secrets.'† These persons could not

* Lady Sale's 'Journal,' p. 184 † Ibid. p. 80.

have been Asiatics. They might have known English, but certainly no Asiatic knew French and Latin. No English officer could have deserted, if he wished to do so, without its being known. No private soldier is likely to have been such a linguist. Therefore, unless Russians or other foreigners were within the town of Kabul, it is difficult to account for the fact that letters in French and Latin were read by the Afghans. The Afghans are of so fair complexion that an Englishman or Russian, wearing their dress, could pass unnoticed and unchallenged. It is certainly improbable, and even impossible, that any Asiatic could read Latin.

Lord Auckland was on the point of leaving India, after his five years' vice-royalty, believing that Kabul was as peaceful as Kent, for Macnaghten was continually writing to him of the good feeling that prevailed. When the disastrous and wholly unexpected news reached him, they say his agony of mind was pitiable to witness.

Elphinstone lived four months in captivity, in spite of his sufferings from rheumatic gout. He, with the other captives, was carried from one little mountain stronghold to another, over nearly impassable mountain roads or footpaths, on horseback, for months. He longed for death, not as a release from his sufferings, but because the horrors of that retreat were never out of his mind night or day, waking or sleeping. The captives were taken back along the fatal path of the retreat. There they saw the stripped and naked corpses in thousands, choking up the narrow mountain gorges; and continually from among the seemingly dead, men with some life, but stripped naked in that bitter cold, would throw up their helpless arms, would call to their former leaders for help in every accent of anguish. From every side these cries would rise, and their leaders were powerless to help. To a man generous, honourable, and kind-hearted as Elphinstone, those despairing cries and spectral forms could never be effaced from memory. Elphinstone died in captivity, thankful for death, and was buried at Jellalabad.

Eight months afterwards an avenging army under General Pollock marched through the dangerous and gloomy Kheiber, fighting its way inch by inch. He relieved Sale, who held out at Jellalabad until aid came from his countrymen. Nott marched up from Kandahar. The two English forces met at Kabul. The bazaar of Kabul was burnt and the city plundered.

Abdullah Khan, Burnes' enemy, died a violent death by the hand of an assassin, in consequence, it was said, of the English envoy, Macnaghten, having offered a large sum of money for his head.

Vichovich returned to Persia in 1839. He was received with honour by the Russian Minister in Persia, at Teheran, and he was ordered to proceed to St. Petersburg. He arrived there, and called on Count Nesselrode, expecting a flattering reception, for he had been perfectly

22

successful in his 'commercial mission' to Kabul. Nesselrode refused to receive him.

The British Government had expostulated about the conduct of the Russian officials in giving assistance at Herat to the Persians, and encouraging an invasion of India. Nesselrode not only refused to see Vichovich, but said that he was an adventurer, and that his intrigues at Kabul were unauthorised. The young Pole went back to his house, burnt all his papers, and blew out his brains.

For forty years no Englishman has dared to play 'the beautiful game' that Macnaghten wrote about. The policy of 'masterly inactivity' has been popular ever since. And now again the Afghan passes have been re-entered by English troops, and Jellalabad and Candahar are once more in our hands.

Shah Soujah was murdered in the Bala Hissar, and that fortress fell into the hands of Ackbar Khan for a time. All Shah Soujah's women and children returned to Loodinanah.

But the evil of the Afghan war did not end in 1841; it left, like many other evils, numerous heirs. The blow to English prestige in India was terrific. For 120 years the people of India had never seen our arms fail; they considered us invincible; but after Kabul it was said in every bazaar, 'The English are great soldiers, but they could not hold Kabul.' The Afghan war assisted greatly in the birth of the Mutiny or rebellion of 1857. By the English nation the Afghan disaster and the Walcheren expedition are alike equally forgotten. But it is not so in India. Afghanistan is a near neighbour, and is close at hand.

Nor is it possible for the Indians to forget the unspeakable misery that befell sixteen thousand Hindustanees. These people, who were lost in Kabul, left relations in India, who do not know to this day if these lost ones are dead or yet living in hopeless slavery among the Usbegs. Many of the camp followers were sold to the Turcoman at four shillings a head, and some still exist among them as slaves. The English Government exerted itself to try and recover such of their miserable people as they could, but with doubtful success. In the retreat some of the camp followers hid themselves in remote caves among the mountains, and for weeks subsisted by cannibalism, until they perished a lingering death from frost-bites and starvation.

Our prestige in the East to this day has never recovered the blow it received in Kabul.

Dost Mohammed was permitted to return to Kabul in 1842, and was by the Afghans restored to the throne.

In 1842, on October 1st, Lord Ellenborough, the new Governor-General, issued a proclamation from Simla, exactly four years after Lord Auckland's proclamation of war, stating: 'To force a sovereign upon a reluctant people would be as inconsistent with the policy as it is with the principles of the British Government. The Governor-General will leave it to the Afghans themselves to create a government amidst the anarchy which is the consequence of their crimes.'

APPENDIX.

THE HOUSE OF TAMERLANE (TIMOUR) IN CENTRAL ASIA.

A.D.

1336 Tamerlane, King of Samarcand, Badakshan, Turkestan, Afghanistan, Hindustan (as far as Delhi), all Asia Minor, Syria, and Egypt. Died 1405.

1367 Mirza Miran Shah, third son of Tamerlane, King of Samarcand. Killed 1408.

Sultan Mohammed Mirza, King of Samarcand. The exact date of his birth and death not known.

1427 Sultan Abuseyd Mirza. Killed 1469. King of Samarcand.

1456 Omar Sheikh Mirza, King of Ferghana (the Russian province of Khokand).

1483 Sultan Baber. Mounted the throne of Ferghana at the age of eleven years; conquered Kabul, Kandahar, Badakshan, Ghuzni, and India. The Usbegs occupied Turkestan, Samarcand, and Ferghana.

HOUSE OF TIMOUR IN INDIA.

1526 Baber ascended the throne. Died in 1530; buried in Kabul.

1530 Humayon ascended the throne; is expelled by Shir Shah.

HOUSE OF SUR.

1540 Shir Shah Sur ascended the throne. Killed in action, 1545. Civil war.

HOUSE OF TIMOUR.

1556 Humayon restored. Killed by a fall inside Purana Keela.

1556 Akber succeeded. Died in 1605.

1605 Jehangire succeeded. Died in 1627.

1628 Shah Jehan ascended the throne. Deposed in 1658.

1658 Aurungzebe (or Alumgire I.) Died 1707, aged 89.

1707 Bahadur Shah succeeded.

1712 Jehandar Shah succeeded. Put to death by his nephew and successor. Civil war.

1719 Mohammed Shah. Died in 1748.

1748 Ahmed Shah. Deposed and blinded, 1754.

1754 Alumgire II. Murdered by Ghasi-oodeen, 1759.

1759 Shah Alum.

Akber Shah.

Bahadur Shah. The Mutiny of 1857 saw the end of the Timour dynasty.

THE PROVINCES OF THE INDIAN EMPIRE UNDER SHAH JEHAN, 1628.

	Revenue.
Delhi	£3,125,000
Agra	2,812,500
Lahore	2,812,500
Ajmere	1,875,000
Dowlatabad	1,718,750
Berar	1,718,750
Guzerat	1,651,250
Bengal	1,562,500
Allahabad	1,250,000
Malva	1,250,000
Khandeish	1,250,000
Oude	937,500
Mooltan	875,000
Orissa	625,000
Kabul	468,750
Cashmir	468,750
Balk	218,750
Badakshan	125,000
Tillingana	937,500
Buglana	625,000
	£27,500,000

The last five provinces were added to the empire by him.

The number of his forces, as they were paid out of the revenue in 1647, amounted to 911,400, horse and foot.

THE PROVINCES OF THE EMPIRE IN THE TIME OF AURUNGZEBE, 1707.

Delhi.
Agra.
Ajmere.
Allahabad.
Oude.
Mooltan.
Kabul.
Cashmir.
Guzerat.
Bahar.
Scinde.
Dowlatabad.
Berar.
Bedr, capital Zafferabad.
Bengal.
Orissa.
Hyderabad.
Vijapore.

Revenue - - - - - - £37,724,615

The provinces of Balkh, Kandahar, and Badakshan had been lost.

CHRONOLOGICAL TABLE OF THE ACQUISITIONS OF THE BRITISH IN INDIA.*

Date of Treaty.	Districts.	From whom acquired.	Remarks.
1661	Bombay.	Portuguese.	Marriage portion of Catherine of Braganza.
1756	Bankote.	Peishwah.	Mahratta: the Nana was his representative.
1757	The 24 Pergunnahs or parishes near Calcutta.	The Viceroy of Bengal.	Mohammedan.
1759	Masulipatam.	The Viceroy of the Deccan.	Mohammedan.
1760	Burdwan, Midnapore & Chittagong	The Viceroy of Bengal.	Mohammedan.
1765	Bengal and Behar	The King of Delhi.	The Great Moghul—chief Mohammedan power.
1765	Company's Jaghire	The Viceroy of Arcot.	Mohammedan.
1766	Northern Circars.	The Viceroy of the Deccan.	Mohammedan.
1775	Benares.	Viceroy of Oude.	Mohammedan.
1775	Island of Salsett.	The Mahrattas.	Hindoos.
1778	Nagore.	Rajah of Tanjore.	Hindoo.
1786	Guntoor Circar.	The Viceroy of the Deccan.	Mohammedan.
1786	Pulo Pinang.	King of Queda.	
1792	Malabar, etc.	Tippoo Sultan, of Mysore.	Mohammedan.
1799	Coimbatoos, etc.'	Conquered from Tippoo Sultan.	Mohammedan.
1800	Districts acquired by the Viceroy of the Deccan from Tippoo	The Viceroy of the Deccan.	Mohammedan.
1799	Tanjore.	Rajah of Tanjore.	Hindoo.
1801	Carnatic.	Viceroy of the Carnatic.	Mohammedan.
1801	Gorruckpoor Bareilly.	Viceroy of Oude.	Mohammedan.
1802	Districts in Bundelcund & Gujerat.	Peishwah.	Head of the Mahrattas.
1803	Cuttack & Balasore	Rajah of Berar.	Hindoo (Orissa county).
1805	Delhi, etc.	Scindiah.	Mahratta, Hindoo.
1805	Districts in Gujerat	Guicowar of Baroda.	Mahratta, Hindoo.

* Black's Atlas of the World.

Date of Treaty.	Districts.	From whom acquired.	Remarks.
1815	Kumaon.	Nepal.	Hindoo.
1817	Saugur, etc.	Peishwah.	Head of the Mahrattas.
1817	Ahmedabad Farm.	Guicowar.	Mahratta, Hindoo.
1818	Kandeish.	Holcar.	Mahratta, Hindoo.
1818	Ajmere.	Scindiah.	Mahratta, Hindoo.
1818	Poonah, Southern Mahratta county	Conquered from the Peishwah.	Head of the Mahrattas.
1818	Patna, etc.	Rajah of Berar.	Hindoo.
1820	Lands in Southern Konkun.	Rajah of Sawuntwarree	Hindoo.
1822	Districts of Beejapore.	The Viceroy of the Deccan.	Mohammedan.
1824	Singapore	Rajah of Johore.	Hindoo.
1825	Malacca.	Dutch.	
1826	Assam and Arracan	King of Ava.	Burmese.
1834	Koorg.	Rajah of Koorg.	Hindoo.
1835	Jynteah.	Rajah of Jynteah.	Hindoo.
1836	Loodeeana.	Lapsed territory.	Sikh.
1836	Feerozpoor.	Ditto.	Ditto.
1838	Part of the protected Sikh States.	Ditto.	Ditto.
1840	Jaloun.	Ditto.	Ditto.
1841	Kurnool.	Rajah of Kurnool.	Hindoo.
1843	Khythul.	Lapsed territory.	Hindoo.
1843	Koloba.	Ditto.	
1843	Sinde.	Conquered from the Amirs of Scinde	Mohammedan.
1845	Serampore.	Danes.	Christians.
1846	Julinda, Dooub.	Dhuleep Sing.	Head of Sikh nation
1847	Part of protected Sikh States.	Annexed.	Sikhs.
1848	Satara.	Lapsed territory.	Hindoo.
1849	Punjab.	Annexed.	Sikh.
1849	Jutpoor.	Lapsed territory.	
1850	Sumbhulpoor.	Ditto.	
1856	Oude.	Annexed.	Mohammed.